THE SOURCE OF CIVILIZATION

THE SOURCE
OF CIVILIZATION

by

GERALD HEARD

'Heaven arms with Pity
Those whom it would not see destroyed.'

TAO TÊ CHING
Waley's Translation

WIPF & STOCK · Eugene, Oregon

Wipf and Stock Publishers
199 W 8th Ave, Suite 3
Eugene, OR 97401

The Source of Civilization
By Heard, Gerald
Copyright ©1935 by Gerald Heard
Copyright restored under URAA January 1, 1996
Copyright transferred to The Barrie Family Trust

ISBN 13: 978-1-5326-5515-9
Publication date 4/11/2018
First published in England by Jonathan Cape, 1935
Previously published in the United States by Harper & Brothers Publishers, 1937

Photograph of Gerald Heard by Jay Michael Barrie, copyright © The Barrie Family Trust

CONTENTS

CONTENTS

CONTENTS

7

CONTENTS

To

C. W.

Thanks especially to Hannah Harris of Wipf and Stock Publishers, and Craig Tenney of Harold Ober Associates for their valuable assistance in bringing this series into print.

For more information on Gerald Heard, visit geraldheard.com, the Gerald Heard Official Website.

John Roger Barrie
Literary Executor of Gerald Heard

PREFACE

THIS book concludes a trilogy. It is the third part of an inquiry into the foundations of society. These three books, *The Ascent of Humanity*, *The Social Substance of Religion*, and this final one have all been prompted by one desire, the hope of discovering what it is that has held and holds human society together, why it is that men manage to live socially. Our age has learnt to look for the forces which control human action and shape behaviour below the level of consciousness. Prior to this all studies made by modern men (though they were possessed of much archaeological and anthropological information denied earlier thinkers) were vitiated by the rationalist assumption that individuals created society either out of mutual convenience-co-operation, enlightened self-interest (the Social Contract) or were kept organized as societies by the enlightened self-interest of one despot who coerced them by violence or debauched them with spoil.

WHAT HOLDS SOCIETY TOGETHER?

We now realize that human society has no such rational beginning. As each individual man almost imperceptibly becomes conscious that he is growing up in a family, so, in pre-history it seems certain mankind, as gradually and unawarely, awoke to the fact that he was living in a society with his fellows.

The problem, then, is to discover not how men came together — they find themselves together as soon

PREFACE

as they become conscious — but how, when they have become conscious, what was once an instinct — the gregarious instinct — is carried over into rational life. Physical force does not hold human society together. For short periods it may give a spear-point to frenzied disgust with monotony, desire for change and efforts to expand. No settlement can be made with it. The penalty of force, as of all artificial stimulants or drugs, is that the dose has to be increased until the patient dies of it. It was Talleyrand, the diplomatic genius, who had unrivalled opportunity of watching force directed by supreme military genius (and directed against effete incompetence) and himself being given the task of making permanent what force had erected, who concluded, 'You can do everything with bayonets save sit on them'.

PRE-HUMAN SOCIETY NOT HELD TOGETHER BY FORCE

Nor is this the unsupported opinion of one man who may have lost his nerve in too great a gamble. We know, as was not realized then, that man is a social animal and the social animals are not held together by violence nor — save in a few morbid cases — do they attack members of their own species. The more natural, the more primitive, the more 'wild' man is, the less then does he depend on violence to keep his societies together. Social animals do not need even policemen. Lately our exploration of our own natural history has gone further and we realize that not only are we social animals but derived from a stock far more receptive than aggressive, far more sensitive

12

than imposing. This point will be developed further in Chapter II of this book. Here it is only mentioned to show that it is clear we must look in human society for some binding, other than physical violence, to account for social cohesion.

BUT TO-DAY INSTINCT DOES NOT UNITE US

It is not, however, enough to say that men hold together out of instinct — this gregarious instinct. As it is clear that human society did not begin with a consciously debated and sworn social contract, so it is equally clear that during the historic, prehistoric, and indeed all periods since man has been capable of what we call invention, discovery, and the elaborate procedure of civilization, he has not been dominated by a gregarious, or any other instinct. The very variety of his social forms and craft-discoveries is evidence enough of that. No animal ruled by instinct can show such variation of behaviour. It is clear, also, that societies have not only been too variegated and changeable to be the outcome of such a conservative force as instinct — the lack of instinct has been shown even more by the instability of societies, by their constantly breaking down and going to pieces. If there was, in the real sense of the word, a social instinct among men then they would have had the profound unconscious happiness of a people who have no annals — a state which only animals have ever enjoyed. Even when man has attained peace, that peace has not been torpor but an intensity of balance, a daring and energetic reconciliation of opposites, the holding of two knowledges in one focus of action, an effort which, however victorious, is as great as any exercise of violence.

We must then seek for some force deeper and less intentional than physical coercion and yet not so deep and blind as instinct, to account for human society and its survival after incessant vicissitudes. We must look for some power which wanes — when we have disruption, oppression, anarchy — and then waxes — and we have once more order, agreement, co-operation.

In my first speculation — *The Ascent of Humanity* — I thought such a force could only be the relic of an instinct — the persistence of the animal group-consciousness right on into historic times. The historical hypothesis then runs as follows: that while no doubt the persons at the top of society were self-conscious individuals, the vast mass remained unself-conscious and thus capable of an unquestioning cohesion which was the real social cement, or to use Walter Bagehot's phrase, the binding in 'the cake of custom'. I still believe that to be a factor underrated or completely disregarded by historians who never doubted that their own acute self-consciousness was and always had been possessed by every man, civilized or savage. Further reflection, however, showed me that this cohesion is not great and in many societies for thousands of years has certainly not by itself been sufficient to prevent social dissolution. It was necessary therefore to look for some conservative force which might have power to appeal to primitive feelings of group loyalty and recreate a less self-conscious and competitive frame of mind among associated men. Religion was inevitably the answer.

NOR IS IT RELIGION

In my second essay of inquiry, *The Social Substance of Religion*, I therefore attempted to see whether the history of Religion would give evidence of this. Was Religion, *au fond*, a method whereby men aroused in themselves an emotion of self-forgetful loyalty? Could there be under all Rites this psychological purpose? While men had pursued the specialized functions now become possible and necessary in the complescent community, their intuitive sense of loyalty had lapsed into the subconscious. The main achievement of Religion was to make the individual able to recover his symbiotic relationship with his fellows. Such an authority as Professor Royce has described the energizing force, in so successful a religion as Christianity, in its earliest and most successful years, as being 'devotion to the beloved community'. Indeed there can be no doubt that much of the intuitive — perhaps one might almost say instinctive — interdependence of a primitive pack may be recovered by people, far advanced toward complete self-consciousness, if they will come together in small groups to concentrate their minds on a unifying idea. That Religion has a very large social substance and that one of the chief reasons for the survival of religions, whose cosmology and theology have been discredited, is the social satisfaction the coming together of a congregation can give its units, is, I think, now accepted by most sociologists. Further, the more modern sociologists allow, and I feel sure are right in allowing, that this satisfaction is not rational but arises from the assuaging of psychological needs which exist now in the subconscious. Part of the spirit of the self-conscious individual is neither self-conscious nor individual but requires a linkage with his fellows in order that he may be whole. That part, however, has become separated off by the growth of self-conscious individuality and the formation of an insulated 'limen', or threshold of consciousness, between the self-conscious individuality and the subconscious.

Nevertheless religion — the meeting together of individuals to recite certain common formularies and share traditional group rites — is not itself a sufficient cause of social cohesion, though it may assist such cohesion. The formularies increasingly either offend or, perhaps worse, are felt to be completely irrelevant to modern emotional needs and intellectual opinions. They are defended psychologically as Mantras, word patterns wherewith the conscious mind is soothed and so the subconscious psyche is permitted to emerge. If they are Mantras they are peculiarly unsuited for this purpose. A Mantra is a sound rhythm expressing a simple idea — one which is either simply ethical or one which raises in the mind's eye an image as restful as the sound that swirls against the ear. The service books of Western Europe are almost exclusively tribal songs of a people who was in anything but a meditative mood when it composed these lays, outbursts of hatred, despair or equally violent relief and delight. In brief, European religion tries to make meditative patterns out of historical records of intense action — epic, comedy and tragedy. In consequence, it failed. Latin which had become a hieratic tongue, in which Chronicle might in time have been transmuted into

16

Mantra, was cracked away from religion at the Reformation and it was found that the Chronicle had undergone very little transmutation. Indeed had the original Hebrew record been the matrix or raw material out of which Mantra could have been manufactured, the Reformation would probably never have been able to bring to an end a process which had it been working could not have been arrested.

The group rites have also offended as much as they have assuaged; the sacraments themselves becoming the centre of the acutest differences between the religions. Since then, except for the Quakers, religion, whether sacramental or pulpital, has been increasingly intellectual, the approach of a creature who thinks of itself as being nothing but a self-conscious individual to an equally defined self-conscious individual creator, a relationship of bargaining or conversation, almost never of union. Religion has, at times, attempted to call the whole species of man to a sense of its common kinship and union. But it has been the religions with the widest appeal which have themselves fissured into the most distinct — and often the most hostile — sects.

The rise of this intensified self-consciousness which marks and causes the modern age and accounts for its distinctive religion, shows that religion cannot be the tie which has kept civilization together during these three centuries of revolutionary thought and action. Nor can we look to traditional religion to save our civilization now it has reached its gravest crisis. The very fact of intensified self-consciousness means that religion itself must become self-conscious, men would dread 'letting go' and permitting a tide of emotion to sweep them over the limen into the larger, but to them, darker world beyond the sharply-lit limits of their individuality. Hence the horror the eighteenth century felt for 'enthusiasm' and, as during the nineteenth the self-consciousness of the few spread to the many, the gradual slaking of the emotional fires even in those sects which had started up in the dawn of the modern age to oppose the growing good sense and rationalistic individualism of the established churches. Even the Quakers became sensible.

If then men are to explore the subconscious, cross the limen, and make the vital contact that exists beyond individual self-consciousness, in a self-conscious age they must do it deliberately, self-consciously. This, of course, sounds a contradiction in terms, an impossibility similar to using the will not to will, or, in clear wakefulness, to resolve by an act of consciousness to lose consciousness and fall asleep. Yet it is here, in this process and in its possibility that the solution of our problem lies.

THERE IS A WAY OF SOCIAL UNION THROUGH PSYCHOLOGY

Therefore into this apparently insuperable difficulty this book will go at some length, for here, it seems, the solution of the larger problem, the continued cohesion of an individualized society, must be found. At this point it is enough to say that it is clear that that cohesion depends no more on the co-operative impulse generated by traditional religion than on the survival of an adequate gregarious instinct and we must look elsewhere for the necessary binding.

A third source of unifying power must be discovered: and, further, it appears as though that power, although belonging to what the individual consciousness calls the subconscious, must nevertheless be reached by an effort of consciousness, by a deliberate technique. For though the subconscious cannot be commanded, it itself cannot, when self-consciousness has arisen, fully and effectively assert itself unless the self-conscious will permits access to the outer world.[1] It can create, but access to the stage whereon it may work is debarred unless the individual can give right of entry. Hence it would seem we have to search in history for some process whereby men gave themselves a power of making contact with their social and greater self.

It may be necessary to repeat that many undoubtedly found this process *in* religion but not necessarily *by* religion. Approaching the problem of their individual nature and its needs, and their social nature and its demands (frequently conflicting demands) they sought in religion, that is in formularies and practices which are mainly psychological rather than economic, a reconciliation. They found it through psychological means but these means were often repudiated and never sanctioned by organized religion. The mystic is generally suspect: the psychical researcher hardly ever escaped condemnation. Hence it is necessary carefully to distinguish between what was probably discovered through the arch of religion and by going -beyond it, and what remains under the dome of religion — the established practices of sacraments,

---

[1] It will appear later that a more accurate term than 'the outer world' would be 'that construction made by the objective mind and which is accepted as the outer world by individuals'. At present the simpler, though less true, description may stand.

creeds, dogmatic teaching, corporate petition and praise.

The exploration and the gradual elucidation of such a process; how it was slowly purified from magic, convention and anthropomorphism, how men realized that their true task and problem was to change themselves and then, with a changed consciousness, to see whether they still required to change the universe, whether in a complete psychology they would not find both the cosmology and the theology they needed; the account of how this happened would be the most essential history that could be written. For all history, we increasingly realize, is only the shadow cast by the growing and defining spirit of man. I believe the first brief sketch of that process, the first hypothesis of that course can now be made. Seldom referred to and often then heavily disguised, there are, it seems, in our records now sufficient statements of practices wherein we may recognize the gradual discovery and ever clearer definition of a technique whereby the individual can make himself race-conscious, re-mend the fissure in his own psyche and so see himself and his community, it and Life, and Life and the universe as one.

THIS WAY MUST BE MADE CLEAR. OTHERWISE VIOLENCE DESTROYS CIVILIZATION

This, then, is the thesis of this book, and one which seems not merely of considerable historical interest (as giving us a deeper clue than we have so far had as to why human societies cohere and go into dissolution) but also to point out a possible escape from the dilemma which now seems to confront civilization. That dilemma is caused by the search for the defensive security of law, order and culture through a continual increase in armaments. These armaments always endanger, and when used to capacity — as competition necessitates — can destroy the very values whose persistence (it is said) are only possible under the protection of this unlimited violence.

This is to claim much and to have to answer many objections. In the essay that follows the argument will be developed first from the practical point of view. The modern dilemma will be stated in an introductory chapter. There it will be made quite clear why the writer thinks civilization is at present pursuing a mistaken and fatal course (a conclusion with which an increasing number of people agree). The following chapters will then turn to history. There only can we discover how to-day's crisis was prepared and where the departure was made, the commitments accepted which have led to the present impasse. For though so many are now convinced that we cannot, with anything but a growing certainty of destruction, go on as we are going; few, very few, think there is any practical way of stopping the descent and averting the collision. To contemporary people of goodwill it seems that they are born fatal heirs to a growing sequence of disaster. They feel they can do nothing effective to avert the collapse because processes pursued by their ancestors have now brought about tensions which a touch will precipitate. Yet they do not wish to blame their parents. They seem to see, as they look back down the corridors of time, how each generation appears to have acted to the best of its powers. To understand all is to forgive all but, if you are the last comer, that understanding of others' unavoidable mistakes does not excuse you from having to pay for them all. Force it is true grows by a natural progression: but where could it have been stopped? Force is in the nature of things. Hobbes said 'Fear and I were born together'. Modern man thinks mankind's values were born, like a Siamese twin, inextricably incorporated with violence.

VIOLENCE AND VALUES ARE IRRECONCILABLE

That conclusion, to any thinkers not as involved and as distracted as we are to-day, would surely appear suspiciously odd. Indeed it has been suspected by some moderns who felt themselves detached. They, however, faced with the fact of violence, have called violence the reality and values only the lovely shadow which lies on the safe side of that grim barrier. All man's agreements, co-operations, self-subordinations, loyalties and devotions, the natural values of his human life, the native emotions out of which every beauty of his culture has grown, are not ends, preserved at the sad price of violence. That is to invert the picture. The true relationship is that loyalty, love and devotion, admiration and compassion only exist to make violence more efficient. Virtues exist to make brutality succeed. For man is a gregarious animal, the pack is the biological, the natural unit, and in order that packs may compete with the utmost effectiveness, the pack-constituents must subordinate themselves to it. The nineteenth-century doctrine of

Natural Selection reversed Mandeville's epigram for now it was seen private virtues made for public vices.

For this reason alone, we must then if we would base firmly a new view of history and a new source of sanctions, start with Natural History. We must, before we study man's acts, decide by examination of earlier evidence what may be his nature, his character, his temper. For it is on that to-day that there turns increasingly our judgment: whether we think man's internecine misfortunes are characteristic or accidental. Is he a creature who wants civilization and through ignorance overturns society into chaos or is he a creature who wants chaos but who in moments of exhaustion relapses into civilization? Surely the problem has only to be stated to be solved? But no: The present paralysis of Liberals, the present paradox that while an increasing proportion of civilized men want peace, civilization ever more hurriedly prepares for a civil war which can destroy not only civilization but humanity — can only be understood if we realize that we are now reaping in practical action the consequences of the abstract thought of two generations ago. When we urge that man does not want to destroy himself, but to enjoy using his creative faculties co-operatively with his fellows, we have all nineteenth-century biology, the study of natural man against us. In consequence we have the 'Autocrat of all the Soviets', sure of his benevolence but equally sure of his sad responsibility and of what sorry material it is out of which he has to make the new order, saying to Wells: 'You think human nature is good. I know otherwise', and Wells himself, while in the very act of striving for peace and with Stalin's challenge fresh

23

in his ear, saying at a great pacifist rally at the Queen's Hall in London on November 20th, 1934: 'Those who say that war is in the nature of society have a very strong case and therefore to strive to abolish war is to propose to reverse the whole trend of humanity.'

THE NEW VIEW OF LIFE AND OF MAN SHOWS VALUES TO BE NATURAL

The new view of history must begin then at the beginning with man as a natural animal. That is clear. Once there, however, we find that even this foundation is not basic. Behind man, behind man's earliest stock, lies life in simpler and simpler forms. It were wise then to decide what is the fundamental nature of the force which has driven life, of which man's stock is only one variant. We might leave so vast an issue aside, content with the fact that our subject, man, has undoubtedly succeeded, and that therefore specifically human characteristics are obviously natural because they have best withstood the test of time, and competition with other animals' equipments. We are, however, forced to go 'on and back' because nineteenth-century biology based the conclusions which made out man to be a desperate fighter, winning by force and cunning, on a survey not merely of man's ancestors but of all living forms.

Our outline of History must then begin with the earliest Natural History. All Human History must be seen as an epitome of Natural History. The first chapter makes a preliminary inquiry whether any direction can be perceived in Evolution and, if there is a direction, by what means the end was striven after and the present station attained. After that we shall look more closely at the early forerunners of man. Next we can examine the evidence of man's earliest ancestors: Prehistory will lead us to proto-history and thence we can survey the historic record itself down to our present critical generation.

So it is hoped some of the evidence may be ordered which tends to show first that Life is not a constant, unremitting contest but that quarrelling and fighting are no more normal than are disease and accident. Most of the time Life is peaceful. Advance is accomplished by creative not destructive forces and, though such destructive forces exist, they do not help forward the Life process but are sporadic interruptions, morbid aberrations, exceptionally noticeable because of their exceptional and dangerous character. When advance ceases and decadence supervenes then the creature narrows into suspicion, ill-will and death.

Secondly, the evidence will be arranged which suggests that man himself is an advanced form of this peaceful Life process. With him, as with Life at large, there are periods, moments of aberration, when he becomes violent, distracted and destructive. These moments are, however, unnatural to him, that is to say such moments retard and imperil, instead of advance, his evolution, and he feels ill at ease when so behaving. For he comes from a stock which is not at home as a pirate or a parasite but has won the way through sensitiveness and superior awareness.

This picture of the stock from which man himself is derived will be succeeded by a third study, giving the evidence which tends to show the same evolutionary process — the constant growth in heightened sensitivity and awareness — working — as indeed it must if it is natural — in man through his prehistoric, proto-historic, ancient, medieval and modern periods.

Thirdly, the evidence will be brought forward to suggest how and why it is that man has developed at times and in certain strains of his culture, the specialized, aberrant, morbid conduct we call warfare; how this grew from, and is a projection of, a peculiar specialization of part of his consciousness and how that may be healed — and so the expression ended — by man adopting a technique which will develop that side of his consciousness which has been retarded and atrophied (while part hypertrophied) and so he may recover the sanity of a whole psyche and continue to progress, saved from the suicide that otherwise awaits him.

Our crisis need not necessarily end in disaster. We can choose the other alternative, an advance as radically constructive and creative as its alternative is destructive and chaotic. Up till to-day civilization has time and again been wrecked by the monomaniac war-specialist, but never mortally wounded. Such specialists have been rare and short lived. Humanity as a whole has clung to compromise — never wholly trusting its inspiration and intuition but never wholly daring to repudiate the apprehension it called conscience. To-day the development of a specialized, partial aspect of the mind, and a neglect of any other mental technique, has led to such an unbalanced increase of physical power without spiritual insight that the destruction of civilization is possible and the probability of it being attempted grows ever higher. Because this development appears to the ordinary person as both inevitable and yet insane it is clear only the discovery of a radically new way will save us. Nevertheless as that way exists and can now be seen, even though it must mean a revolution as drastic as the Industrial Revolution, as man successfully made the one there is no reason why he should not achieve the other. Thus a new outline, an alternative — and it is believed — a truer clue can be given to history, and so, with a truer idea of the past, with a truer reason shown for human advance, a new and real hope for our human future.

This sketch can only be slight and very imperfect in presentation. Each chapter calls for authoritative statement. The excuse for one inexpert hand attempting such a new ordering is that the matter is desperately pressing. When a house is on fire and all the onlookers say it is its nature to burn and, when pipes are pointed to, the appeal for action is dismissed because 'everyone knows those pipes do not contain water but gas', then surely a person must not wait until he is an accredited authority on piping, hydraulics and communications before saying 'The old opinion that those pipes contain inflammable gas and are feeding the conflagration is untrue. They contain water.' That metaphor, of course, means that it is necessary for practical men, politicians and statesmen, to realize that the nineteenth-century view of human nature as a fiery and destructive essence is no longer supported by evidence, but that, on the contrary, human nature is, because of the way it has been evolved, the very thing — a true and natural humaneness — on which we must depend, which we must trust and tap (for now it is buried) — if our burning civilization is to be salvaged from destruction.

INTRODUCTION

THE DILEMMA

OUR problem can be stated as briefly as an ultimatum. The world has always been seeking for sanctions. The ordinary man is certain that there is only one sure, immediate and final sanction — violence. The scales of Justice are ineffective unless enforced by its sword. Men — so runs the ordinary man's judgment — cannot or will not attend to an impartial verdict, a matter of fact. Truth cannot affect them if their interests are involved.

JUSTICE VERSUS SANCTIONS

Whether this is true or not, we need not immediately discuss, for the first fact we have to face is that such an assumption does not extricate man from his difficulty or solve his problem: how to sustain a just social order, an equable relationship between himself and his fellows. Justice, pure justice is not sanction; sanction is an added and awkward necessity. Justice, pure justice would exist whether it were enforced or no. Roman law, a code heavily encrusted and corroded with violence, nevertheless accepted and enshrined the maxim *Fiat justitia, ruat coelum.* Not only if there is no force behind, does Justice still remain eternally valid; it is true even though nature leagued herself with men, and lawlessness could not only raise all life against law but drag down the heavens to crush the principle of right. The sword is then no part of pure justice but only a practical sequel, something which, kept in the background while the precise and patient balancing of claims is settled, is afterwards unsheathed to enforce the finding, with the establishment of which it had nothing to do.

THE DECLINE OF JUSTICE

That procedure exposes, however, a practical and grave difficulty. It was a practical and grave difficulty which first admitted the sword to rise beside the scales. It has been said the first commandment ran 'This do' and the fiat was so powerful, the advice so obvious, the authority so undoubted, the communal suggestibility so strong, that it was done. 'This do' was enough — 'and thou shalt live' marks a later gloss — a rise of questioning which thus is answered. If this is true — and anthropology seems to support the conclusion — then it is clear 'This do or thou shalt not live — thou shalt be cut off' marks a still later decline from the immediate and effective recognition of Right. We are then faced with evidence of a degenerative process. An homogeneous organic co-operation decomposes into a conscious adjustment of mutual self-interest. This further decline is into a balance of power increasingly unstable and needing ever more frequent and abrupt correction. It is clear then that such a disease is active and — each state of derangement being more grave than the one which preceded — it also becomes clear that we are viewing a rapid decline — each stage lasting less long than the one it superseded and being in itself more unstable and more violent. In short, we are viewing in the history of human justice and the putative attempt to preserve it, an ever accelerated descent into chaos. The sword, it becomes clear, is not an original and essential partner of the scales. It is a sign and cause of their decline. 'It was not so in the beginning.' It is so now. It must be more so in the future. Prescriptive custom, draconian code, martial law: So runs the sloping road to destruction.

This is not pessimism but merely detached observation. Justice takes the sword and perishes by the sword. For the sword — advanced as the essential bar which prevents a tentacle of violence from touching the scales weighing conflicting claims — the sword itself is violence. 'Who guards the guardian?' (another of the ruminating questions of legal genius) raises that awkward issue. The only answer must be still another question:—Can you hope to shelter health from infection by interposing a screen or shield that is itself highly infective? The very shadow of the sword disturbs the exact balance of the scales, the wind of its stroke perturbates them and as it approaches nearer and nearer to them, like a magnet brought near steel, they are permanently deflected. The sword which was to defend the scales is, in the end, their ravisher. Brought in to keep a finger from touching them, a breath of prejudice disturbing them, so that they might poise regardless of interest or consequences, the sword renders them finally suspect and deranged. Justice cannot be done as long as the beat of the harpy wings of human violence can sway the scales by hovering closer upon them, drawn by the ever more urgent need of sanctions. The sword which first arose behind the scales in the end cannot be kept from throwing itself (as did that of the Brennus) into the scales.

WHAT OF INEVITABLE PROGRESS?

At that grave conclusion the practical man brightens. It is true it is he who talks of the necessity of sanctions, who laments, if a little perfunctorily, the hard necessity of stern measures and with a regret, which may be partly sincere, points out that all men are not as just as himself and quite a number must be made to fear what he freely approves. Force, violence must be employed or justice would be helpless. Extreme force, unlimited violence must be at hand, threatened, yes and loosed on his fellow men if they will not submit to findings which have been found against them by their fellow men, and even by the party opposed to them in the disputed matter. Still he refuses to take a gloomy view of the situation. He does not believe things have become worse, injustice multiplied, and violence increased. Indeed he looks upon weapons — although they have become more destructive and indiscriminate — as a relic of earlier, cruder authority. He still maintains that the ultimate appeal must be to this unlimited and indiscriminate violence, but he believes that it is less and less necessary to go to extreme measures — the sword must be there, it must every now and then be drawn and flashed before the people's face; the canister of poison gas must be raised, like a chalice, off and on before their eyes as a solemn benediction. But there will be — so the practical man hopes — no need to make the people actually drink of that cup. It serves if they know it is full of poison, which will exterminate them like weeds from off the Earth's face. For he — the practical man, the cautious conservative — believes, when it suits him, in progress. He may mock at that faith when it encourages progressives to advance with inconvenient haste toward social betterment. He adopts it when the serious consequences of holding on the present course are presented to him. Then he will maintain a natural, inevitable evolutionary progress so as to escape from the dilemma of deliberately turning from the present course or running on the rocks. Nature shall somehow save him and make him safe without his having to take any risk or abandon any weapon.

In this argument, of those who will not face facts, sanctions, force, violence then become only temporary expedients, the shuttering put around the soft concrete of the peoples' will until that will sets in accepted custom and prescriptive right. And people are becoming more sensible, more humane, more inclined to see the other fellow's point of view and the justice of his case. Even the most conservative, the least favourable to the modern world will maintain *that*, when the alternative is accepting the fact, not merely that violence has failed to support justice — that sanctions are the confession of justice's failure — but that violence must continue to encroach until it has destroyed justice, until might is right and whatever is is law. The customary Catholic defence of the Inquisition is that considering the time and the place, the savagery of the people, the brutality of contemporary customs and procedure, you could not expect

c

the Holy Office to be more merciful in its penalties or more just in its methods. Inquisitors were removed for corruption — for putting to death, with no defence permitted, men whose property they wished to acquire. Torture was used to extract confessions from victims never confronted with their accusers. Such admitted miscarriages of justice and imperfections of procedure are nevertheless dismissed as being in no wise the most extreme examples of deflections of law in the thirteenth century. We must remember the time, when judging the code and practice. The rational conclusion of such an argument is that to-day the world is morally better, less violence is needed to preserve right, less terror to overawe the evildoer, and the general sense of fair play and goodwill makes it not only easier for the judge to be just but for the tempted, if not to escape becoming criminal, at least to fall less far, to be more easily recalled and to have a less disastrous effect on his fellows through his example.

ARE WE GETTING BETTER BECAUSE WE ARE OLDER?

Is this defence of the practical conservative valid? Is the world growing better? Are both sense and sensibility gaining? Is it a misjudgment of the facts of history that violence not only must increase but must encroach ever further upon justice and right? This question is the gravest we can face. Nothing then must be extenuated and nothing set down to dish a Whig or disconcert a Tory.

Two things so far have become clear. In the first

place we have the ordinary man's assumption (be he conservative or liberal) that justice ultimately rests on violence. In the second place we have his further assumption that though the means of violence, the extremities to which it can go, have been increased, the occasions for such employment are becoming less. It is clear to any social historian that these two basic opinions show the triumph of a Hobbesian outlook. The argument runs: Man began with his hand against every other man. He raises an authority to give him the best he could hope to get:—Justice against his fellow at the price of justice against himself. This great Leviathan had to be given arms to enforce its judgments. Hence the armed State. But as man grows in good sense he sees the limit of what he can hope to get for himself. Increasingly therefore he complies with justice as a matter of enlightened self-interest. All the central power has to do is to keep strong and firmly hold the stakes. Then the constituents will learn by habit that justice pays and injustice is ruinous. Better the loaf divided between you and your neighbour than no bread.

Such a picture of history is, however, made by a very partial selection of the available evidence. We shall look into that later. At this point it suffices to ask: Does it even give us a picture of a general design of civilization to-day, as it actually is? In Europe now we are not witnessing a steady advance toward the realization of an obvious mutual self-interest. Nationalism is becoming more, not less acute, and nationalism is the negation of general law, and general convenience. No one Leviathan seems appearing. Rather a number of Kraken-creatures, their lethal tentacles hopelessly entangled with each other, each attempts to drag the other into its maw and devour it. For inter-individual anarchy we have exchanged inter-social anarchy and, in the gigantic violence of these struggles, civilization is on the brink of dissolution. The individual is helpless to check the collapse. His individual self-interest which would urge him against this suicide cannot extricate him. He cannot secede from the social organism in which he is immersed. He is made an involuntary altruist acting for a selfishness beside which his greatest display of greed would be innocent. His individual goodwill, which would urge him to aid his fellow, is exploited, through his national loyalty, to make him destroy all other of his fellows divided from him by a frontier — but united by humanity. His none too strong goodwill is choked by constant appeals to this greed and fear and doubt of strangers. He is made, it is true, more obedient, and so internally there are fewer small breaches of the peace, but he is not more peaceable.

NATIONALISM, CLASS WAR AND ARMAMENTS ALL INCREASING DANGERS

Hence we see the decomposition of civilization. Nor do the multiplication of occasions, in which unlimited violence may be used, cease with the international anarchy. The retreat from a common agreed order does not stop short at the frontiers. Within even these restricted bounds cleavages of violence are being driven. The Leviathan himself not only fails to make a general human order: his own body is rent with fissures. Vertically divided from his fellow Leviathans, he is horizontally split in his own organs. Classes now feel justified in advocating against each other 'relentless war'. Has not every individual been taught that when 'right' is at stake then any violence, any wrong must be used? Hence unlimited violence extends not only along the inflamed frontier but between the factions of one State.

Nor are the instruments employed to coerce your neighbour more merciful and more exact than those of the past. Flame warfare and gas warfare — the gases being chosen because they are peculiarly painful — are not only weapons which yield to none in their brutality, but, because they are almost impossible to localize when they have been loosed, and must be loosed from such great heights that exact aim is impossible, of necessity they cause the maximum of damage. What advocated itself as coercion becomes inevitably extermination.[1]

Our present international and inter-class situation does not therefore seem to point either to fewer occasions on which men may think resort to unlimited violence justifiable nor to that unlimited violence being less destructive and cruel than in the past. The reverse seems nearer the truth. On this showing it would seem man is becoming more not less savage and the justice he would strive to maintain becomes in itself more confused and more tainted with the sanctions it employs.

Some, however, would say that international and inter-class rivalries are in some sort atavisms. They are passionate outbursts which we have not yet learnt

---

[1] If anyone doubts whether civil war would be as violent and inexact as international war let him read an account of Oviedo in Asturias after the class revolt in the autumn of 1934. And when one 'class' gets another in its power we see the degree of violence considered necessary to confirm the victory from the accounts of Kulak liquidation in Russia, and concentration camps in Germany and the islands of banishment in Italy.

37

to curb — passionate outbursts which arise from neglected wrongs, injustices (which we shall settle), whether of ancient territorial rights or new social claims. Such an assertion seems more of the nature of *a priori* hope than an impartial expectation. Certain it is that if the parties to these disputes are questioned we find them convinced that only the use of unlimited violence on their part will permit them to gain those improvements in their condition which they call their rights. They will never rest content with what a third party, anxious for peace, may concede them as a compromise with their adversary. They must assert the limit of their claim, they alone be judge when it is satisfied and they therefore be free to use any means to establish it.

The advocates of compromise, those who believe violence may, like drug-taking, be 'tapered' until, without any risk to the patient — i.e. the social order — the last element of coercion is removed from law, these gradualists are however not answered by the above objection that nations and classes seem to be increasing their demands and also their means of obtaining those demands by violence. They fall back on the defence that justice, though it may be abandoned by nations and classes, is growing among individuals. The state itself is giving more justice between man and man and this must grow until class and class and nation with nation agree.

ADVANCED DEMOCRACIES RELAPSING

This claim must be examined. Is individual justice growing and is the sanction needed to enforce it becoming less? To start with the largest Democracy, a state specifically founded in the ir´ ests of the individual, the United States: is the ju. ле individual can there obtain better and less tai than at the time of that State's founding some ᶜ , gᴄ.ierations ago? It hardly seems so. The Supreme Court is the only one in the country which has not been openly charged by responsible citizens with corruption. The State courts it has been claimed have been bought time and again by gangsters, by the thieves of the Navy's oil reserves (Teapot Dome scandal) by anyone who had enough money. The police have been charged time and again with racketeering, and their connivance of and alliance with the bootleggers, drug traders and prostitution agents has been proved. And not only has the police been proved corrupt, they have been proved to be cruel. The extraction of evidence under such duress as to amount to torture has also many times been established. Beside these 'third degree' methods, with those undergoing or about to undergo trial, there are also on record the cruelties committed in prison on the convicts.

Nor are the people better than their officials. Corrupt and cruel as the law may be, it has frequently to fight small civil wars with the citizens to prevent them killing — generally in cruel and ghastly ways — negroes who are charged but not yet tried and sometimes only suspected. On this showing it seems clear that Justice in the world's greatest democracy, founded to defend individual rights, has become gravely infected with the violence it employs — so gravely as to throw doubt on almost the whole of it.

The second great democracy, that of Great Britain

also cannot feel easy about the degree in which violence used as sanction for justice has infected the justice it sanctions. Though much has been done through the attempts of idealists — most of whom repudiated violence altogether — to remedy the prison system in some important particulars, there has been not progress but retrogression. Scourging — a form of severe torture — has been brought back into the criminal law, although every penal expert was aware that it was useless and protested against this atavism.

THE NEW-MODEL STATES MORE VIOLENT

When we turn to the States in which the new self-consciousness has appeared we find, however, not so much a decline as a collapse. In Italy, Germany, Spain and France political crimes have become again high treason. In France, men who objected to military service, though of the highest moral character and of social usefulness, have undergone and are undergoing indefinite sentences of imprisonment under conditions in which the final breakdown of health is almost certain.

France, however, is lenient in comparison with the other countries. In Italy and Germany opinion is punished ruthlessly. The right of a sane and responsible man to express his judgment as to the best interests of his country has become a crime. Nor can we dismiss this as a flare up of reaction. These states are advanced, progressive, 'new model' societies framed purposely to be the last word in efficiency and self-consistency. The increasing adulteration of justice with violence in these countries to-day is not due to confusion and corruption or to the ignorance of the supreme power as to what is done in its name, but to a deliberate policy and a consistent realization that without the sword the scales will not weigh; the creaky beam must be made work with the sword as lever. Once that is allowed all else follows, as necessity compels consistency. No historian of our age should blame unduly these latest developments. They are only the fruit of what lay and was let lie by our fathers in the seed.

That this is so, that it is the modern self-conscious, efficient world — and not blind tradition and reaction that is destroying pure justice, the most advanced of the modern states proves most fully. No state has attempted more radically to remake itself than Russia and in no state is free and pure justice further to seek. The Soviet Government openly boasts it does not intend to deal fairly with those it rules to be outside the law and any whom it accuses of questioning its absolute right is for it such an outlaw. Russia is ruled not by justice — a balance of rights between the State and its constituent, such rights being guaranteed by the State and adjudged by an independent judicature. Russia is ruled by fear. The sword has usurped the place of the scales, for the tribunal is judge and prosecutor, law and execution in one. As long as the individual can be considered as prompted only by personal and private motives, so long he is viewed with indulgence. He may be enlightened, converted. But if, growing in understanding, he would think for himself, not merely greedily but socially, then he becomes a political criminal and for such there is no justice; they are outside the law. The safety of the State is the supreme law that sanctions all these 'divine state's' outrages. Who is to judge, however, what is a matter of political safety? Russia has lately ruled that to be an intergrade and remain unchanged is 'an offence against the State' and so to be outside the law — Russia which claimed that it left the individual's private life absolutely free.

EFFICIENCY, IF VIOLENCE USED, COMPELS BRUTALITY

This it must be repeated is not savagery, it is consistency, it is efficiency. Mussolini quotes Machiavelli: 'The prophets who have disarmed have always been destroyed'. It is not true, but what he means is that the man who has a message which preaches force must depend increasingly on force. That is true. The new states, whether Fascist or Communist, have no prescriptive right and are based on the *coup d'état*. That is not to say that much in their programmes is not effective and noble. It is only to point out that the dyer's hand is subdued by what he works in and that the means used, in the end dictate the end attainable. Once law is made depend on violence then every move toward efficiency of necessity is a move toward more violence. You have seized the state by violence in order to bring about the better order you preach. When then you have won power there can be no law but your law. *Le loi c'est moi.* You alone hold the light — all the rest lie in darkness. So he that questions you, throws doubt on the light itself — on truth and justice. You have to strike ruthlessly, for you are not fighting for yourself but for truth and if you perish it perishes. The sword has become the knife edge on which alone the scales can swing. You end a tyrant brooding over a land which you dare not trust and against which you must act ever more sharply, a tyrant who never dares step outside his frontiers, a prisoner of your own chains.

GROWTH OF SENSIBILITY ONLY INCREASES SUFFERING

Further it must be recognized, that as this degenerative development is not necessarily due to the ends these leaders envisage, (that the social betterment that Stalin envisages, the heroic Italy Mussolini prophecies, the mystic Germany Hitler foresees may all be noble prospects and able to inspire in many of their followers intense devotion and self-sacrifice), as the descent into chaos is not due to (nor to be prevented by) the aims but is due to the means, so also it is no reply or comfort to say that the people themselves are growing in feeling, in sensibility. This may well be so. There is indeed much evidence which suggests that millions are beginning to feel war to be an outrage against their conscience and against the purpose of life. But if this is true, then our situation is only more grave. For pure sensibility — just feeling that it is intolerable to have to massacre your neighbour's children — will not prevent men having to act as they believe to be the only possible way to act; any more than the leaders, because of the nobility of their aims, find themselves released from having to use unlimited violence to obtain them. The fact that the peoples feel acutely will not save them but only make them suffer more exquisitely — just as the splendour of the goals their masters indicate make more tragic, more squalid the crimes they commit.

That then is the world to-day. It is the modern efficient states which have got rid of pure justice and they have done so in the name of consistency. The more ancient democracies hesitate. Their Liberalism makes them unwilling to accept this harsh consistency, this facing of the fact that justice must have sanctions because men are individuals and that those sanctions must steadily be increased until no longer does justice call on the sanctions but whatever the sanctions effect that is justice — the scales simply register, after the event, that balance of power the sword has allotted. Conventional optimism still clings to the fact that we no longer have to witness a crucifixion or *auto-da-fé*. We have to remind ourselves that we are still living in the Sunset of Liberalism. At present it is considered sufficient warning to state that 'All the accused were shot immediately at conclusion of trial'. Of what takes place in dictatorial prisons where it is necessary to bend the will of a stubborn protestor we have evidence from Italy, Germany and Russia. It was not a sadistic disposition but legal responsibility that made Ulpian, the Stoic and codifier of Roman law, state the necessity of torture. The same necessity drove Inquisitors to employ the same means. The great Legalist was defending Roman civilization, light against the darkness of barbarism. The Holy Office was defending church and faith, salvation against the blackness of the damned. To-day Mussolini is defending his Italy and his great Fascist idea, Hitler his Germany and his

Nazism, Stalin his Russia and his Communism. If summary shooting will not produce its effect — and it is clear from other ages of violence that violent death, when it becomes sufficiently common, soon ceases to be a deterrent — then examples have to be made.

ARMAMENTS RACE MUST LEAD TO ATROCITIES RACE

As behind imprisonment most liberals feel there must stand 'the supreme penalty', so dictators and other practical and efficient persons know that the supreme penalty may lose its point, but behind it are things, regrettable no doubt but, as indubitably, more efficient, slow deaths to warn others and tortures to make the victim repent. To break the will is more effective than to kill the body. Killing can only be a threat to the will: torture can be the real thing. The terrorist states cannot therefore stay where they are. The dictators are not superior to Ulpian the Stoic or Dominic the Saint. The downward way these predecessors went, searching for a sure sanction for authority, the men who to-day are determined to find such a sanction must also go. Yet it must be repeated — or the reminder serves no purpose — to describe such things in plain words is not to indulge in denunciation. It is merely to make a diagnosis. As Luther said, so the dictators can say: *Ich kann nicht anders*. The whole degenerative process is inevitable if you allow the initial assumption of sanctions. If justice has no inherent basis then it will melt away if put to rest on violence, as a lump of ice put to rest on a stove.

The ordinary man's conventional optimism is shown then to have less and less basis. Under our eyes things are not getting better but worse. Justice is being eclipsed and swallowed up by the forces which were permitted to act as its guards. Was the hope of progress then nothing but an illusion and must we now wholly despair of human society?

THE REAL PROGRESS

The thesis of this essay is an attempt to answer both those questions and to answer them in the negative. It is hoped to show in what follows first that though what was called progress was misdescribed there has been a force working in and through man, that that force made for righteousness but shunned violence, established justice but was untainted by the use of fear and pain and was the real unificator that kept human beings united and co-operative and has never wholly deserted mankind. On the contrary, there have been times, in periods of direct illumination and more often at others by a reflected light of authority, tradition and prescriptive right (a light which if not replenished will die) when this creative force has made possible a pure justice and given a sure non-violent sanction to well-doing. Secondly, it is hoped to establish that it is this force and this alone which to-day may save us out of our present quandary, into which our increasing self-consciousness, efficiency and consistency have thrust us. Another way, a more excellent way, must be found, for in attempting to establish the rule of law through the use of violence we have destroyed law, in striving to protect the light of reason with the extinguisher of force we find ourselves plunged back into the realm of Chaos and Old Night.

In a phrase our dilemma is that we want peace and justice but seem only able to attain these values by acts which destroy them. Values without sanctions are only dreams, but in attempting to make the dream come true we destroy it and reality also.

Is there some other force which can implement ideals, except the unlimited violence which destroys them? That is our riddle. Pacifist and militarist have both been ignorant of such a possibility. So the pacifist has hoped good intentions, good resolutions would create peace. He has failed to check the militarist. The militarist, pushing aside the pacifist, has destroyed what he maintained he alone could preserve. The first has failed to take a real hold on peace and justice: the second has caught hold of them and crushed them to dust.

Nevertheless a force which is both real and yet non-violent does exist, a power which can meet both the requirements of our case.

Its nature, its manifestations and it relationship to human civilization and human warfare it is the aim of the following chapters very briefly to outline.

CHAPTER I

THE NEW NATURAL HISTORY
OF ALL LIFE

I. THE END DOES NOT JUSTIFY THE MEANS

WE have seen that our dilemma to-day is due to the fact that though we wish to preserve values, humanity, civilization, we cannot see how we can preserve them without the use or at least the threat of means which if employed destroy that which such means were employed to protect. We repeat, and it is experience which has taught us the lesson, the end does not justify the means. We have learnt it is the method we use not the aim we propose which decides the value of our action and how far its resultant is of worth to humanity. This is a platitude, but however often spoken is so constantly followed by the very action the futility of which the platitude exposes that it is worth quoting the latest finding of its truth. Mr. Chamberlain is an author whose studies of Soviet Russia and its great attempt to achieve Communism are justly well known. He has at length concluded twelve years' residential study of this experiment. He began his residence as an observer convinced that Communism alone could save civilization and that Russia was achieving that social order. He ends convinced that though the aim is obviously ideal (and much material success has been meanwhile achieved) the aim itself is as far off as ever. More, it will never be attained, not because it is itself impossible but because the method which is being used to attain it is, though it seems the shortest way, in reality a path which leads from, not to the goal. His summing up runs, 'I think the overwhelming weight of historical evidence is to the effect that the means determine the end and that an idealistic goal pursued by brutal methods has a tendency to disappear from view. They brutalize the Society which is taught and forced to look on them with indifference and even with applause. I have often felt that even more terrible than the commission of these atrocities was the fact that no voice could be publicly raised against them in the Soviet Union' (p. 374, *Russia's Iron Age*).

This is clear. Expressed by one who hoped that in Communism in general and in the Soviet in particular he had found the solution of our anarchy it is highly significant. It states the dilemma and will not let us escape it. It does not however take us one step toward solving it. The Government of the Soviet is new and original. It promised more in welfare to the unpossessing, it threatened more in punishment to the possessing classes than any other government. What it does with the employment of violence shocks then more sharply both those who are already frightened by its threats and abuse, and also those who have already waited long with hope deferred for the new order, not merely of plenty but of justice, mercy and peace, which these sympathizers thought Communism would shortly achieve. Soviet Russia is using the Terror as the French Revolutionary Government used the Terror and for the same reason. As Hilaire Belloc pointed out in his study of the French Revolution, Revolution must use Terrorism: it is only Martial law appearing among the civil population and through the whole country-side, because the whole country is split into a war-frontier horizontally, in short there is civil war everywhere.

What then we are seeing done in Russia — which we realize is a method which must defeat the ostensible aim, may be different in intensity but is not different in quality from the methods which are used by all modern societies to-day. It is true the use of violence can, as a society gains in prestige, be gradually restricted. Innate force of custom takes the place of imposed coercion. The difficulty however is not solved but shelved. Should any maladjustment in social growth take place, should, as must happen, 'the cake of custom' crack either from its own age or through outer pressure, then automatically law and order fall back for their sanction on violence. The very fact of progress therefore gravely imperils progress. Arrested societies can gradually let fall into disuetude even the simple instruments of violence they once employed and, as none can any longer conceive any other way of life, the law is kept freely or at least without conscious conflict. Progressing societies are always creating conditions and situations to which custom supplies no rules. The issues are all unprecedented and in dispute. Tensions are therefore bound to arise. Nor is this all. There is a demand for overruling sanctions, that decisions in which the party which loses (and which must feel itself wronged or at least have some right to that feeling) shall be made submit. At the same time the very changes, which give rise to the new confusing situations and counter claims, also give rise to new forces, new weapons. The society has become large, disorganized, powerful: the central power must balance those disruptive forces, that weakening of social loyalty, that strengthening of local power and individual force, that difficulty of seizing the wrongdoer in a society which is so huge he can hide in it as in a jungle, and so indifferent that it cares as little to help the central power as it does itself to try the criminal. New weapons are therefore forced on governments just when the modern confusion of all other social growth aided by invention, makes the occasions on which weapons may be called for much more numerous.

The so called capitalistic societies, the countries which have not as yet attempted by a violent Revolution to abolish classes, are then in reality in no more morally stable conditions than the U.S.S.R.

Both divisions depend, to maintain their state, on unlimited violence and both have to increase that violence because (1) there are more and more occasions, in their new and constantly changing circumstances, when violence alone can decide, for custom is helpless and no other sanction is supposed to exist, and (2) there are also new and constantly increasing weapons which others may hold and with which, because they have as yet not been tried out, none can say without trial where the limit of security may be.

In brief all that the doctrine of class war necessitates in Russia, the doctrine of nation-war compels outside. If violence is the only sanction of values then violence must be increased unlimitedly. The constant increase in aeroplanes, the failure to reassure any nation as to gas and incendiary bombing of open cities are proof that all civilization is getting ready to do to itself what Russia has done to herself. Justice is to be maintained and based on the supreme principles of injustice: that the accuser, judge and avenger may be one and the same person, and that innocent and guilty be destroyed together.

We are drawn back once again to principle. 'The ends do not justify the means' we repeat. There however the Ends exist — safety, peace, order, civilization, humanity. We must attain them. 'The Means determine the Ends.' True, but what other Means are there of reaching the goal? It is little use pointing out that the accustomed way does not lead there but over the precipice. 'A more excellent way' must be found. If you warn castaways that on no account must they drink sea water however thirsty they become, for if they do they will not quench their thirst but go mad, your warning will not save them. Water they must have even if it be deadly water. So if we can show men no other way of sanctioning law and order save by law and order's denial, violence, to violence they will turn.

Nor have they thought until lately that such a step was to put out of their reach the very thing which that step they imagined must put within their grasp. It is only because unlimited violence has lately become so rapidly extended and unconfined, so that it may destroy even the hand that uses it, that the ordinary man has begun to ask whether it really effects what he was told it alone could. As long as it stopped short of that, the fact that always innocent suffered with guilty and the 'guilty' were not seldom held guiltless by impartial onlookers, weighed hardly at all. Till the weapon became (as science has made aerial and gas and fire war) a weapon all edge and no haft, men were content to say that not only was there no other sanction except violence but violence had obviously time and again secured peace, vindicated justice, protected the weak, supported mercy, established order and materialized law.

Such has been the obvious answer all down the ages to pacifism. Violence delivers the goods and nothing else does. This case which falls into two parts needs then a double answer. Has the End justified the Means? For if it is violence which has done as common sense claims then the ancient platitude had better be discarded. When we have settled whether that is so we can then examine the second part of the case whether or no there is any other sanction which can secure values.

2. HAS VIOLENCE SANCTIONED VALUES?

The case for believing that violence has ever sanctioned values when it is examined is found to rest far more on assumption than proof. What is clear is that while on one occasion violence has been used, peace has followed — though it not seldom resembles the Tacitan peace which is really desolation — on another apparently similar occasion defiance has been inflamed. It looks as though some other unrecognized factor may be the real effective agent — sometimes sufficiently effective to give quite a high proportion of peace in spite of the initial violence. Some vital nourishment may have been given the body politic

54

so that in spite of the septic injuries inflicted on it by violence, and restrictions imposed by threat of further assault, it recovers and becomes orderly. The belief that when peace has followed violence, peace has been caused by violence, may be no more than *post hoc, propter hoc.*

We have however in modern times never really inquired into the possibility of such another factor, because we have been fully convinced that science has shown that such a factor could not exist, for violence alone is the cause of evolution, we are wholly animals and so the only natural explanation of order, justice, mercy and peace is that they are such biologically advantageous subordinations of the units in the pack as to render that pack more formidable in those constant and violent struggles with other packs. So Natural Selection, the *vera causa* of evolution, exercises its elevating influence.

There can be no doubt that the belief that man has risen by successful struggle from bestiality to civilization has not only made sociologists blind to the fact that some other factor than violence may hold society together but has actually made practical thinkers less inclined to believe that the end does not justify the means. If Natural Selection, the struggle to survive and the survival of the fittest, is the explanation of all evolution and of man's progress in particular, then virtues are a real handicap — they are 'biologically immoral' — if they are allowed to do anything but make that struggle more acute.

This has of course been pointed out by many influential authors. General Bernhardi did much before the war 'to justify the ways of Brute to Man',

55

to make the influential specialists, the army staff chiefs
— still many of them, in their general philosophy,
stuck in a puzzled, inconsistent Lutherism — see that
Darwin had proved that war was Life's way and only
way to higher things, that you must be brutal to
become fine. Of course those biologists who were
aware that their principle was being recommended
as a guide to practice, practice which might be
gravely inconvenient to quiet scholars, began to
mutter that after all they had never defined what 'the
fittest' might actually be. The phrase might only
turn out to be harmlessly tautological: The fittest to
survive were those who survived: what survived was
most fit. So Nature, dragging itself up out of the
slime by tooth and claw, red and raw from the
incessant blind efforts of each to scramble on the back
of all, that was perhaps a little too dramatic a picture.
Still the practical thinker could point to Natural Selection and maintain that the first great evolutionists had
declared that this force accounted for evolution and
the rise of mankind and that Natural Selection was
defined as the derivation of every and all features and
capacities solely because they serve physical survival
in a world of incessant struggle.

Here again an increasing number of 'subapostolic'
biologists attempted to qualify the great masters'
rashness. As Thomson and Geddes, for example, in
their study of *Evolution* for the Home University
Library series pointed out, Natural Selection turns
out, on more careful examination, to be not a positive
but a negative force, something that cuts life back as an
east wind cuts back new shoots. It tells us, then,
nothing about the *vera causa* of Life. In fact, owing to

some unrecognized prejudice, the first evolutionists had evidently made the facts stand on their heads. Natural Selection was a shears not a seed. It had as little to do with life and progress as had inter-stellar night. It was clear that it was when the struggle to survive was modified and called off that then it was that Life became most inventive and various and dared explore and experiment.

Such a profound reversal of judgment was however only an academic affair. The old misconception was still taken as the unbiased finding of science by practical thinkers. If the new view became known it was easily discounted. Had not the great genius of Darwin, impartial and sublimely indifferent to consequences, found the truth, and were not the lesser later biologists, infected with morality and afraid of the practical application of pure fact, trimming their sails before the blast?

3. WHY EVOLUTION THOUGHT TO BE BY VIOLENCE AND CUNNING

This objection was also faced and answered by expert study. It became clear that even on this ground —where the actual arguments advanced by authorities are not weighed but the sincerity of the authorities themselves is at issue and permitted to count largely in the final conclusion — even there the case was not as the practical and ruthless thinker supposed. Darwin was no 'purer' a thinker for example than Thomson or Geddes. He himself was just as much subject to unconscious prejudice which leads to unconscious selection of facts to support theory. It is now known that Darwin himself owned how much he was, at the beginning of his life, influenced by Malthus, that the question of human population-pressure sent him with a thesis in his mind (the blind struggle of creatures breeding to the limit of subsistence) to study life. There he found — always a dangerous discovery in science — what he was looking for. Being a man of sensibility (he would not become a doctor in that pre-anaesthetic age), of property (he inherited considerable wealth and lived a life always free to pursue his own interests) and living in the acutest period of the misery of the industrial revolution when the huge increase of population was least provided for, and *laissiez-faire* was unloosing even those inadequate ties an earlier, smaller order had imposed, his emotional and moral position was extremely awkward. He wanted to live his own life, to travel, study, think and write. For all this he required a life of considerable resources, far more than were needed to keep himself in modest physical comfort. Hence, as any psychologist can now point out, the particular interest to which he devotes himself and the particular conclusion he reaches are foregone. He will inevitably become interested in the struggle to survive and he will as inevitably find that struggle to be essential, that those at the top should be at the top and those who fail are rightly being eliminated. In short he will give the appearance of a scientific setting to *laissez-faire* and will find that 'what ever is is right'.

Darwinism is therefore not impartial and in the particular generalization, the law of evolution through the struggle to survive, the Natural Selection which produces every power, gift and faculty through acute competition between creatures, Darwinism is a reversal of the facts. Further, this reversal is caused by a keen if unconscious wish of a man of considerable feeling faced by the problem of justifying his own position of privilege in a period of widespread suffering and the dislocation of customary ways of life.

Nevertheless just because the Darwinian explanation was so apposite, so suited to save the comfort, physical and moral, of the educated and the rich, and yet seemed so vast and detached, it is immensely hard to get such a judgment reversed. The Survival of the Fittest may be shown to be nothing but a Tautology: Natural Selection may be established as a force which imperils life as plagues, famine and war imperil it, instead of stimulating and inspiring it: Darwinism may be proved to be 'the defensive mechanism' of men whose sensibility was growing just as the distress of their neighbours was also growing: to-day Natural Selection may be used to advance and sanction destruction as generations ago it seemed to sanction 'Progress'. All this may be — it *is* true. Yet practical thinkers will go on feeling that any other theory of life and of evolution, of the energies in living nature and human nature must be too good to be true. Not merely reactionaries but progressives are agreed that force is the only remedy.

Thirty years ago powerful Liberalism used to cry loudly 'Force is no remedy'. To-day the men who are striving to make a new world and convinced that they alone can make it, the Trumpet men like Shaw, the Sword and Trowel men like Stalin are one with the reactionaries in calling for force and still more force, as human nature refuses to prove itself good in their eyes by going into the particular arks they have designed for its conveyance. A socially convenient misstatement dressed up as a Natural Law takes long to die. Yet we can hardly wait for its slow withering. The truth is too grave. For if it is true that the end does not justify the means, if it is the means you use not the ends you indicate that reveal your true nature and direction, if it is true that there is something in human nature and all living nature which (whether it can reveal its real way of life or not) can bring to ruin any other way and make order imposed by violence collapse into anarchy, then no duty is more urgent than to persuade men where the real way lies.

So great has been the prejudice, so convenient first to conservatives and *laissez-faire*-ists and now to revolutionaries, has been the false belief that life had to rest on violence and was most 'biologically moral' when it competed and strove most ruthlessly, that it is not enough to show why that false belief arose and how among experts it has been modified for years and is now abandoned.

4. WHAT FORCE HAS ENERGIZED EVOLUTION?

We have to attempt to show this other principle in action. It is not enough to say, negatively, Natural Selection, the blind struggle to survive is not the force which has caused Evolution and achieved man, that the blind struggle only cuts back life and when struggle pauses then Life progresses most quickly. We have to state positively what this force is. Darwinism permitted its Natural Selection to be translated into human terms, to be found expressing itself in human relationships through ruthless commercial competition and in warfare. Man, using his physical violence and those vast additions to it which his cunning gave him, was, in sharper and sharper business and more and more efficient war, showing on his own scale the continued play of the force which had evolved him and all life from slime that crawled upon and suffocated its fellow slime.

That picture is gone: but what are we to put in its place? Until we find a principle in Life equal to the part Natural Selection was intended to play, as the explanation of how evolution worked in the past and is working among us still to-day, practical people, out of habit, will fall back on Natural Selection even though they know it to be a baseless support. The mind must have a principle with which to work and if the new facts are not put into principle-form, men will fall back on the old principle-form, although almost every one of the facts around which it was originally framed and which gave it its shape and strength have disappeared from out of it.

It is worth pausing a moment to see why, though Biology, Natural History, has discarded for some time Natural Selection, and the struggle to survive, as the explanation of evolution and vital advance, no other explanation, no other general principle has been put in its place. That is mainly due to two things: practical prejudice and specialized interest. When Natural Selection had to be discarded as the explanation of evolution some biologists feared that teleology would come back into Natural History and that religion would counter attack on this failure to establish that Life was wholly blind and accidental.

Specialized interest, on the other hand, was indifferent to any theory whether materialist or animist. For this expert attention was concentrated on the interest of the discovery which had upset Natural Selection. That discovery was Mutationism, the fact that the cell itself contained within itself power to change spontaneously. The pressure of outer events could only very gradually modify a species. These changes would at first have to be so insignificant as to be of no value in helping the creature to survive or in handicapping it in competition with its fellows. Such minute changes therefore could never give rise to more efficient types. A change to be sufficient to be distinctive must (and it was proved did) suddenly arise in the germ itself. 'I wish,' said T. H. Huxley, made cautious by much controversy, 'that Mr. Darwin would not repeat so often, "Nature never goes by leaps".' We now know how wise was that wish. Nature it appears, up from electron and photon, never really goes otherwise. Live Nature is no exception to the rule of 'all or nothing' and it now seems clear that unless the force can be generated which will jump a process out of its rut, any gradual continuation but deepens the groove.

This discovery of Mutationism was however so startling and caused such keen controversy among Biologists themselves that they had little time to attend to the larger issues of Evolution and Natural History. William Bateson, championing and extending the work of the Abbé Mendel, had to meet with acute opposition from the Elder Biologists who still clung to evolution by innumerable small modifications, sifted, preserved and built up by their survival-value — the orthodox

Darwinian view. Bateson and his fellow genetists held that all Evolution was due to the germ cell's spontaneous capacity to mutate: everything was in the cell — the genius of Beethoven, the monstrosity of the decapod — the environment only permitted this creative capacity to unfold.

In maintaining this power of the cell as the source of creation the Genetists had naturally to stress its infinite variety. Reacting from the former biological outlook, wherein Natural Selection produced those forms of life which were most utilitarian, emphasis was now laid on Life's incalculable extravagances. In establishing Life's autonomy, after the long time during which it had been considered merely a mould resulting from the pressure of events, attention and emphasis were concentrated on its caprice. The cell was king and a king after being long considered a nonentity may be held to be most royal when most arbitrary. 'Life gives rise to forms which circumstance modifies so that they can fight and win', said the earlier evolutionists. 'Life can give rise to almost anything', said the genetists. The cell chooses, and circumstances only have a voice if the choice is obviously extravagant, 'unviable'. You must not then search over the body trying to tie a utilitarian label on to every organ and feature and characteristic. As long as the ship will float it may fly as many flags as it pleases. The bunting is not to make it more buoyant and necessitated by the sea but because the ship's captain having settled the problem of keeping up, is now free to enjoy himself as he likes.

This restatement of Life's rights had to be made and the accent placed with compensatory emphasis on the initiative, against the secondary and reactive role, which Darwinism had allotted it.

Yet this change of stress, though proper in the biological dispute, did not itself leave a satisfactory picture of the Life-process. It had established Life's freedom but in doing so had underrated or disregarded Life's purpose.

5. THERE HAS BEEN A DIRECTIVE ENERGY IN LIFE

It is however quite clear that though Life has in it an infinite capacity and might give rise to practically any variety, in point of fact it has not done so. On the contrary it has produced but few fundamental types and with one (and it would seem only one) of these it has succeeded, after persistent and protractive refinement, in producing a creature which while preserving the main lines of its original structure has attained to a mobility, freedom and capacity which place it obviously on the threshold of completely new developments, powers and apprehensions. In brief we can then say that Life has a purpose. In spite of all the possibilities contained in the germ only a certain direction has been taken. Whether by accident or design there has been progress. Some creatures have remained unchanging — the cockroach for instance does not seem to have modified since the laying down of the coal measures. Many have become extinct. But among those who have gone on there seems present evidence of an urge which has driven them toward a constantly extending capacity. And moreover the highest types it would seem are on the whole types which have comparatively lately come to dominance.

We have then to add to this fact that progress has taken place, the discovery of the genetist that it has taken place not through outer accident but through some inherent capacity in the living cell, in life itself.

The problem therefore which now faces Natural Historians is to define some principle in Life itself, some inherent power, capacity and process which may account for the fact of progress. Faced with that fact, the Darwinian Evolutionists still attempted to explain it through Natural Selection. Natural Selection discarded and the power of change and advance found in Life itself, it remains to find what is the main character of the drive which from within the cell, within the organism, directs it so that Evolution is accomplished, higher types appear and in the end one type, which becomes self-conscious, realizes its evolution and itself undertakes its development deliberately.

In the first place it is clear that if evolution is true then, though there may be accident, breakdown and occasional miscarriage, a single and successful process must be discovered running through the whole sequence from amoeba to man. The main driving principle must be the same. It may — indeed we might expect it should — become refined and clarified. What is not possible is that it should be reversed. Man cannot in his deepest nature and profoundest feelings be unnatural and perverse. It is not possible then that his firmest devotions should be 'biologically immoral' and that his values, which he realizes alone make a life beyond his individual satisfaction worth while, alone make him able and willing to recognize his part in a general life process which stretches beyond his private existence, that these ideals should be not only unreal but fatal to Life's purpose.

We have then to look for some principle which has manifested itself throughout Life's History, weakly it may be at first but with sufficient insistence to direct and carry upward those organisms in which it played. This same principle we can then expect to find at later stages more fully expressed until finally it should reach self-consciousness in man and become his principal driving force, or, as we should say, his supreme value, his categorical imperative, his ideal.

Such a principle has now been discovered. It is one which reconciles the newly established autonomy of the cell with the old conviction that values could not be biologically immoral, and it supplies an alternative explanation of evolution, to take the place of natural selection — a real inner urge instead of an outer inhibition.

6. AWARENESS IS THE PRINCIPLE OF EVOLUTION

That principle may be called awareness. The growth of consciousness may be asserted to be the method and aim of evolution. How this principle has worked may perhaps best be illustrated by Dr. Robert Broom's thesis set out in his essay on Evolution called 'The Coming of Man'. There he shows that when we consider the whole process of evolution, as now known to us, certain principles become clear. Life starts in the sea. There it attains to an extraordinary efficiency. The fishes give rise to types which are so successful (such for instance as the sharks) that they have lasted on unchanged until to-day. The path of ascending evolution did not however lie in this direction. In Evolution Dr. Inge's aphorism is probably always right. 'Nothing fails likes success.' A creature which has become perfectly adapted to its environment, an animal whose whole capacity and vital force is concentrated and expended in succeeding here and now, has nothing left over with which to respond to any radical change. Age by age it becomes more perfectly economical in the way its entire resources meet exactly its current and customary opportunities. In the end it can do all that is necessary to survive without any conscious striving or unadapted movement. It can therefore beat all competitors in the special field but equally on the other hand should that field change it must become extinct. It is this success of efficiency which seems to account for the extinction of an enormous number of species. Climatic conditions altered. They had used up all their resources of vital energy in adapting to things as they were. Like unwise virgins they had no oil left over for further adaptations. They were committed, could not readjust and so they vanished.

7. THE ASCENT OF LIFE THROUGH KEEPING SENSITIVE

If then we are to find out the path of Evolution we have to look for some species which never became such a success, for it is such a species which would always have in hand a balance of unused energy and capacity for change. As we can only study form, and generally only skeleton, in the evolutionary record we have to look for a structure which retained unspecialized certain fundamental features which coming down from the earliest times have been preserved to-day in the highest forms of life as its distinctive instruments of expression.

We are here only examining the record of the vertebrates for it is out of that line that man has arisen. At the level when life was confined to the sea and the fishes were developing, they threw up forms which evolved a spine and so represented the vertebrates in the highest form then evolved. From the spine there spread out on each side, to aid the head, that fan of feelers which in them became the fore-fins. In the shark, and almost all the fish, these feelers were specialized so as to become no longer feelers but paddles, amazingly efficient flukes for bringing the creature headforemost on its prey. Rapid reaction was everything, patient negotiation nothing, and these flukes not only ceased to be testers, explorers, examiners: they became increasingly efficient for water movement and for nothing else. It looks as though pre-piscan pre-vertebrate life must have lived in warm shallow pools and perhaps always have been in touch with the floor, as to-day the gurnet by its feelers keeps contact with the solid bed. Once, however, swift unpremeditated movement became everything, specialization drove the fishes out into water where they lost touch with the bottom and all solids; and water, which till then had been really no more than a bearing or lubricant to carry them over the solid surface which they were constantly exploring, water then became their only element. This meant their power of being stimulated by new circumstances was greatly limited for they were becoming, as afterwards the birds became, creatures who have gained movement at the expense of incident and, unlike the birds, domestic ties did not bring any (but such oddities as the sticklebat) home to roost.

That type of fish, then, which gave rise to the next advancing order of animals, must have been a creature which did not adopt this extreme specialization of the fin. For, first, it must have been a creature which kept in touch with the floor and so remained more variously stimulated, than the fishes which lost touch with a solid environment. And, secondly, it must have been a creature which for the same reason kept in touch with the shallows and kept this touch by means of fore-limbs, which, because they could not therefore become wholly specialized, as water-driving flukes, retained a more generalized, 'inefficient', exploratory and tenta-tive character. The skeleton of such a creature has been discovered, a creature whose forelimbs are, it might almost be said, rather clumsy hands than proper fins and through these members it looks as though the transition from shallow pool to flooded shore was made, the deep sea was left behind, the land was invaded and the amphibians arrived.

In this transition we can also recognize the working out of other details of the principle of evolution which will be noted repeating themselves at the succeeding similar great steps in the ascent of Life. The creature which effects the transition is itself transitional. It has retained an unspecialized structure and when the time comes it attempts what we may call an anabolic effort while the efficient types go in a catabolic direction. It takes to the land, where stimulant, difficulties, dangers, and, apparently, handicaps will all be immensely increased while the fish push out to sea where conditions will be easier and smaller effort will lead to increased movement. It makes the transition and then disappears. The type seems to have itself become extinct or perhaps it would be more accurate to say that because of its power of adaptation to alien conditions this type changed still more rapidly when it established itself on land and in consequence was taken up in, assumed, transformed in some still more progressive species.

What is certain is that once the transition from fish to amphibian is made, the door of opportunity seems closed. Never again does any fish give rise to an amphibian, though, as Dr. Broom has pointed out, there has been time enough for all the other higher types of life to appear. Twice more is this tremendous step taken and a creature representing one way of life manages to pass over into a completely different form and function. As an inefficient fish, which had retained generalized factors and capacities, gave rise to an amphibian; so too an inefficient amphibian, which in its turn had clung to the capacity for a wider awareness at the price of poorer immediate success, gave rise to the reptile. In its turn a reptile of the same capacity gave rise to the first mammal.

From this simple large-scale pattern it is then clear that we can discover something about the evolutionary urge and fill the gap left, in the effort to explain ascent of Life, when Natural Selection had to be discarded.

The creature which ascends is a creature which somehow chooses sensitiveness, awareness, a constantly widening focus and new experiences which it cannot master, rather than preparedness, narrowed purposiveness, an outlook which only sees what it can use and an environment in which it can express ever more exactly its particular powers of action.

When we come to the transition which particularly interests us — from the reptile to the mammal, our own great division of life — these principles become with every new palaeontological find more vividly illustrated (*see* Dr. Swinton's *The Dinosaurs*). First we discovered that the giant reptiles were themselves hopelessly decadent before the rise of the mammals. There was no hope any longer for this great third step in Life's advance. They had begun small, mobile and lively creatures. They grew so vast that these land ironclads could scarcely move and many had to remain all their time awash in pools where water would bear some of their otherwise crushing weight. All their energy seems to have gone into their bodies and their brains remained practically non-existent, in many cases the spinal column hardly enlarging when it entered the skull. Their heads were no more than periscopes, breathing tubes and pincers.

Meanwhile as they slowly swelled and hardened up to their doom — until it seems with such a genus, for example, as Triceratops, bone growth went on of itself, a huge degenerative accumulation of rigid tissue — there was already being fashioned that creature which was to leap the boundary and limits then set for life and start a new stage of energy and consciousness. And nothing could illustrate more vividly the principle that life evolves by sensitiveness and awareness, by being exposed not by being protected, by nakedness not by strength, by smallness not by size.

71

The forerunners of the mammals have now been discovered in the Cretaceous, the age which ends the age of the reptiles. These transitional types are minute rat-like creatures. In a world dominated by monsters the future is given to a creature which has to spend its time taking notice of others and giving way to others. It is undefended, given fur instead of scales. It is unspecialized, given again those sensitive feeling fore-limbs and, no doubt, those antennae, the long hairs on the face and head, to give it irritating stimulation all the time. Ears and eyes are highly developed. It becomes warm-blooded so it may be constantly con-scious throughout the cold when the reptile falls into anaesthetic coma, kept alive in discomfort that it may be constantly taking in, and its consciousness, in the end, may have to go on comparing conditions it remembers enjoying with those it now endures. So its consciousness is blown upon and developed. The varied continuous stimulant is reacted to with varied answer because the creature being unprecedented is capable not of one but of many replies, none of which can settle the question for it.

Here then we have the sensitive shoot, 'the tender plant out of a dry ground' from which we are sprung.

We can then conclude this brief illustration of the newly recognized evolutionary principle — intensify-ing sensitiveness, awareness and consciousness — with the rise of the mammals to complete dominance.

There seems now to be agreement among palae-ontologists, comparative anatomists and embryologists that the proto-mammals must have resembled some rat-like creature but a creature possessed of something more than the sensitiveness and agility of the rat and mouse family. The animal which is considered the most probable approximation to the creature who won against all the immense saurians and gave rise to all the mighty and dominant forms into which the mammals developed — not only to the elephant and the mammoth but also the 25 feet high Baluchitherium, horse, camel and giraffe, lion, tiger, boar, wolf, cat, dog, ape, and man — the proud ancestor of so many mighty breeds was a Tree Shrew.[1] This little animal has only one thing in its favour as a successful competitor in the struggle to survive — it is undifferentiated, unspecialized, and so more widely sensitive and uncommitted than any other animal. Yet, had any human intelligence been permitted to look down with comprehensive vision upon the whole scene of life as the vast Middle Period closed and Life itself seemed turning to defeat; as the saurians — Life's triumph of that period — sank into decadence, disuetude and death — could any mind of man have pointed out where the new hope lay, and have dared imagine that out of a small timid scurrying creature in the tree tops there would be raised up first a new order of beings and then on the crest of this tremendous array at last the being who would begin to understand?

Creation behaved as the legionaries when Gaius was murdered; our stock found itself like the poor Claudius who having fled into hiding found himself dragged out not to death but on to the very throne before which he had quailed. The tree shrew won because it was a creature of response, with feeling hand and

[1] An Insectivore of the Tupaioidae. See PROF. LE GROS CLARK, *Early Forerunners of Man*, p. 222.

73

sensitive face. Its one point was that of all animals it was most aware. That was all it could claim, but such a claim was valid and raised it to the throne of life. Such is the supreme importance of feeling.

8. THE DIFFICULTY OF KEEPING AWARE WHEN SUCCESSFUL

Yet once the mammal stock, through this ancestor, who was nearly all potentiality and hardly at all in actuality, had come into power and had the world as its inheritance, it too behaved as all life before. It 'waxed fat and kicked'; it sold its primal sensitiveness for specialized efficiency which should yield it the comforts of power, protection and plenty; and once again the real Natural Selection, the test of feeling and awareness had to be applied. Once again choice had to be made of a creature who had as yet enjoyed nothing, had carved out for itself no kingdom, who was master and authority in no sphere.

As it is at this point that the story of unconscious Life's third stage closes and we come to the foot of that particular gradient which will lead to self-consciousness, to man, this chapter must end. We have seen that Natural History so far discloses a constant remarkable process. The real line of ascent runs from helpless amoeba to timid tree shrew. At each stage we can form some idea of the potential power residing in the sensitive exploratory point of progress, by looking at the mighty forms which, as soon as the potentiality loses its mobility and sensitiveness and precipitates into efficient form, appear at each distinctive stage.

In the Archaeozoic — Life's first great step — we have the rise of the monster fish — sharks more terrible than any to-day and even the harmless fishes throwing up giant forms. One of the latest finds of these is a mackerel six feet in length. In the great Middle Period of Life we have seen the rise of the prodigious saurians. Yet here again the creative power was, we see, shown not to be at full pressure but actually ebbing away as these impregnable forms added still further to their strength.

And once again in our own age — the age of our stock, the mammals, we see the same process repeated: the hands of the mighty find nothing: the monster form, which seems the throne of dominant authority and purpose, is not a throne but a prison, a mausoleum in which the spark of creative fire is choked and quenched. The history of our own great stage recapitulates in detail the sifting process which was carried out before on fish, amphibian and reptile. In this our third stage, as in the stages before, a small, sensitive, unspecialized form gives rise to an innumerable array of powerful and efficient genera and species who each establishes its authority and, within its field, becomes dominant. Then having won their particular kingdom and having spent all their inherent inventiveness, having specialized out irrevocably all their general capacity, having directed and concentrated all flexibility in certain restricted channels, they are perfected and are become living fossils. For the perfectly efficient is the perfectly finished. All finish is fatal to full life. It is the exchange into the faultless machine from faulty fertile vitality — an exchange which, obviously, hardly any living creature refuses when the choice is offered. It is the exchange of trial and error for unerring instinct; doubt and distress, uncertainty and tentativeness for conviction and dogma; the constant strain of knowing you do not know but must know, for the relaxation of believing you have at last found certainty, you are right and all the rest are wrong: the misgiving that you must go on never knowing when you will reach your goal, for the realization that you have arrived and are at last perfectly at home.

No wonder we, who so inevitably are drawn down through comfort and security to unreflecting instinct, sleep and death, found it hard to discover this hard lesson of Life. With what hope we may welcome the fact that, in spite of all our natural prejudices, the discovery has at last been made. Perhaps there could be no better surety that the creative force has not yet deserted our species and we may still be allowed to suffer, feel, become still further aware and so more creative and created.

Nor were the clues put plainly in our path. Searching for the way Life has actually advanced and what particular capacity and urge has driven it, it was all too easy to overlook the traces of the actual ascent, so faint they were. It was all too easy to think that mighty form must lead to mighty achievement, as Samuel assumed the elder robust sons of Jesse must be designated for the Crown of Israel.

Those bodies wherein the vital force has silted up most completely are the bodies which leave the vastest and most indestructible fossils. The saurians were so material that they left not only their bones but even sometimes their armoured skins. They were so little alive that when they died death could destroy little of them. They were almost fossils before they ceased to move. The minute creatures in which Life ran most fully and freely, not only were too nimble often to become bogged and entombed — a common and natural fate of the Saurians. When the fluttering leaf of their slight bodies fell to the ground it quickly withered away. The large eye perishes completely; the frond-like feeler, the shell-like ear last little longer; sensitive skin crumbles and the slender bones are easily crushed. The wind passes over it and it is gone and the place thereof knows it no more nor keeps any record of it.

So we see that the more vital a form is, the less we may hope to discover its record and impress. Life, when advancing most certainly and swiftly, treads almost as lightly as on air. It is only when it stumbles heavily down toward death that we cannot overlook its plodded spoor.

Yet in spite of the difficulty of tracing the authentic print of ascending life, in spite of the fact that that path, when we detect it, we find to be one of continual subordination, insignificance, risk, misgiving, nakedness, patience, it has been traced and confessed.

Natural History now recognizes certain principles which make our search more clear and life's method more defined. Two such may here be stated, one negative, the other positive:—(a) 'No giant ever gives rise to a giant'; a huge and dominant form is sure evidence that here is a shunt off the main line, a blind alley, a tip and rubbish dump, a creek where stagnant silt and scum have accumulated and heaped; (b) the direction of Evolution is marked by 'foetalization', by the advancing creature becoming not more specialized and efficient but more generalized, receptive, malleable, sensitive. The importance of the Foetalization principle will be brought out later (page 113), here it can only be mentioned.

With these principles and this path discovered, running from the first forms of life up to the threshold, from which man himself arose, we can now turn to this the latest chapter of Life's History. We have seen at this level there is laid a firm foundation for man's Natural History. We have seen that sub-human life and the way it has advanced shows that, though brutality and violence have dogged Life's ascent, far from stimulating it they have been forces of decay and death; threatening, ineffectively, those creatures which dared feel, suffer, experience and respond; paralysing and suffocating the very animals which fell back on such cowardly methods.

In short the lesson of all sub-human life is that the meek do inherit the earth and however many times the descendants of the meek become untrue to the nature they inherited and, losing vitality and nerve, specialize in defensive violence and parasitic cunning, Life will not be cheated of its purpose to bring forth a being who can understand because it dare feel. All the expert and ruthless specialists, because at heart they are frightened and want security, safety, comfort, insensitiveness, are let choose their downward path, are let spend their precious birthright of doubt, misgiving, pain, uncertainty and wonder, on knowing how to answer and silence their immediate problem and distress. For the day they succeed; and those who would not defend and resent seem their natural prey.

But Life turns the page and they are not found and what they thought to be their victim may reign in their stead — if only he will still wonder, suffer and realize that he must go on unprotected that he may be constantly changed.

CHAPTER II

THE NEW NATURAL HISTORY
OF MAN

Now that it seems clear that all Life has advanced only so far as it has retained sensitiveness, and that it has been destroyed when it lost that power of feeling and suffering, we can see how such a Natural History makes a Natural Philosophy and man's values show themselves to be no longer biologically immoral but a natural development of such a growing, essential power of feeling and finally of sympathy. Man has not to 'defy the cosmic process' — certainly a hopeless and biologically unsound procedure. His task is consciously to avoid losing his power of feeling and awareness, to keep on casting the skin of his mind and the callous on his emotions, to avoid the danger of safety and security and to dare, to dare, and yet again to dare to understand and sympathize.

In this chapter we have to trace the evidence which links up this Life process, carried on since Life appeared perhaps one thousand million years ago (the report of the Committee on the Measurement of Geological Time 1934 gives the Uranium-lead reading for Laurentian as being one thousand and forty million years) with our specifically human development and adventure. For it is still open to those who wish to prove that man must and can only advance by violence and cunning, to say that, though all unconscious Life, it is now clear, did advance by maintaining sensitiveness and developing awareness, yet man, because he is conscious, does and must go otherwise. For better or for worse he is the unnatural animal. True he is unarmed; but see he has made himself arms beside which the armanent of Saurian and carnivore mammal is innocent. This is suddenly to reverse the old naturalistic argument but we must be prepared for it. Undoubtedly, as the new evidence makes the old standpoint of excused brutality untenable, we shall have the forces of the reaction and decay falling back on this position.

And it is true man is undoubtedly faced with the possibility that the fate which overcame all fishes, all amphibians, which has overcome all mammals save him alone, will also engulf him. He may choose safety, security, comfort, defence. It will need a keen creative effort if he is not. Has he still left in him this power of fundamental daring or will he hide from himself his lack of nerve and so lose his destiny by pretending that he is brave and strong and so he must crush and shatter? What is clear is that this is the choice before him. He can see it now: he can choose. It also grows austerely, vastly clear that, as he chooses, may decide the fate not merely of his species but of all life. For this picture, of Life ascending by sensitiveness, has shown us that each time only one species got through and gave rise to a new stage of Life, a new intensity of consciousness. All the other rockets fired, but failing to cast their life-lines on to the cliff edge above, fell back toward the sea. As we view life to-day, in this lightning-flash moment of self-consciousness, what we see then is all fishes, all amphibians, all reptiles, all mammals, except man, no longer progressing.

The curve of their potentiality has ceased to rise. Some seem still to carry on without losing ground. Many are already diving toward the black sea of extinction. Only one still climbs — man. The whole huge battery of Life has already fired its shower of bolts; they have all spent the initial drive which might have carried them into a new order of being. Man alone is still on an upward trajectory.

I. WHAT WAS MAN'S ANCESTOR?

For the sake of discovering what our fate may be and of discovering what the purpose and meaning of Life may also be, we have then to see whether man has good reason to choose the painful way of becoming still further alive, aware, sensitive. The first question is, has man since he was singled out to be the supreme creature shown a growing specialization and an abandonment of the sensitiveness he inherited and because of which inheritance he was given Life's headship?

The answer here is far more hopeful than till lately Natural Historians thought possible. For until the principle, 'No giant can give rise to a giant' was recognized it was maintained that man arose from a large and powerful ape. Looking for actual apes which might represent such an ancestor, man came on the gorilla, the orang and the chimpanzee. Obviously the gorilla was close to man in structure and the reports of his monstrous strength and ferocity confirmed the belief, natural when struggle and cunning were assumed to be the directive factors in Evolution, that here we had a picture of primitive man. Let us settle then the greatest of the apes before we go on to the others and see on which side — on the side that man must have evolved by violence or by sensitiveness — the evidence adduced from it, inclines. First, we have seen the gorilla is a giant, often weighing as much as two men.[1] Secondly, it is as highly specialized as it is huge. This tells against it being an ancestral type as much as, perhaps more than, its size. Specialization is irreversible. Special features cannot again be remelted into indeterminate, general capacity. The die is cast; the choice made: 'Even the gods cannot recall their gifts.' The specialization of the gorilla is so advanced that the animal cannot be far off from extinction and indeed unless rigorous protection is extended to it, it will become extinct in this century. In almost every important particular it is fatally limited by specialization and even while still in the womb the foetal gorilla begins to grow decadent. Before it is born it has begun to lose generalized character. The foetus at one stage resembled roughly the human foetus. Then as birth approaches the hand becomes more hook-like, the brain is compressed as a keel of bone forms along the skull and on this keel are attached the huge muscles to work the heavily fanged muzzle that is sprouting from the face.

The gorilla then is no ancestor of ours, but a parallel line showing not what we were but perhaps what fate may be in store for us if we fail to retain our sensitivity. Yet even the gorilla, slowly being strangled in his timid adaptations, is not the monster we supposed. In him, too, we see that the choice of force and violence is always a choice prompted by a fundamental timidity

[1] The ten-year-old gorilla in the Berlin Zoo weighed 37½ st.

or failure of nerve. It is now known that the gorilla
is really no more savage than any other anchylosed
creature — man or beast. It has been proved that it is
only dangerous with the negroes who want to attack
it for its flesh and is quite harmless with the much
weaker pigmies whom it can realize have no wish to
molest it. Because of this fact whites wishing to study
gorillas are now instructed to take pigmies as guides —
for their own safety and that of the animals.[1]

The orang and the chimpanzee are equally highly
specialized, equally advanced variants of a basic type
which in man alone has kept unspecialized undifferentiated. And what embryology argues, palaeontology
sustains. From the Siwalik Hills in India, from the
Nile delta, and from Bechuanaland in South Africa
have come the fossils of many extinct types of apes
and several of these such as Australopithecus, Siva-
pithecus and Dryopithecus, more lately again such
new finds as Ramapithecus and Sugrivapithecus from
the Himalayan foot hills (see report of Yale North
Indian Expedition 1934) are more advanced than
any ape to-day. Sugrivapithecus has a jaw with well-
developed chin, a feature lacking in all surviving apes,
and Australopithecus has a brain case much superior
to that of any other ape.

It is clear then that man arises from no ape. He
and the apes have perhaps a common ancestor. How
far back must we go to find the place and the type
from which branched ape and man?

The monkey, it has been long recognized, cannot
serve as that junction for it too, though not a giant,

---

[1] The Berlin gorilla also only seems dangerous because it is so timid,
always construing every approach as attack.

is highly specialized — neither the old world monkeys nor those far lower, smaller and probably more primitive types, the new-world monkeys, such as the marmoset, can then be ancestral to man. Not only are ape and monkey specialized but fossil evidence shows that they attained to this pitch of specialization so long ago that no junction can be made with a pre-human stock until both types have been traced back to a degree of generalization where all specific simian characteristics have yet to appear.

2. THE ANCESTRAL TYPE WE HAVE TO FIND

In our search then into man's past, to discover what features and expressing what temperament his original nature may have shown, we have then to search for a creature which will be smaller than the apes and less specialized than the monkeys. Before attempting to follow further that clue it is perhaps necessary for us to remind ourselves that even at the stage the inquiry has now reached the evidence tends to support the belief that in man's earliest ancestry, as in all life that advanced, it was sensitiveness and receptivity, not strength, pugnacity and formidable-ness, that gave him power of progress and, in the end, supreme success. For we have seen even the great apes, far sunk in specialization and decadence as they are, are not ferocious; only tending to become as they age, suspicious and 'crusty'.

Even the gorilla, which has specialized in strength, is not offensive. And if we consider as a whole the primates as distinct from all other animals, it is clear from their equipment that apes and monkeys are creatures which have preferred to be more generalized than specialized. Their hands with their small nails, useful as forceps, useless as knives, are the most striking evidence of that. Their binocular vision — and incidentally the fovea of the eye and its large equipment of cones as wells as rods — also shows a power of taking interest in a larger world than that immediately referable to appetite. In some degree they can all take a general interest.

Even the marmoset, which has claws, uses these it would seem not for offence, but as 'scaling irons' to permit so small a creature to scale trees and branches on the boles of which so minute an arm could get no purchase. And as far as the emotional nature of this poor little clawed primitive is concerned we fortunately know that, though the mind may be very limited, the emotional life is highly developed, these creatures generally dying if kept separate in captivity unless their keeper can show them constant affection.

We may then perhaps add to our description of the missing-link as a creature small, unspecialized and sensitive, the additional item that it was probably capable of considerable affection and needed both to give and to receive this opposite of violence if it was to live to its full capacity.

With this general description in hand we may begin to search for animals which may approximate to it.

There is one small ape which can act as a guide, if he himself cannot lead us right to the spot where our main line passed on its way up to our present unsteady station. That is the gibbon. Where gorilla, orang and chimpanzee all have to be dismissed as lines that long ago sloped away from the main gradient of ascent, the gibbon may be held as more conservative. He may have stayed on, not advancing but not descending, still loitering within a short distance of the junction when ape went on and down and man went on and up. For the gibbon has many significant features about him. To start from his feet, he really walks like man. All the other apes slouch and shamble. Their weight is too much for the bones of their feet and this, as Professor Le Gros Clark[1] has pointed out, is an important piece of particular evidence indicating that man attained his 'ortho-grade' and fully upright stature while he was still a smaller and a less specialized form than that of any of the Great Apes.

The gibbon is then an obvious rough model on which to try and reconstruct the form of man's ancestor at the time when he and the ancestors of the Great Apes all were still 'in for the competition' as to which could (which, through some profound uncon-scious vitality, and courage, would) dare longest, and against all temptations of danger, comfort and power to remain unspecialized, alert, sensitive.

For besides its carriage the gibbon also has two other gifts which the great apes and monkeys lack — it is friendly and also has a real delight in making sounds; it chants and yodels for the love of playing on the air. These two psychological factors are of great importance. For the great apes not only very

---

[1] *Early Forerunners of Man*, p. 138, PROFESSOR W. E. LE GROS CLARK. 'The evidence of foot structure which very convincingly indicates that the forerunners of the Hominidae diverged from the forerunners of the large anthropoid apes at a point in Evolutionary time when the common ancestor had not exceeded the body size of the Gibbon.'

seldom make any sound except under emotional stress; they seem to have no interest in the range of sound.[1] It has frequently been pointed out that a human child is ready for talk because of its love of pure sound and vocalization. The gibbon possesses this. The gibbon, however, as it is, is not at the junction through which went the line of human ascent. For in one outstanding particular the gibbon is intensely specialized — in its long arms. When it runs it has to hold these half-flexed, half-extended to get these great grapples out of the way and not trip over them.

We must then, in reconstructing our ancestor when he had shrunk back to gibbon-stature, think of a creature walking upright, perhaps a couple of feet in height, with arms and hands much as ours, with short muzzle and well-aligned eyes, and in character, curious, friendly, adventurous, social and already enjoying his choruses and arias.

Strange to say such a society has lately been discovered still further down the tree of life — the new-world Howler Monkeys, long known to be socially minded and given to tremendous glees. Study of them (by Dr. C. R. Carpenter, of Yale) has revealed that though they are a primitive type of monkey they have not only the rudiments of a language, no less than nine voice sounds already having been found current among them, but their social state deserves the name co-operative as they do not fight each other, have no 'old man' dominating them and do not desert either the injured or the old.

---

[1] DR. KÖLHER's, DR. KLUVER's and DR. YERKES' numerous psychological studies of apes and the DRS. KELLOG on their study, *The Ape and the Child*.

To return to the search for our line of ascent, we see that, with growing certainty, it can be plotted, passing up through a small, two-foot high creature, slender, agile, sensitive, with what we should call human, if manikin, features.

Indeed the more we try and focus on this ancestor, the clearer it seems to be that as he had to be unspecialized and we have retained that unspecialization, the difference between him and us turns physically mainly on size and psychologically on mental capacity. Emotionally and physically he was a model of us, intellectually he was probably a rudiment though of what degree of simplicity we can never be sure.

3. THE SENSITIVE WHO ENDURES

And behind that? First we must remind ourselves how far we have already gone back. The gibbon type it would seem, the unspecialized gibbon whose successful children we are, while the unsuccessful ones are the gibbon of to-day, goes back to the Eocene — the dawn-age of the mammals when all of them arose from the unspecialized insectivore. Now quite apart from the immense time that this must mean — some fifty million years ago — if our unspecialized gibbon- or manikin-ancestor is Eocene two further remarkable and even startling facts have to be faced. Our unspecializing stock instead of being a creature of a moment, a sudden fine outbreak of delicate nobility rising out of the mud of violence and flowering in the face of a hostile universe, a creature whose very fineness proves that it cannot last and must be marked for swift destruction (unless it will climb down and fight, as all must, to live), this creature which seemed the destined victim of any brute, has in point of fact outlasted them all and preserved unchanged his impossible sensitiveness, while they have tried every shift and change to survive and most of them are already extinct. It is he who is master to-day, and the bull, the tiger, the boar live at his pleasure and because he delights to preserve his crippled fellows. In that is the real significance of our way of survival and theirs — of all the other mammals. And it is that which brings us to the second fact which our unsuspected antiquity reveals.

We are as old as all the other mammals. In that Eocene — the dawn age of the mammal period when Life started its third vast experiment — once again (as we have seen) the new order was to be derived from a small generalized sensitive creature. This ancestor of all of us mammals was what we each are, if from us was taken our stature and every expert specialization and feature of mind and body. Reducing us to a common being we get this tree-shrew, half squirrel, half rat, handy, alert, responsive.

Then, the field open to mammalian life (because of its wonderful efficiency when faced by the sluggish reptile, the water-bound fish and the handless bird and the instinct-shackled insect), mammalian life began to exploit its vast inheritance. The better to carve out Kingdoms — as we have seen — the irreplaceable birthright of generalized structure was sold right and left. On one side was the snare of speed, the trap set for the growing hand by the hoof. Here fell the Ungulates. The horse, wishing for speed, sacrificed one after another of its digits, growing in size and strength and power of exultant speed but fatally tied to the Earth which, could it have thought, it could not but have imagined it had spurned beneath its hoofs. So, too, all the oxen. The hand, precious guide, true 'Hand of Glory' whereby, up the dark stairs of life, we may grope and reach and draw ourselves to even higher stations, the hand, the essential minister and staff of the advancing brain,[1] was bound in the shackles of the hoof. On the other hand the other 'superordinal division of mammals' the Unguiculates, those who chose the specialization of claw instead of hoof, made as evil a choice, selling the birthright for a sorrier pottage. For though the hand was not quite so crippled as in the hoof, the claws made it a weapon, no longer a universal instrument. And the mind so served, caught in a vicious circle, dwelt more on prey and violence and, spreading fear all around itself, became a creature increasingly narrowed in savagery and fearfulness.

Hence every one of the mammals might have attained to self-conscious intelligence, but none, save man, could cling to the essential unspecializing sensitiveness without which that width and intensity of intelligence could never be reached. Every other mammal has descended by constant shifts of specialization down from its primal weakness and creative freedom to its present efficiency, strength and evolutionary impotence. They are all imprisoned in their expert power. Man alone remains with full feeling and so with the future. Man alone remains physically no more armoured than when he began, and so, because in himself he is helpless, and as a child repeats

[1] The many studies of SIR GRAFTON ELLIOT SMITH on this subject have made this connection clear for all time.

each life his utter receptivity and defencelessness, thus he does homage to the supreme principle of Life, and so long as he offers this fealty, to him is given the heirship of the world and the vicegerency over all his fellow creatures. All the strong animals are literally crippled by their specialization and tied as captives to their particular way of life.

Man may preserve them but even he probably will never be able to unlock those bonds and free them from the servitude of the addict into which they have fallen body and mind.[1]

Between this humanoid manikin, this unspecialized gibbon creature and that ancestor of all the mammals, the tree-shrew creature, lies of course a great maintenance — a great effort at continuous retention — of the

[1] There is, however, one example of the power of affection (emotional symbiosis) to make such a tie between man and animal so that the carnivore actually recovers something of its primal unspecialization and flexibility. This is the case of the dog which it has been shown is the foetalization of the wolf. Step by step as the dog came to depend no longer on its lupine habit of parasitism on vegetarian animals, its structure has been modified in a foetal direction. The wolf-dog, the shepherd's guard, is still near the wolf. A number of reductions can be and have been made until the highly specialized carnivore muzzle is wholly reduced, the skull correspondingly released, from the cramping musculature such a jaw requires, the forehead and the brain develop, and a type is produced of which the Pomeranian, the smaller spaniels and the Pekinese are gradual examples, wherein the head has adopted a foetal character retained into full life — a character of flexibility and unspecialization which the wolf has in the womb but which it loses before birth. Such an animal can live on a vegetarian diet and adapt its life completely to the complex and varied conditions which it shares with its companion man. It also recovers psychological flexibility being able to direct to human beings in the form of affection – i.e. varied emotional response – the emotional urge which in pack-hunting animals is specialized and restricted to spontaneous reaction with the pack. It has often been noted by naturalists that though a unit of a pack may show great distress (indeed Köhler noticed the same thing with his chimpanzees) when separated from the pack, there is practically nothing that could be called affection – a positive resourceful and varied response and reciprocation. For the pack shows no corresponding distress at the excommunicate member's misery and, more, as soon as he can reach the others his misery vanishes but no positive expression seems to take its place. Affection at that stage is negative. It merely becomes conscious as a want and vanishes on satisfaction. It does not lead to more varied and continuous experiences.

balance of generalization. At each earlier epoch the stature is less until we reach a proto-mammal form not larger than that of a dwarf squirrel. This creature must, we see, have been as unspecialized psychicly as physically, as widely sensitive emotionally as it was generalized in its bodily structure.

Into that immensely deep shaft of backward time one window seems to open as we peer. One creature to-day seems to show us what the intermediate form may have been between the proto-undifferentiated mammal and the manikin. We can find a midget form to put as a link between the two others. That is the famous Spectral Tarsius. This creature is the sole survivor of an order of mammals which fossil remains seem to show much resembled its present form in the early Eocene, the dawn of the mammal age. It still remains, with few striking specializations. The most evident of these are the eyes. It has become nocturnal (a retreat from the full pressure of living) and so has evolved immense 'gig-lamp' eyes for night seeing. The hands, too, have specialized a little, probably. The finger tips have become flattened to such an extent as to make them look like discs. This of course is an evolutionary trend opposite to that taken by all the other mammals — save the primates — which, as we have seen, have all tended to narrow the digits into claw or hoof, not to splay them.

If then we reduce these specializations we are left with a midget — (it can crouch comfortably in the human hand and with its hands hold on firmly to the massive pallisade made for it by our Brobdingnagian fingers) — curiously human, but in height hardly a foot, if it stood upright.

The question of carriage is of course important. As it is specialized to-day, it crouches with flexed thighs in the branches on to which it holds with its hands, while it searches for its food. The thigh and leg however are more favourable to the development of upright walking should the creature have come to the ground. With our present knowledge we cannot be sure whether this particular stock ever returned to earth (after the tree-shrew ancestor of us all left earth and had taken to the trees) or whether it has remained aloft with no more than the anatomical promise that it could make good would it dare to come down into the full battle.

What however the evidence at present accumulated does seem to show is that here, if we can re-generalize the structure of this little creature, as the evolutionary principle shows we should, we have the scale and general outline of 'mid-Eocene man'. What we have to look for — should the fossil record ever grant it us — is in this period (some forty or forty-five million years ago) a being who may or may not have left the trees but who in any case probably often sallied out into the open, prompted by curiosity and adventure, if he had to scamper back home and scramble up again into safety.

One further point, but one of the utmost importance to our inquiry, can be learnt from study of the tarsier. That is about temper. The gibbon type we saw is more friendly than the other larger apes and has social possibilities not only in its vocal capacities but also in its emotional nature. The tarsier is far more timid. But here again we see that the primal capacity is sensitiveness — not violence and cunning. Of course a toy creature clinging to the tree tops could never be an awe-inspiring beast. But it is more significant to learn that its temperament confirms the direction of advance imposed on it by its physique. The tarsier is so sensitive that up to the present no one has succeeded in keeping it alive in captivity though kept in its own country — Malaya — and supplied with its proper diet and physical conditions. We have seen with that proto-monkey, the marmoset, what care has to be taken if its emotional needs are not to be starved and it die in captivity — the death of its mate nearly always being followed by the death of the companion should no other form of affection be substituted.

The same seems to be true of the tarsier: it too must have psychological as well as physiological care and this is due to the fact that its principal psychological faculty is sensitiveness.

4. WHY LIFE HAS SO MUCH VIOLENCE: BECAUSE ALL BUT ONE STRAIN ARE DYING

We have then answered the second question of our inquiry. The first was what is the principle which has driven Life throughout its evolution and has made it progress? That principle was found to be the retention of generalization, the avoidance of specialization: and this retention of the open door and avoidance of shackling has it seems been effected, and was only able to be effected, by sensitiveness. To feel rather than to impose, to be aware of as much as possible, not to know just and only what you want and concentrate wholly on getting it, this seems the way of Life and here seems the choice every living creature has through all time to make and go on making.

This is not to say the World is really filled with types so striving and doing. On the contrary. Sooner or later almost all fail. The impulse to go on tires and they retreat. This is the true Natural Selection: only one thread, one nerve of life has gone on growing in capacity. All the rest have shrunk, withered and hardened into death.[1] It is their death agonies and convulsions that devastate the world and drag down all but the most vital in their train, into counter-violence and destruction. The world, then, is far more full of anachronisms and atavisms than of those who are fully alive and are able to grow to their full capacity and to whom therefore the future belongs because they alone are not afraid to understand, feel, suffer. The world therefore at first sight looks a place given over to the tough, the callous, the violent and the crafty. That is the hasty view which assumes the battle is to the strong, the race to the swift. Evolution, the Natural History of Life, at first glance seemed to confirm that conclusion. Now it reverses it. Violence is always fundamental cowardice and therefore a confession of defeat. The creature who lives by attack, and even the creature who concentrates on defence, both are already doomed by their own actions to the fate which they falsely imagined they alone and only by their violence, could escape.

The first question so answered, as to Life in general, it was not likely that Life's final product man would

[1] cf. 'Every created thing when it is alive is supple and soft but becomes brittle and dry when dead.' Tao Tê Ching. WALEY's translation (*The Way and its Power*), Ch. LXXVI, p. 236.

prove to be an exception. And that second question the evidence has shown can also be answered as was the first. A common principle works in man as in Life at large. He is the resultant process yielded by the one and only mammal which dared retain its un-differentiated form, which is the expression of the primal sensitiveness and defencelessness. That seems now certain beyond any further attack on the part of those earlier students of evolution, who supremely, if unconsciously, anxious to show that the competitive chaos in which they lived — though it wounded their feelings — was natural, inevitable — had to pick the facts to show Life grew by violence and man must be the supreme expression of that violence.

How much further the discovery of our earliest ancestry may go no one can say. We have seen, one by one, all the powerful apes put aside, the monkeys, the lemurs. Even the tarsier is only a rough, and it may be an animalized, if not brutalized, decadent sketch of what the proto-man was at that dawn age of the mammals. We cannot avoid the conclusion that man is no newcomer. On the contrary he is, because of his unspecialization, far the most retentive of all the mammal forms. We cannot therefore rule out the rather startling conclusion that the man-type may have lasted right through the mammal age[1] keeping his precarious generalized condition, his undifferentiated form, through his sheer power of sensitiveness. The type-form of man would then run up, from reptile to fully human, through humanoid

---

[1] We should also note that the giant forms of mammal life quickly reached *their* goal. The Baluchitherium, largest land form, attained its development in the Eocene and soon became extinct. The Whales, the largest of all mammals and perhaps of all animals also, very early attained their goal.

tree-shrew — an animal with delicate hands, quick eyes, alert senses and gentle ways — given to affection and to play — through a foot-high midget, sallying out increasingly on the ground to explore, wonder and investigate, a creature curious and affectionate — on again through a two-foot manikin, mainly on the ground, always busy with eyes and hands, happy, in an endless curiosity about the vivid world around it, and in its group life with its fellows, to whom it was tied by its other dominant emotion, affection.

So man may well have climbed, increasing in power, with all its temptations — growth of physique, growth of society, growth of instruments — until at last he looked round and saw he alone was King — all the beasts only lived at his pleasure.

This chapter must however conclude, with this second point argued and the evidence shown: man — as all Life grows by sensitiveness and affection and dies through fear and callousness — man is no exception. He has become man and the supreme creature because he, too, in turn did as had done that one strain of Life, which achieved each earlier transition to a completely new and higher order and so made him possible. As it did, so did he, fulfilling it in full natural obedience. He dared go on feeling, responding and so entered a new kingdom of capacity and creativeness.

CHAPTER III

PRE-HISTORY

In this chapter we must make the transition from Natural History to physical human history, pre-cultural history, or pre-history as it is more generally called.

It is a difficult transition to make and further discoveries make it no more easy. For, first, we have seen man's pre-history completely overlaps the history of the mammals. Until lately we could cling to the old neat ascent of man. In that all too simple picture 'the Phylógenetic Tree' stood up, one fine bole, branched, perhaps, where the hoofed and the clawed, the Ungulates and the Unguiculates, thrust out, but running straight in the trunk which went up undeviating through dog-lemur, monkey, ape, to the final leader-shoot — man. If we want a chart of ascent to-day we are faced with something much more like a banyan-tree. Puzzle, find the trunk: for we trace out, running parallel, more and more genera, which we once thought successive. It is more confusing than attempting to sort out early Egyptian or Sumerian dynasties — so many lines which we thought were ancestral are really contemporaneous. Further and further back we go looking for the point of divergence. The stem becomes shorter and shorter. It almost seems to have reached ground level — the level at which we find the proto-mammal — and yet we have not brought in and convincingly bonded all the divergent branches in the one common stock.

And, of all these problems, man, who was thought to be the least difficult, because he must come latest and last, is now seen to have been completely misconceived. The last is first. The very fact that he is supremely generalized, supremely aware, means that he is fundamentally supremely unchanged and primal.

We have then to start with the hypothesis, the working probability that man is an immensely ancient type. More, we have also to assume that because he has been able to endure by means of his undifferentiation, he is a type which must always have shown great flexibility of behaviour. We know also that he is a gregarious animal. Add these two facts together — his freedom from instinct and his gregariousness — and how far back have we to go to find the beginnings of the social tie which takes the place of instinct — tradition?[1] When we add the further fact that it is sensitiveness, which becomes in a creature which has an inborn capacity for social relationships, affection, which is his main social tie, what form of society are we to expect in the immensely far past?

It is clear that those doctors who thought 'the myth of the Golden Age' was dead, signed the certificate prematurely. There was, it appears, a middle way between the dilemma — either an age in which all our powers were theirs, *quod est absurdum*, or the Hobbesian Solution, original human life must be 'poor, nasty, short, brutish'. Man, when an animal, may most likely have been an intelligent, happy, affectionate creature. The life of sensitiveness has not only the

[1] Tradition and teaching certainly can go below language level. Naturalists have noted how much the carnivores teach their young – cats if not taught to catch mice by the mother do not do so. Horses can teach their young to avoid wire: birds not only make the fledgling fly but teach it what to fear.

promise of the future, it can be most of the time more enjoyable than the various degrees of desperate conflict, paranoia and guiltiness which the offensive-defensive decadents all have to suffer. The Life of the callous and brutal may have a peace but only the peace of decline, the unconscious torpor in which the numbed lie.

I. THE CHARACTER OF PRIMITIVE MAN

We must then expect pre-history to carry on the two principles of natural history. The stock which is to succeed continually keeps sensitive. It is always curious about the outer physical world, always touched by the inner social world. Its consciousness is constantly developed by the reciprocation of that understanding which is the sympathy of the mind and that sympathy which is the understanding of the heart.

And, beside this one successful stock, are an immense number of others, all the other stocks which are being eliminated and which illustrate the second principle, that to specialize, to become callous and to shrink into violence is the path down which always the vast majority of creatures are being sifted to anachronism, atrophy, and extinction.

2. THE EVIDENCE OF MAN'S EARLY ORIGIN

Does pre-history, or the physiological history of man since he became full-scale man, sustain this thesis? Undoubtedly it does, and so startling was the evidence that for a considerable time it could not be accepted.

Indeed until evolutionists were able to split almost to the root that Phylogenetic Tree, it was not possible to fit in these fossil men. On the evolutionary record they were far too old; man turned up in the picture indecently soon. At first however the fossil men themselves did not present the main difficulty — indeed for a little while they seemed to make it on the whole less acute. The problem began when flint tools were found in geological formations which showed here was not merely a tool-using but a tool-shaping creature existing long before any orthodox evolutionists imagined any human being to have possibly existed.

A couple of examples will show the distress and consternation awoken. When Harrison found his 'dawn-tools', his eoliths, in Kent, authoritative opinion was almost unanimous in declaring that the whole collection was merely chance-fractured flints. Even when the successive strokes along the cutting edge made accident look far too like design, still the principle held — man could not be of the age which some of these stones (specimens found *in situ* in geological 'horizons' which left no doubt of their immensely ancient date) must be. Later when Reid Moir, following up this work in East Anglia, found many more such unmistakably fashioned flints, and gave the proof that they must come from deposits laid down in the early Pleistocene, an age then held to be long before the appearance of man, his competence to judge these horizons and even whether the flints had actually come from them was in turn long and stubbornly challenged. Dr. McAlister remarked that if such tools had been made intelligently and not accidentally then they must have been made by 'mermaids', or at the date presumed this land was under the sea. Nevertheless the discovery of hearths with stone tools scattered about them and the whole site sunk in deposits which showed the site must have been occupied by some tool-using and fire-making creature in the Pleistocene period — perhaps half a million years ago — left no further doubt that some man-like creature must have existed far further down the Phylogenetic Tree than had been deemed possible.

Still he may, indeed must, have been distinctly sub-human, that was the conservative belief. It was here that discoveries not of the tools but of the fossil bones of prehistoric man seemed to help. As far back as 1848 the Gibraltar Skull had been discovered and though not studied for a good many years it seemed clear here was a missing link, here was a creature half-ape half-man, and so exactly what the old notion of evolution required, that man arose from a brutal-ized form, clumsy and powerful. The Gibraltar Skull itself was that of a female. Soon however the typical skulls of this species were found, discovered at Nean-derthal and also at Spy in Belgium and Krapina in Jugo-Slavia. More, at le Moustier it was made clear that a special type of stone weapons made from big flakes of flint were made by this creature. It seemed that the whole puzzle of prehistory was about to prove quite simple; all the pieces fall into place; each distinctive fossil species fit neatly with a type of flint tool; species and tools show a progressive refinement; and so there would be provided every step, from the brutal slouching ape man up to the slender and refined homo sapiens, hence derived, and lately derived, from the brutal beast.

It certainly was clear that the Neolithic cultures, the small and efficient flint knives, many of them polished, were associated with the modern species of man. So the prehistorian climbed down the rungs which led to where those Pleistocene tools lay. He found the skeletons of the latter palaeolothic tool-makers. He correlated the Azilean craft with the Azilean skeleton, the Magdalenian Craft, the Solutrean and the Aurignacian crafts with skeleton remains. The physical type was changing a little but all these men with their different crafts were to be classed as modern, neoanthropic, the same species as man to-day. Then with the next lower craft, the Mousterian, came the distinctive species — the beetle-browed, muzzled, bent-legged Neanderthaler. Everything was going according to plan. For behind the Mousterian flints lay in geological and typological order, in order of age and of skill, the Acheulian cleavers made, not from a large flint flake, but from a whole nodule, and, behind these again, the Chellean tools, still more simple, pre-Chellean ruder still, and so back, with ever growing simplicity, to those 'dawn-stones', pebbles which have been given only a few flakes to make them yield a clumsy edge.

It seemed clear that alongside of these tools, to match them must be found at each stage the fossil bones of creatures increasingly more ape-like than the Neanderthal, as their workmanship was successively cruder than the Mousterian. This hope however was first deferred and now seems becoming increasingly fainter, until perhaps to-day we may post it as abandoned.

First, doubt was cast on Neandethal's relationship

with our species. Granted he was the ogre cave-man, which the old Natural Selection by violence seemed to postulate in our ascent, he could not claim to be that actual ancestor. He was highly specialized and his features, such as the huge distinctive brow ridges, marked him as a species set, like the gorilla, for extinction. He was at an end and would give rise to no more species. Nor, considering how late he lasted on, was there time for him to have done so and now perhaps no anthropologist would assume such an evolution possible.[1] It is also worth remarking that we have less evidence of his ferocity than we have of the gorilla's. His teeth were taurodontic, that is approximating to the milling teeth of vegetarian and graminivorous animals. It looks, then, as though he were not carnivorous.[2]

Secondly there has been a failure so far in Europe to find fossil types of men to match with the types of tools (Acheulian and Chellean) which precede those Mousterian tools used by Neanderthal man.

There have been found a few fossil skulls in earlier deposits than those in which are found the Neanderthal bones but these fossils have created far more difficulties than they have solved. In the first place none of them have as yet been found associated with the Acheulian or Chellean tools. In the second place nearly each fossil has presented peculiar difficulties of its own. The famous Piltdown skull and jaw is probably early Pleistocene. Skull and jaw probably

[1] Dr. Hrdlička was the last to maintain this.

[2] For vegetarianism as a factor in non-aggressiveness see Dr. Katz's work done at Rostock on the diet of children and the effect on character. The children chose their diet owing to what Dr. Katz believes are inherent tastes. The reflective had an inherent aversion from meat. The diet then tends to strengthen an inborn psycho-physical tendency.

belong to one another but the skull has been badly shattered and is capable of varying constructions from the far from complete number of fragments which remain and the jaw is as strongly simian as the skull itself seems to be human. Again it looks as though we were faced with no ancestor but an aberrant specialization which became extinct.

Indeed wherever we search among these fragments we seem to find the notice 'No road'. In fact when we get down to the Pleistocene we seem to find our genus doing in its turn what the apes probably did in the early Pliocene or late Miocene. Then, as we have seen, the apes gave rise to many large and advanced species some of which (proof that this was the apes' opportunity, at this point their tide flowed, and they missed it) were better brained than those few species which to-day hang on sinking into disuetude and waiting for extinction. Our turn seemed to have come in the late Pliocene or early Pleistocene. Then the hominidae, the mannish animals also produced many types of which Neanderthal was only one, perhaps, the-most-successful-but-one — ourselves. Then, the man-type shot its bolt, as the ape-type had in the period before it, and all the other mammals in earlier periods. What we view in the Pleistocene seems the carrying out in our own human stock of that final sifting which has always marked a supreme crisis in life. Here, something between a million and half a million years ago, was repeated on our human stock that testing and sifting which when life passed from fish to amphibian, from amphibian to reptile, from reptile to mammal, meant that all save one should choose toughness, facility, specialization and one, the one who alone should win, should choose new awareness, fresh sensitiveness, a wider receptivity.

Continually the fossils of such human variants are being found. The Pekin fossil men, dated at a million years old, possessed fire and could flake simple stone and bone tools. They have some Neanderthal features but are not as highly specialized as the full Neanderthal. It does not seem however that they are ancestral to modern man though they may be close to the main stem.

3. THE ANCIENTNESS OF MODERN MAN

Far more serious and indeed confusing was however such a skeleton as the Galley Hill man. It was found as long ago as 1888 in the 100-foot terrace of the Thames which terrace contains in places Chellean flint tools. Was this then the maker of these early tools? This skeleton was unfortunately removed from the gravel bed, in which it was found, before it had been examined by every authoritative expert who could question its authenticity, though it was viewed *in situ* by highly skilled geologists who maintained the skeleton had not been intruded. Also there was and is no doubt as to the age of these gravels. A consensus of opinion among authoritative experts however was much required because the skeleton was that of modern man and the gravels were Chellean. The question had to be settled, Was this an intrusion, a burial of some sort, or were the gravels and the man laid down together? As it was at that date so startling to find, or to imagine finding, a modern man in mid-

or early-Pleistocene circumstances, it was necessary such a find should be vouched for and its actuality put beyond question. As it was, the Galley Hill man went, and had to go, to a suspense account, where already was waiting such another seeming anomaly dug up even twenty years earlier in geologically similar terrace deposits at Clichy near Paris. They would weigh in for something when, if ever, any other confirmatory evidence of modern Pleistocene man should be forthcoming.[1]

Now in the last couple of years such evidence has begun to accumulate rapidly. It had long been suspected that homo sapiens, our own species, was not at home in this climate during the Ice Age. He had probably been here before, during the temperate and tropical conditions which preceded the cataclysm; and when the Ice-sheet withdrew, he certainly quickly returned. It was therefore obvious that search should be made in the south. The Sahara was long known to be plentifully sprinkled with stone tools of nearly every type.

That search, as every student of pre-history now knows, has been rewarded remarkably. Dr. Leakey near the Nyanzas in Central Africa has not only discovered in unbroken series the full tale of the successive stone tool types, he has also found associated with them skeletal remains and there seems no doubt that, as the finds at Galley Hill and Clichy suggested, the maker of the Acheulean and Chellean tools is not a creature more ape like than Neanderthal man but is our own species. When Dr. Leakey brought these

[1] Mention should also be made here of 'the Foxhall jaw', a mineralized fossil which was maintained to be modern and from early Pleistocene deposits but which was lost.

skull fragments to be examined by a competent committee of geologists, palaeontologists and anatomists, they agreed that with such evidence as he had put before them they must conclude not merely that Chellean tools were made by a modern type of man, our own species probably, but that this modern type seems to have been existing in the Pliocene, a million years ago. It has, then — if that is so — at least outlasted several species of mammals and kept its form while they changed theirs.[1]

This latter conclusion is for the moment not as unquestioned as it was, as one expert geologist sent out specifically to examine the sites has reported against accepting at present in full the conclusions Dr. Leakey drew. He is doubtful whether the geological ages attributed to the sites where the bones were found can be established, though the skull fragments themselves are undoubtedly of great age, because of their complete mineralization. However this controversy will conclude, it is anyhow clear that the case for supposing the maker of the first fully shaped flint tools was no ape-like creature but our own unspecialized species grows rapidly in strength.

This then is the picture of pre-history with which we are left to-day: our unspecialized type of man is traced running back beside all the submen or intermediate men, as we to-day exist contemporaneously with the surviving great apes. The intermediate men are not missing links. They are blind alleys. They are proofs of how often life fails. They are a warning we too may become extinct. They are all stages of

[1] This is important because an authority such as Sir Arthur Keith writes: 'Reject the geological evidence rather than believe the human body can remain unchanged for say 50,000 years.' *Nature*, May 4th, 1935, p. 705.

descent to that dead level to which at length they all came — extinction. All of them probably had a day when by their specialization they seemed more efficient to face things as they were, then and there, and so no doubt they felt more comfortable, natural and at home. If they had such feelings of security they were fatal. Probably they lost feeling more and more. What is certain is that they all perished and the creature that never quite fitted, that never felt wholly natural or comfortable — which had instead moments of incomprehensible hope — went on to complete supremacy.

We may then add the finding of Pre-History to the findings of the whole Natural History of Life and the findings of the particular natural history of our Class, the last great Class of Life, the Mammals. In each three cases we see the same sifting process at work. Many are called: all but one make the choice which seems to give efficiency, authority, security: one chooses to know rather than to shape, to wonder rather than to master, to feel rather than be safe. All the others are doomed; are first imprisoned and then entombed in their habitual success. One goes on to an unknown destiny, inconceivable even to itself, only allowed to know this, first by intuition and then by knowledge, that as long as it dare feel it will be let live and as long as it dare explore, and realize it does not understand, its vision shall grow.

CHAPTER IV

PROTO-HISTORY

WE start then the study of history with an understanding of the creature which has made it. This unique animal we have seen is nevertheless, though unique, not unnatural. His peculiarity, to which he owes his paramountcy, is that he has, latest and last and with a final perseverance when all the other animals deserted and declined, held to the specific quality of Life. That quality is the aliveness expressed by awareness, sensitiveness, curiosity, impressionability. His body is, as is natural, the materialization of these qualities. His brain, his eyes, his hands are all proofs of his generalized and receptive nature. His brain is 'the largest mass of unspecialized tissue in the body' yet it is his distinctive organ: it, if anything, is his specific specialization. His mental and visual centres have dominated and eclipsed such a centre as the olfactory — the centre of the short range sense of smell, and the sense most highly charged with emotion. Increasingly he takes in a wider world with which he is less and less passionately involved. His hands become increasingly universal joints of indefinite flexibility to which he fastens whatever particular extensions may serve an immediate purpose. Always he retains the primal undifferentiation brought to still greater flexibility.

I. MAN'S DUCTLESS GLANDS PREPARE
HIM FOR PEACE AND TO BE
CIVILIZED

This has now been realized for some time. Only lately however has the study of the ductless glands given further proof in favour of man's receptive, against the earlier assumption of his violent, nature. This is all the more important because the ductless glands, it is agreed, make the secretions which influence and, at animal level, tend to shape the emotions. Indeed so far has the linkage of gland and its secretion with temper and its expression now gone, that the suprarenal glands are often called the glands of conflict. For the secretion, adrenalin, undoubtedly not only makes the body ready for struggle — by increasing the normal pressure of energy and making the blood (against possible lesion by wounds) inclined to clot more quickly when exposed to air — it also makes the mood one of high irritability and increasing emotional defiance. The creature charged with adrenalin is charged like a mine and the slightest outer stimulus may throw it into that state of rage Homer describes when he speaks of the 'Anger which rises in a man's mind like smoke' (smoke stinging, lurid, blinding) 'and is sweeter in his mouth than honey'. It is worth then inquiring what animals show these glands to be highly, dominantly developed within the endocrine system, the linked series of all the ductless glands. It is found that those with dominant suprarenals are the carnivores — those highly specialized mammals which have become completely parasitic on other mammals. Man, on the other hand, is found to have an endocrine system which tends to be dominated not by the suprarenals but by the thyroid, the gland not of the sudden spurt, the spring, the hit-back but of sustained effort, of foresight, then, of endurance, patience and receptivity.

2. HE IS FURTHER STRIPPED FOR ADVANCE

Man is then endocrinely attuned and physically equipped for the part which Life calls on him to play: to retain still the primal awareness and to extend even further his capacity to explore and to be impressed. Nor is that all: there is one more fact lately discovered about his nature which is of even greater significance for the light which it throws on the way of his ascent and the prospect of his future. That is the principle of Foetalization, a principle which we have seen is present as a character essential to progress at any stage of Life's advance (see page 78). Man has not merely tended to retain a certain primal flexibility, awareness, sensitiveness. He has done and had to do more, if he was both to go on and yet avoid the fatal commitments and specialization which ensnared all other forms of life, his fellow mammals, his fellow primates, his fellow anthropoids and the hominidae as well. He had to find some way of casting his nature as it became too rigid, as a snake casts its skin. He had to find some way of being born again. It was not enough for him just to keep countering decline — then he would have stayed a tree-shrew, perhaps outlasting all the other animals but in the end to perish also and never to give rise to a new order and way of living. It was not enough for him just to manage to avoid entanglements, to keep his poise. As the Red Queen said to Alice, 'Really to keep your place you have to keep on running as fast as you can'. Really to avoid becoming gradually, imperceptibly ceremented by custom and efficiency, the creature which would live must constantly be unwinding the gossamer clinging shroud which its own effectiveness continually, like an autotoxin excretion, throws out on itself, to harden if left into the rigid shell of its sarcophagus.

Man's success because it is so great is, of course, his greatest peril. 'Power always corrupts, absolute power absolutely corrupts' ruled Lord Acton, perhaps the wisest of historians. Man the sensitive, the easily impressed, has to-day power of imposition, no species calloused and brutal ever had. He has to take the utmost care that he does not become so impressed with his power that he forgets it has come to him only through his sensitiveness, and so he, too, fall into the snare in which all other life is now trapped and become imprisoned and finally entombed in his own too effective force, too expert power.

But can he hope to escape this which seems the inevitable fate of everything which has lived? Must not success lead to the inescapable failure which completes it?

Whether he will or no, it seems clear that, now he has reached the stage of self-consciousness, he will be able to choose deliberately which thing he will do. For he has not only been kept flexible: the coil of circumstance has been stripped from him, the anchylosing by-products of success have been, astoundingly, eliminated from his system. 'It is manifest that in his evolutionary progress man has tended to acquire and preserve states which appear at first as transient conditions in foetal or infantile stages.[1] There has then been present in man a definitely progressive movement whereby not only has he avoided the paralysing danger of a perfectly inherited set of instincts, so that the success of the past would have become the rigid limit of the future, but he has tended to become more generalized, impressionable, sensitive and wonderingly aware.

This in brief outline is then the nature of the creature which has made history and civilization. We can only understand hive, ant-hill or termitary if we study the nature of the insect which builds these forms. We can only understand civilization, what pattern it is trying to express, what goal it is attempting to attain, if we have cleared our minds about the nature of the creature which makes it — man.

3. WHY MEN MISAPPREHENDED MAN

Men have made many assumptions about man. Feeling their inherent strangeness, recognizing that they could never attain to the soothing — and stupifying — sensation of being natural, they first attempted to explain this by saying they had offended the gods and were fallen. The animals are wise and live according to nature, said all totemistic peoples. 'The ox knoweth its stall and the ass its master's crib but my people hath not known me', said the Hebrew prophetic thought attempting to speak for the

[1] Sir Arthur Keith on Human Evolution.

creative power and explain man to himself. 'Live according to nature and all will be well', sighed the Stoic. The Christian Church and its philosophy, realizing that such advice might be good but would not help men so to live, yet hopes by redemption, sacraments and penance to win for men the peace of mind of knowing once again they are no longer wrong and unnatural but living in restored-prelapsarian naturalness, through Grace. As this effort also failed, as had failed Stoicism and Totemism, as no amount of redemption, sacraments and penance would make men natural and without conflict (any more than gazing on the night sky — the stoic recipe — or talking to animals — the recipe of totemism) so the Christian view darkened, and increased violence was used to enforce obedience. The Church was determined to make men at peace with themselves even at the cost of waging war with them. The aim was so philanthropic and the methods so unrestrained that had the closing of this fissure been possible the Church must have succeeded. It failed because, until Nature abandons man for the fossil scrapheap, whatever she may mean for him she does not mean him to be natural, to enjoy the sense of being settled which is denied him only, because of all animals he alone is still advancing. He shall never have the peace of mind of knowing his exact position and what he is — as long as he is the supreme creature. As Plato said 'We are saved by wonder' and in that shock of surprise we must find our happiness, and not our distress, if we are to be saved.

With the failure of the Church's effort, thinkers were however still not ready to see that this was the truth about man's position and the explanation of his distress — he was uncomfortable because he was most alive, he was restless because he alone was growing and so always outgrowing all his circumstances and all his forms.

Men still thought the Church's diagnosis correct, though they increasingly questioned the treatment with which the Church followed up her diagnosis. Hobbes finally gave consistent expression to this next stage of thought. Man was an unsuccessful animal and so haunted by conflict and fear. It was no use trying to change his nature as the Church had tried. Magic does not work on nature. All you could do was to manage matters so that you might balance out man's conflict against his fear — set up a supreme umpire, the Great Leviathan and so give men as much comfort as was possible, by reasonable device, to give to a deranged creature. You could not cure its nature but you could prevent its tortured inner nature making it outwardly torture others and itself. Rousseau's brief effort (to make men believe that it was no fault in man generally, but of a few particular men — the Rulers — which made them feel unnatural) had only the momentary success an optimistic but false diagnosis can always have. With the nineteenth century and the advance of biological study there is then inevitably a return to the problem as Hobbes had left it.

Man felt unnatural yet he was a fellow creature of all the other animals, none of which, it appeared, suffered from this profound distress. How had he come by this unhinging unnaturalness! 'God made man upright but he sought out many inventions' said the Hebrew 'Wisdom'. This line of thought lay behind

Greek and Jewish and still earlier speculation. Once man had been all right: there must have been a period when he was as natural as any of the other of Nature's creatures.

Hobbes' originality was that he broke away from that assumption. Man, he divined, must always have been unnatural, ill-adapted, suffering from lack of callousness. There was in his past no Fall from a primal condition of security and comfort. Man had never been at home but always aware of the strangeness of his circumstances, his situation and his own feelings. 'An abominable life, it hurts too much', reflected the philosopher of Fear and thereupon took the immemorial turning taken by every animal which, since the dawn of life, has become extinct. Hobbes is the first great thinker of the West openly to advocate on philosophic ground the use of violence for the sake of safety. From his time therefore we must expect part of the European culture to start becoming increasingly anchylosed, specialized, defensive and decadent. War will cease to be a brutal sport which men are striving gradually to refine by rules and will become the unlimited violence which efficiency demands. Again the diagnosis seemed so clear that the therapy appeared unavoidable. As Payne the revolutionary philanthropist said, frankly nonplussed by the problem, there was 'no getting round that old rascal'. Biology was rapidly to confirm Payne's worst fears. No trace of a Fall could be found, and of its corollary a Golden Age behind it, but every possible support for the Hobbesian belief that pre-historic, pre-civilic man must have been a defenceless, unhappy creature. The Hobbesian conclusion also seemed the only possible conclusion for Biology. Man, if he was to have any comfort or security, must arm himself and set about to toughen himself: otherwise he would be thrust from his precarious position. If, however, in the struggle to survive he could become by far the fittest, then, if he would 'spare, like the Turk, no brother near the Throne', he might have a little ease until, ease made him slack, rivals grew and once again he must hack out for himself his place in the sun.

We have seen how natural it was for nineteenth-century biology so to read the evidence it gathered — and how completely mistaken. It was true that man was 'unnatural' and ill at ease — if by 'natural' is to be held all the rest of life which is sinking down with ever less struggle, in slower, smaller circles toward unconsciousness and finally extinction. However, the two facts — a strange conjunction — of man's undoubted sensitiveness and uncertainty and his even more unquestioned supremacy, might — one thinks — have suggested even then to an unbiased thinker, that this association was not a biological freak and outrage. On the contrary, did not the one account for the other and, in a truly evolutionary sense of the word, was it not natural for man, because he was still ascending, to feel unsettled and ill-assorted, while it was equally natural for all the other creatures to feel themselves increasingly at ease and without inner conflict, as they sank into the comfort of anaesthesia and euthanasia?

We have seen that there was enough in their conditions and their natures to account for the nineteenth-century biologists arriving at the conclusion that ascent was caused by those very activities, violence and cunning callousness and blind strength which are in reality signs of decadence; and that sensitiveness (the real cause of evolution) was, though admirable, only a luxury and must in the end become fatal. To-day the evidence forces a more consistent conclusion on us. We see human nature is not untrue to nature if by nature is meant the power to live, grow and to become increasingly aware and conscious. It is only untrue to the nature of the vast majority which has forsaken life. *Homo contra mundum* is right.

Man is only untrue to that Nature which is already failing and addressed to death. Man has to suffer, he has to feel out of place: as the rest of the shrinking energies of life, as expressed in all other living forms, cannot feel out of place. But he suffers simply because he is most alive, grows fastest and becomes even more precipitately aware of problems he cannot yet imagine solving and of questions to which he has no answer.

4. HOW MAN IS NATURALLY UNNATURAL

So at last we reconcile the problem of man's apparent unnaturalness with his profound naturalness. If we believe in evolution at all, the rest of Life with its dead sureness, its instinct, its perfect adaptation, its lack of doubt, curiosity, wonder, experimentalism — it is all this which is contrary to the drive of nature. This is the failure, and man, with all his tragedies, misfits, mistakes, maladjustments and blind gropings, is still the only being who may be called a success. The dilemma disappears between man's values and his biological morality. His values — love, truth, beauty — these are the hall-marks of the essential sensitivity which has made possible his ascent and which, though he is now beyond where life has reached before and has outstripped even in power, as well as capacity, in efficiency as well as in understanding, all the beasts, promises him still further advance beyond any animal limit. For love is the power to feel for ever remoter lives; truth, to elucidate wider and more complex correspondences and relationships between the laws of his own mind and the Universe around him; and beauty, to apprehend higher and profounder harmonies in the world; until there is nothing that he can perceive which he cannot appreciate.

Here then is the being which creates civilization and makes the last, the briefest but, who can doubt, the most intense, the most significant chapter of Natural History, that chapter in which, as in all master-plots, the whole comes to a head and finds its fulfilment.

5. HOW STONE AGE ART CONFIRMS 'MAN IS BECAUSE HE FEELS'

With the essential nature of that character understood, we must now see how we may interpret his acts and estimate his works.

The outline of man's works has been interpreted in terms of his supposed character. The earliest historians finding relics of the megalithic culture assumed that there must have been a race of gods or titans who piled such holds. Later historians were no freer from prejudice when they assumed all prehistory must have resembled the individualistic, competitive history which was all they knew at first hand. Documents need care, if the reader's frame of mind is not to be read into them. When dealing with cultures which are predocumentary and which have only left scraps, shards and unexplained objects, far more care is necessary.

It has then been far harder for an objective picture to be made of proto-History than to get a correct view of the character of evolution and the force which directed it. The mistake about the real Natural Selection working in evolution, made historians as ready, and for the same reason, as evolutionists, to prove life was a battle and the best fighter got to the top. They therefore assumed history to be far simpler and cruder than it now grows clear it has actually been. Indeed the main view of general history (as far as any such thing can exist among experts, who are all too specialized to have anything beyond a layman's impression of the whole) is that man began as he had to begin, a fighting hunter. He is the cave-man of popular fancy clubbing his neighbour and bullying his family until some son is strong enough to kick him out and take his wives. The discovery of the great cave paintings, carvings and drawings done mainly by hunters at the end of the Ice Age, the Aurignacian and Magdalenian works of art, were naturally received with incredulous surprise. When their date and authorship could no longer be denied, prehistorians were still very slow to make the modification in their estimate of palaeolithic man's temperament and intelligence which such works required.

It was clear however that this person, without agriculture, pottery or weaving, living mainly in caves was nevertheless capable of draughtsmanship which can be compared with that of the most civilized artistry. Further study showed that he was not merely an artist but a thinker, a theoretician. These were magic works, not merely art studies. He knew, because he had an elaborated view of life, that if he could show the beast just as it was he would gain power over it. He was also an anatomist and physiologist. He knew where the heart was, showing its shape and place correctly and he realized that if it was pierced by his arrow the prize was his: it ceased to be a danger and became a blessing.

This realization, that Stone Age man was a magician as well as an artist, however did nothing to raise him in his first critics' eyes. If he was not a brute beast then he was a deluded fool. Still it should have been realized that a man who can make theories about life and invisible powers, when he is still without anything but the rudiments of economic savagery, is not quite the simple problem he was assumed to be. If he had theories of other forces, save physical violence, at play, even in his hunting of mighty and highly dangerous beasts, were it not wise to assume that other forces beside violence played an even more important part in his social life? Here, again, painted evidence supports such a supposition. There is no evidence that palaeolithic men lived each family alone — on the contrary the cave in the hill at Montespan has preserved the traces in the mud of its floor of a host of dancing feet round the model clay bear, still scarred with the jabs of spears, while between its paws was found lying the actual bear's skull. There are many representations of such ritual group dances and there is the famous drawing of the masked totem-istic actor called The Sorcerer.[1] This strange figure opens up another perspective of man's history. For to-day there has been recognized another peace-tie which helped hold the 'stone age' communities together. We have already seen there is an ancient, an animal, linkage of our species — music. Yet so pre-judiced have we been about our past, owing to the fact that we would conceive ourselves as organized solely by and for violence, a fierce pirate pack, that we failed to see this further important pacific evidence. Now Dr. Otto Seewald in his *Beiträge zur Kenntnis der Steinzeitlichen Musikinstrumente Europas*, has collected evidence which shows that Stone Age man already possessed a veritable orchestra. His stringed instru-ments have of course perished, though rippling sounds produced by his comb-like instruments show that the vibrant prong would have led to the vibrant string. Beside these, not only whistles but true flutes have survived and Dr. Seewald is convinced that the same masked totemistic actor mentioned above is not only dancing but also playing some such pipe. We have then evidence not of isolated, half-animal family groups but of a social life and one depending certainly to a great extent on ritual and magic and so certainly not wholly under the sole control of unlimited violence. It was already finding the sanctions for social life, the substitutes for the pack-instinct, in some sort of tradi-tion based on powers which were not material.[2]

[1] From the Cave of Trois Frères, France.
[2] Some authorities have considered that the styles of rock paintings are so distinct over large areas that there must have been schools of artists who travelled throughout widely scattered but united societies to make their magic pictures for them.

Later in the Azilian deposits — the last of the old Stone Age cultures — we get those distinctive marked and barred pebbles. These were puzzling but obviously of some mystical import, and the clue to them is probably given by one of the few recorded utterances of those now extinct aboriginal Tasmanians, the earliest of all the backward peoples which survived down into the last century. An old woman of one of these tribes, questioned as to what similarly barred pebbles which her tribe made and she guarded, represented, explained that they were 'absent friends'. Here then is quite possibly a development of thought which will lead to sacramentalism and the conception of the human psyche as something generally associated with, but able to be distinguished and perhaps detached from, the body.

It is clear then that the palaeolithic man had, before the invention of any but the hunter's economy, realized, however indefinitely, that his life was in some mysterious way linked with other forms of life, his society was something more than the physical unit of the family and that the social unit can be preserved by ties which are neither those of unconscious instinct nor physical coercion but of ritual and probably tradition.

When we add to this construction of the evidence the fact that we know man to be a highly social animal, sensitive, suggestible and affectionate, one who required co-operative help, moral support, praise, advice, encouragement and criticism, it seems that we should expect to find the hunter to have found, long before he hit upon those secondary discoveries of economic inventions, those primary discoveries of social and psychological arrangements whereby his corporate life might endure.

This then must conclude the review of pre-history, of that immense transitional period between the instinctive animal, secured firmly in its pack (though here we must remind ourselves that instinct can never have been an iron compulsion in the species which above all others retained its generalized nature, its flexibility and impressionability — it were wiser then perhaps to speak of the unconsciously suggestible animal) and the fully human personality. As that period passes man advances, because he gradually but successfully brings out into the definiteness of ritual and social function those co-operative relationships and mutual emotional ties which hold society together. These relationships need deliberate emphasis if they are to endure against the outward stresses caused by changed conditions and the inward torsions resulting from intensifying self-consciousness and critical awareness. It is on sustaining this balanced advance of inner and outer powers — always keeping the subjective progress from falling behind the objective progress — on preserving an equal consciousness of the reality of values as his consciousness of his means grew — on this has depended the success of man's transition from animal to man: as to-day, on the self-same balance, depends whether civilization shall continue and man survive.

CHAPTER V

PROTO-CIVILIC HISTORY

I. CIVILIZATION IS CRISIS

IT is clear that with the rise of what was first called the Neolithic age man underwent a revolution perhaps as severe as any he has endured. That name indeed gives so little notion of the complexity of even the economic changes then made and endured, that it will probably be discarded. For man at this time discovered in the economic field: agriculture, domestication of animals and dairying; in the fields of the craft-arts, building, pottery and weaving; and in the field of thought, analysis. His mind must have undergone an immense change and strain, whether he infected himself or was infected, whether one mind made this revolutionary advance or many. The economic discoveries meant that he was to settle down and so would have far more time to ponder his problems; the same place would recall his train of thought, the same object would repeatedly provoke his curiosity and tease his power of speculation. Often after good harvests he would have plenty and the first full and careless leisure. The very strangeness and success of the work he was on, the tending of the living corn and the living cattle, would raise endless speculation in his mind. Increasingly all that mattered to him, it was clear, took place out of his sight in the deep of the earth or the dark of the womb.

Nor was his new relationship with his beasts one

that starved his emotions or made him brutal. It was
clear that dog and goat and oxen all responded to him
on a basis of affection. The relationship was symbiotic.
These creatures served him best when the tie was
most friendly. His dog was his friend — backward
peoples — anthropologists have noted with the surprise of the economically-obsessed — are always
littered with pets — but goat and cow were also so
close to his emotions that he could only think of their
essential spirit as divine. Cow, goat and sheep are
among the earliest and most lasting of gods. Man is
grateful to them and in early days often felt they were
too sacred to be killed. They yielded milk and wool.
Was not that enough? man often thought. Why kill
a co-operative companion?

The craft-arts meant a constant development of
inter-acting sensitiveness of touch and sight, that inter-
action of brain and hand on which (here again Elliot
Smith's classic studies of the development of the brain
must be referred to) so much of man's mental development has constantly depended throughout his evolution from animal to artist. The delicate thin black
burnished and rippled pottery of those proto-Egyptians,
the Badarians, showed how soon man brought to real
refinement his touch on the clay. Weaving also is a
constant drawing out of another delicacy of touch until
in dynastic Egypt and perhaps far earlier were woven
muslins the thread of a few square inches of which
would stretch a furlong and which can compare with
those Indian muslins which till hyper-delicate machinery was invented could only be spun and woven by a
hand trained to touch almost as lightly as the spider's
foot tries its stretched web.

Such evidence of constantly improving skill and fresh and even faster invention is proof of intensifying consciousness. Indeed when we put in typological order all the Stone Age cultures we see a constant acceleration of discovery. The Chellean and pre-Chellean flints improve so gradually that their development is more akin to the evolution of a species than the inventive addition to the efficiency of an instrument by a conscious mind. Thousands of years pass and the stone tool remains as true to type as the bones of the hand which shaped it. Then gradually the speed of change begins to accelerate until, when we reach this neolithic or agricultural phase, we have something which can be called by our modern term invention.

2. ECONOMIC REVOLUTION EVIDENCE OF PSYCHOLOGICAL REVOLUTION

Evidence of this change is however most unmistakably seen not in the industries, crafts or applied arts but in pure art. To have proof of a change in consciousness it is necessary to compare the Aurignacian and Magdalenian drawings of the Old Stone Age with those of the New. It was the late Roger Fry who first draw attention to the great significance of the change. The first impression received by anyone on looking at a Magdalenian and Neolithic drawing is that the cave man had learnt to draw and the much later and more civilized successor had never learnt or had no skill. A moment's reflection takes us much further. Consider first the Old Stone Age picture. It is nearly always drawn and painted on a dark part of the cave wall, often where artificial light must have been used to see at all. It often makes use, in the most curiously ingenious way, of juts and bosses in the natural rock, so that a skilful touch or two of charcoal or red paint turns the lump into the humped shoulder, the massive flank or the bent head of a bison. Yet the naturalism is perfect. So the creature stood; so it charged. These sketches, everyone who has studied animal form realizes, are anatomically certain and they express function more satisfactorily than photographs. These facts taken together suggest very strongly something about the mentality of the artists — they were pre-analytic. They did not think and draw, they saw and drew, they saw as they drew. In the dark of the cave the jutting rock, its mass made loom in the pin-point light of the animal-fat lamp, became the charging bison and all they did with shading and line was to set their vision, etch and define it before it faded. Like magic calculators, if they had stopped to analyse how they put down the whole sum of it, how the legs were related to the head, how far the head should bend to look natural, what was the rightful contour of those flexed muscles, they could have put down nothing, the whole vision would have melted away. They saw all the better because it was dark. In the full light of common day the rock would have shown itself to be only rock.

This unreflective vividness of vision, when it attains a certain intensity so that the picture appears to be objectively there on the wall and the seer can, and only has to, outline it with crayon, as though he was working through tracing paper, such hallucinatory power is called power of eidetic imagery. It seems often

130

present in children and seldom to last on into adulthood. Analysis interferes with it.

Now if we return to the Neolithic drawing and hold in restraint our disapproving disappointment that art has made so little progress, has actually declined, when economic advance should have made possible far greater triumphs, we discover that these crude little drawings are nevertheless clear proof of a progress of a sort. For these drawings are the sort of drawings every child nowadays makes naturally. They are analytical. They are made by persons who think at once in terms of detail and parts. They put together these details and so composed an object which is very unlike any particular animal or man at any particular moment and particular position. As art, therefore, the drawing is a failure but it is a tremendous success in quite another direction, which art never attempts, but man has to attempt if he is to gain power over the outer world and extend his capacity of consciously communicating with his fellows. It is the discovery of generalization and abstraction. So it will lead to further conscious analysis, to symbolism, to writing and to numeration.

We see then that in the Neolithic drawings with their little figures stiffly composed of heads, arms, bodies and legs — no longer organic forms as the Old Stone artist could see them — we have proof of a new degree and intensification of consciousness. Man has moved so fast in his inventions that at last he has woken up to the fact that he is moving. This leads inevitably to a new interest in the thing which is always at the centre of his apprehensions, but never seen — himself. It is significant then that whereas

the Old Stone Age artist hardly ever draws man —
save when he shows him as the sorcerer or the dancers
at a group rite, and then generally disguised, and
woman is only shown as a faceless lump of fecundity,
expressionless plenty — Neolithic drawings are chiefly
concerned with human beings.

All this bears closely on the growth of man's consciousness. Such an increase of analysis and power of
reflection must have put an immense strain on the
natural, hitherto unquestioned cohesion of the social
group. Man was breaking the traditional ways
through discovering new technical processes. That
alone would provoke questions in his mind. He was
becoming increasingly aware of himself as a discreet
person. Inwardly and outwardly, to and fro, he was
being worked loose out of the matrix of the tribe in
which he had been securely embedded. His natural
suggestibility would be shrinking within him at the
very same time that the voice of authority of the group
would be growing increasingly qualified, as the immemorial unchanged way of life and all procedure
broke up about it.

3. THE FIRST MORAL CRISIS: AT THE NEOLITHIC

It was natural then for social historians who have
considered this first great crisis on the threshold of
history, to say that the Neolithic period marks the rise
of property and with property the necessity of new
laws and penalties within the community and a new
organized defensive-offensive towards other communities — deliberate war. It is at this point that the

need of sanctions is first clearly recognized, the sword has to be brought up and put beside the scales. Henceforward violence and values will be inextricably confused, values having to call on violence to make them real, and violence, in the attempt to materialize them, making them vanish. In short, the modern dilemma. Such a view of history is however pre-psychological. It assumed that man makes discoveries through some sort of outer economic necessity. That certainly is untrue — a survival from the earlier notions about evolution when it was thought that every change in the species was not produced by inherent mutations but by external pressures in the environment. Man, true to nature, makes his discoveries, as life has made its advances, by inherent originalities. Further, as life seldom makes real advances so man also seldom makes discoveries. As only one species at each great step up the staircase of life seems to have won through and then given rise to all the genera and species of the next — the narrowing crisis and the general expansion repeated as we have seen three times until for a fish we have man — so man it now seems only once discovered civilization. All these radical discoveries coming together — crop-raising, dairying, pottery, weaving, the beginning of symbols, look like a single outburst in creative originality. We take for granted that any human being will blunder on such finds which are such ancient commonplaces among all of us throughout the world to-day. It is not so. Men do not make discoveries as hens lay eggs.

Such an assumption, that the great complex of discoveries which we call the Neolithic culture could have arisen spontaneously in widely scattered areas, we now see to be so contrary to what we know of the working of the human mind-body that we can call it unnatural. The prejudices of nineteenth-century archaeologists, arising from an unconscious or uncritical acceptance of that century's first crude conception of the main force behind all evolution, such prejudices made it difficult for them to accept any other alternative of discovery and invention. Man blundered on small finds and these finds somehow coalesced — as the minute and random changes of the organism had, according to Darwin's mistaken notion, gradually been sorted out and the valuable ones accumulated by Natural Selection. So at last the general corpus of traditional, cultural knowledge came together and extended throughout mankind. To-day we know such a process to be inherently highly improbable. That is not the way evolution has worked and man's advance must be, because he is a creature, along the same lines; different in intensity but similar in essential character to the natural force which has derived him — the final form of the animal most responsive to life's essential urge.

Another reason which would make us doubt that first crude hypothesis as to the way the first pattern of civic behaviour was precipitated, is that that culture integrates too well — the parts fit together with too great completeness. This culture pattern is not the resultant of a series of colliding discoveries. It is rather a series of discoveries resulting from a new integration of experience, a new insight into the environment and a new extension of outlook over time. These discoveries are all discoveries based on foresight. Agriculture, dairying, weaving, pottery, and symbolism, all need a power of abstraction and patience, a power of envisaging an end when the means bear no apparent resemblance to that end and the end itself will not be seen for a period which, for instance, to the mind of a hunter (*his* attention continually held by the continual reminder of the spoor, wind and sight of the quarry) seems inconceivable. Civilization has been defined as the power to postpone pleasure for the sake of purpose. The saving of seed, then planting and leaving it for months out of sight. The slow preparation of clay and then, after shaping it, the patience to leave it for the necessary dry-out without which firing will not preserve but destroy the pot. The patient carding of the rough wool and then from it spinning the firm thread until there has accumulated a great mass of spools necessary to weave even a few feet of cloth; the 'setting up' of even the simplest loom: these fundamental Neolithic processes all call for a patience only possible to people (who have had no experience of seeing their work surely rewarded) if they have, instead, been taught each part of the process as a ritual sequence having its magic worth because *laborare est orare* — the particular process not merely leads to bread, raiment, vessels but integrates with the whole cultural complex. To do the particular part well is one's duty, to fulfil the Will which gives one's life its meaning. So one is bonded with the group not merely economically but psychologically, not merely with daily needs of life but with the whole natural sequence of day and night, men and nature, life and death. In short the Neolithic culture is not merely a series of economic inventions.

These are merely the relics, the skeleton. The co-ordinating and expanding life-force, creating the culture and informing it, was a complete outlook on existence, a *religio*, a faith of which the economic crafts were the resultant works.

Here then — as with the 'Neolithic' culture we have the first rudimentary illustration of it — is the place where this principle can be enunciated as a sociological 'law'. The evidence herein collected suggests that man is by his animal nature a social creature whose whole existence (let alone his advance) economic as well as psychological depends on spontaneous loyalty to and affection for his species. As he advances, by use of that section of his mind which is analytic and self-conscious, through the intentional mastery of his environment so given, he must lose his intuitive sense of kind-ship and his spontaneous power of social behaviour. The self-conscious mind which permits him to question and alter his relationships with his surroundings, also permits him to question and alter his relationships with his fellows. The self-conscious mind is, *ipso facto*, ignorant of the intuitive sense of kind-ship. This (to use Pascal's terminology) 'mind' can find no reason for the 'heart's' reasons. Hence the sociological 'law' runs: A society which advances economically (in invention and powers over outer nature) must become unstable and collapse through that advance unless, through an equal advance in psychology, it can gain a proportionately self-conscious knowledge of its inner nature. Self-consciousness in one outlook must be balanced by self-consciousness in the other. This 'law' stated in familiar historical language becomes:

136

The Society which does not make and continue to make religious discoveries as radical as its material discoveries, must rapidly increase in ill-distributed wealth and power; will generate increasingly neuroses, ill-will and violence; and must finally (if it can so long escape internal anarchy and ruin) become wholly militarized, devote itself to destruction and collapse.

4. THAT CRISIS SURMOUNTED BY PSYCHOLOGICAL INVENTION

The way of evolution, then, suggests that this new great advance by natural man, whereby he reached the threshold of civilization, was a complete complex of discovery, a mutation in some peculiarly fertile and receptive mind, or co-ordinated group of minds, similar to those mutations in those other previous ultra-sensitive and plastic living types, which gave rise to the successive radical advances throughout the ascent of Life. The discoveries themselves suggest a co-ordinated integration which indicates that they are all natural resultants of a new, single and complete extension of outlook on the world and a new insight into the relationship between man and nature.

The proof however must rest on archaeological discovery. It is clear that the earlier archaeologists, as was inevitable, permitted an inaccurate general view of life to dictate to them what might be the motives and the methods which brought together the first rudiments of civilization. We can see that such assumptions were mistaken. Can we however put in the place of those assumptions a picture which will not only be more in accord with our new general knowledge of the way Life as a whole works — and therefore to which man cannot be an exception — but which will also incorporate our new archaeological knowledge and show that that knowledge confirms the belief that man must and does continue to behave according to the nature he has inherited?

There seems little doubt that this is possible. Indeed so remarkable and radical has been the growth of archaeological discovery in the last couple of decades that it is obvious that even if we had not had a new view of evolution to reverse our notions of what is natural and to integrate vitality and values, we should have been compelled to recognize how early it was that man for the sake of his morality began to behave in a way which was a denial of the old 'Natural Selection'.

The latest discoveries suggest that though the Golden Age, when man lived naturally without inner conflict (and so in outer peace) may never have existed, because his nature is always one which must suffer and advance through strain, nevertheless there may have been a time when social peace did exist because values were self-sanctioning. There may have been an age when man discovered how to make a conscious technique of what, among gregarious animals, is an instinct; when men learnt how by psychological knowledge to cross the limen now existing between the subconscious mind, where his values lay, and the self-conscious mind, in which he increasingly had to live because that part of the mind had control over the increasingly economic world.

We must then turn to examine some considerable archaeological material to see the basis of this belief.

CHAPTER VI

THE NUCLEUS OF CIVILIZATION

I. THE DIFFUSIONIST DISCOVERY

THE first radical discovery in modern archaeology was Diffusionism, the generalization that civilization in its origin spreads from one centre. The question is still difficult to discuss because of the heat which was first generated by this change of view. The elder archaeologists, inheriting, as we have seen, their prejudices as to the mechanism of human advance from the mistaken assumptions about evolution as a whole, believed firmly in spontaneous discovery. Like causes lead to like effects and the human mind everywhere makes the same inventions and the same mistakes.

The accumulating evidence did not however establish this. It became clear that new methods, techniques and crafts had spread perhaps from one centre. First it was not possible to imagine that men had twice spontaneously made such un-utilitarian and peculiar inventions as, for example, double-necked vases. The skill needed to make these perversities would have discouraged mere caprice. Here was, then, a design which must have a single place of origin. Further it was clear such defiance of use and convenience by men so little raised above the constant pressure of economic need must mean that with the design had travelled an idea. The pot was utilitarian — all things ultimately are — but the use it served was not a physical but a psychical need. The pot was evidence, not merely of the spread of a curious aberrant of the potter's style, but of psychological ideas — a thought-complex of which the new economic ideas, which were making material civilization, were themselves only consequences and symptoms. This particular bizarre form showed the object itself was a cult-object and it gave a hint of what were the strange quality and the power of the forces which were causing the revolution which was only, in its end-process, an economic revolution.

That archaeology should begin to be influenced by such psychological conceptions was highly distasteful to elder and conservative archaeologists who anyhow naturally resented the change which the conception of Diffusionism by itself must entail. Such changes complicated their study by introducing new and imponderable factors, and to men who imagined — as certainly some of the Frazerian anthropologists imagined — that they were proving the Gibbonesque association of barbarism and religion — it looked as though this new-fangled stuff might not only be resented (as biologists resented change in revolutionary theory) as a needless complexity, but repudiated as opening the door to superstition.

2. HOW PERSECUTION MADE DIFFUSIONISTS DOGMATIC

Diffusionism met with a welcome from elderly authority which combined in its warmth the natural irritation of age with the theological bitterness which suspects heresy. This reaction of those in possession produced in its turn the natural reaction in those who wanted the case given a hearing. They believed that facts had been discovered which gave a new meaning to history and pre-history and which the elderly (clinging to the blessed hope that everything meant nothing and history was as blind and pointless as Natural History: man as mistaken and ignorant as life was without direction or aim) were blindly refusing to recognize.

The Diffusionists often became in their turn dogmatic. It is an invariable alternation — dogmatic denial breeding dogmatic assertion. One school makes a complete and closed system composed of nearly all the known facts. The few that have to be left out are slighted as exceptions which exist to prove the rule. As fresh facts, that will not fit, turn up, they too are shelved until it is clear to outsiders that the centre of gravity is beginning to shift — there are almost as many exceptions to the rules as the examples which prove them. Still the trouble of recasting the principles is too great for those who have long used and may even have framed them. This does not debar outsiders. They realize that the period of abstraction is over and the reciprocating period of hypothesis is due. Now all the facts must be included and if, with such plenty, spare elegance of design is lost, then a larger design must be found even though the present quota of facts does not fill it out fully. This of course is the inevitable and legitimate reciprocal advance of knowledge — from abstraction to hypothesis. Unfortunately the abstractionists too often resist the next stage of natural development and so render it

revolutionary instead of evolutionary. The hypothe-
cators, in their turn, then find it difficult to treat what
should have been a stimulating suggestion on their
part, welcomed by the elder party, as being so much
and no more. It has to become a fighting faith.

Hence in many cases Diffusionism became too
dogmatic and ruled on insufficient evidence, and sometimes even on *a priori* grounds, the exact particulars
whereby the spreading of the primal culture has taken
place. On particular points of evidence the elder anthropology and archaeology were able to challenge the
completeness of the Diffusionist proofs and so on these
local successes claim that the entire front was wholly
unaffected, the hot-head attack had broken down.

This, however, was far from being the case. Far
too many of the claims of Diffusionism had been
established. Papers which have justly become famous,
such as the late Dr. Rivers's 'The Decay of Useful Arts',
showed from evidence from Oceana how an original
culture-wave could pass by modifying the life of a
people, who afterwards could relapse, until only
patient care could detect the traces of a current of
diffusion. The grand hypothesis of Diffusionism
needed then the most careful attention, whether or no
its particular applications should be accepted. That
hypothesis was that civilization is a single original
conception which results and expresses itself in many
co-ordinated activities — it is in the exact sense of the
term a new way of life. Instead then of random economic
inventions resulting in a new outlook on the universe,
new doubts and new beliefs, it is a new outlook which
permits the mind to make new inventions.

This of course is psychologically sound. It is and

must always be the mind and not the environment which invents. Place a limpet in the most favourable situation, it will not rise to its opportunity but grope for a rock on which to glue itself. It is pre-psychological to think otherwise — still pre-psychological thinking is easier and simpler. That general frames of mind gave and give rise to particular discoveries is an unsettling hypothesis, for if that is so, theoretically we have to face the fact that the mind itself mutates: invention, discovery and all progress are much more complicated and mysterious things than our intelligence, seeking simplicity, wishes to allow. Practically we have to face the even more unpleasant, inexpedient conclusion: that if all invention, discovery and progress are resultants of — and only possible if man can make — the new world outlook, a new cosmology — then the religion of the past, which was such a cosmology, was not such unnecessary and obstructive nonsense as had been supposed. If he cannot frame such a cosmology then man will either make no inventions and his society will be safe, stable, sterile (the normal majority state) or he will make inventions and he, being psychologically unbalanced, will be unable to contain them and shape them and they will destroy society. The metal of the gun is too weak for the powder and there is a burst — the present state and peril of our society.

This first step in the Diffusionists' theory had new thought in its favour and old thought against it. For and against were both however still based on *a priori* grounds. The proof or disproof must come not from economic prejudices or psychological speculation but from archaeological research.

3. THE PROTO-CIVILIZATION FOUND IN THREE PLACES

If Diffusionism were true then there must be one centre where the discovery of the proto-civilization was made and whence it radiated. The Diffusionists were ready to provide such a centre, in Egypt. The discovery of a civilization as ancient, in Southern Mesopotamia, was undoubtedly taken as refutation of the whole Diffusionist hypothesis by the conservatives. When, further, still another centre was found on the Indus, a centre which appeared to have autochthonous origins equal in age to Egypt's and to Sumer's, the conservatives' case seemed immensely strengthened. Here were three sites far removed from each other and on each of them is found an original civilization showing all the basic characteristics which have lasted on among men above the savage level. How far back the earliest traces of this culture goes in each of these three places it is too early yet to be certain. It can be said however that all three have been traced back now to dates which, until this generation, were considered frankly mythical. The Badarian and Tasian cultures in lower Egypt: the Jemnet Nasir and proto-Ninevehan cultures in Mesopotamia: the Mohenjo Daro and perhaps still earlier Amri and Kol Deja cultures in the Indus basin are not only the earliest sites at present known of the proto-civilization — they all of them carry back that culture, in a complex and competent form, to epochs where, till our own generation, the learned were certain no such culture could have existed and the stories of it were the baseless romances of men dreaming of a mythical Golden Age.

Still, conservative opinion appeared more to be strengthened by these discoveries than shaken. True there were difficulties to be faced. The cultures showed not merely such similarities as should be produced by 'a common human way of thinking applied to a common environmental problem'. They showed some of those curious non-utilitarian and detailed resemblances which — as in the later case of the two-necked vases already mentioned — suggest a common origin, because of a common speculation about the universe — a common cosmology. These details, however, could be overlooked. What, however, brought them back into a position where they could no longer be disregarded was the far larger and more serious discovery that none of these cultures — with their many strange agreements — seem to be truly aboriginal. When the earliest and lowest levels in Egypt, Mesopotamia, and on some sites of the Indus valley are excavated, they do not take us down to a level whence we can pass, without break to so rude a stage that we can be certain here culture sinks down to the simple unorganized way of life of a hunting people only removed from animals by their artifically manufactured weapons.[1] On the contrary it is found that in each of these places when 'ground level' is reached, where no further lower sites are disclosed the culture stops abruptly. As it is traced back it is not degenerating. This certainly Dr. Woolley believes

---

[1] It should be remembered that study of the palaeolithic cultures, of their art and 'cult objects', suggests with increasing strength that even in the hunting stage man was already much more than simply an animal which made, instead of grew, its armoury.

to be true of Ur where he has dug to the bottom of a fifty foot pit and it is also true of Mohenjo Daro.[1]

We are faced then with these strange facts on all three primal sites: firstly that each culture seems to have arrived already equipped from some other place, secondly all three contain many objects, 'cult objects', that seem to refer to a similar cosmology. Fine pottery such as the Badarian thin black ware, the famous painted pottery from Mesopotamia and the Indus wares, these, though evidence of a long tradition in the potter's art, may be original inventions *in situ*. Each on its own site minerva-like without lower parentage, may have occurred simultaneously to diverse and widely separated peoples. Such things however as the early cylinder seals in Egypt — a seal form which disappears as the Egyptian culture grows on its own — for this seal is very suitable for a clay-based people such as the Sumerians and equally unsuited for a rock, silt and sand-based people such as the Egyptians — these seals which last on in Sumeria suggest that Egypt must have received them from Mesopotamia. The pear-shaped 'mace' is another such object once thought of as a clumsy weapon when found in early Egyptian sites and represented in the earliest carvings — the famous Palettes for mixing cosmetics. Now however evidence goes to show it, too, is a cult object as 'magical' as a seal, for it represents the thunderbolt, a cosmological idea immensely, dominatingly impressive to people who lived under thunderous conditions[2] On the other hand there is no great

[1] See *The Indus Civilization*, E. MACKAY.
[2] Compare the place of Indra the thunder God in Indian theology and later Zeus the sky shining one who nevertheless is powerful through the thunderbolt and who is worshipped in the tree of his favourite manifestation – the oak – as at Greece's earliest great oracle centre Dodona.

thunder God in the Egyptian pantheon and so the mace, like the cylinder seal, is an import which finding no environmental stimulus after a time dies away.

The early seal and mace link that Egyptian proto-civilization with somewhere without, probably to the north-east. This supposition is immensely strengthened when we get the first religious writings of the Egyptians. The Book of the Dead is more to Egypt than the Bible to a Protestant or the Pentateuch to a Jew. It is the crystallization in words of the whole people's sub-conscious and conscious attitude to life. Because the guide from this obvious world to the unseen was made so clear and definite, Egyptian civilization — though it did not know the way to escape them — could endure and repeatedly recover from disasters. Each individual knew his place and process. Here was morality's clear sanction. Why it did not work better, why it frequently lapsed and finally decomposed must be discussed later. Here, what has to be remarked, is the striking fact that this description of here and hereafter which was accepted so completely by the Egyptians, takes all its imagery from some completely different environment.

It may be said by Northern Europeans, who have been accustomed to the same thing, by their sacred literature being also an import, that such a process is always necessary among highly civilized peoples. A prophet or a cult cannot be honoured where he or it originates, because if origins either of thought or imagery are known their impressive quality disappears. This however can be proved to be untrue, from perhaps the greatest religious poem ever written by an acutely self-conscious and civilized man. Every reader of the *Inferno* is continually struck by the way Dante takes his similes quite frankly from scenery close about Florence. Here is no fear that the familiar cannot be made the vehicle of the awful and the terrifying.

Detailed study of the Book of the Dead has shown not merely that its scenery of rocky glen and winding river is certainly not Egyptian. Study has traced this picture to its most likely source. Again we find ourselves taken north-east and the environment which tallies best with the description is a Caucasian site.

Other evidence, that these three primal sites probably were not ignorant of what the others knew is borne out by the discovery of Mesopotamian cylinder seals in the Indus Valley and the evidence of the peculiar and distinctive Indus seals in Mesopotamia. These 'exchanges', if such they were, are found in very early levels just as the cylinder seals and maces belong to an early stage in Egypt.

It looks then as though an exchange of basic ideas about life and death, about the individual and his obligations and rights, was going on between these three primal sites. That is the first fact which it is increasingly difficult to avoid. The second fact however drives us beyond even that position. That second fact is that these cultures, when they are in exchange, are near their beginnings on these specific sites, in fact they are in exchange as soon as they appear on their sites, but they do not begin their cultures on these sites, we find them planted out there with the first stages of their growth already long completed.

4. BUT ONE CENTRE SUPPLIED THE THREE SITES

When these two facts are put side by side it is hard to avoid an alternative and more drastic view. Perhaps these three centres, though they may have continued to make occasional exchanges and have some intercourse, do not owe their curious likeness precisely to exchanges and intercourse: at least over the great distances which divided them and soon, as we know, caused active exchange to cease; each centre working out its distinctive forms and discarding many that it had brought, or which had come from outside. The forms which they later discarded as unsuitable to their actual environment they may have acquired under another environment and discarded when they found themselves in a new and inapplicable position. There may have been no true — or very few and insignificant — exchanges.

The only alternative is, of course, that each of the three centres are centres of colonists. We cannot now avoid the further conclusion that if that is so these colonists must have radiated from a common centre. What we see in Egypt, Mesopotamia and the Indus Valley are three sectors of a widening, diffusing ripple of a common culture, which finally breaks into three separate waves, each spreading up the particular creek into which it poured.

Archaeology seems then increasingly to support the psychological view of pre-history against what has been called here the pre-psychological view. More and more evidence is accumulating[1] to show that the proto-civilization is a fact: that man made at one time somewhere in the Middle East an integrated series of discoveries which completely revolutionized his life, which put for ever a great gulf between him and the animal and which laid the foundation of his present, ever more rapidly developing civilization: that this civilization-complex resulted from a mental mutation, a sudden new insight into things: that its economic achievement was only a symptom of that new radical outlook, and further, the economic achievement was only possible because these economic changes were balanced and integrated by equal psychological discoveries. Man's cosmology and its dependent ethic had to keep pace with his new techniques and power-processes, or otherwise value and fact, worth and achievement would become separated, intense individualism based on physical satisfaction as its only end would ensue and society would collapse.

This view, perhaps it should be repeated, is fundamentally natural for it agrees with our present knowledge of the process and invariable conditions of all successful evolution. Great advances are very rare — the vast majority of the forms of life has never made any advance: indeed advance seems confined and only possible to one strain. So when that strain culminates in man we should expect that fundamental law to remain unabrogated and advance, discovery and invention to remain as rare, and confined to a few profoundly comprehensive minds. We also can see (for it is the converse of the above proposition) why till now

[1] See the brilliant summary of revolutionary finds given in his essay 'The world-wide expansion of "Neolithic" Culture' by A. Vayson de Pradenne, Professeur à l'Ecole d'Anthropologie. Paris. 'L'Anthropologie' 1934 XLIV.

archaeologists were naturally prejudiced against accepting this fact — that the proto-civilization originated in one place, the result of one profound apprehension. Their belief in the older conception of evolution made it as unnatural to suppose this could happen, as the newer view of evolution shows it to be natural.

Diffusion of a proto-civilization, of one complete pattern of culture, must then, it seems, be accepted as a fact suggested by what we know of evolution as a whole, of man's nature and also of the actual evidence which archaeology is piecing together. We have to-day growing before us the picture of the single primal civilization, precipitated as a whole, for each part — from carving seals, to milking and reaping, on to worship and prayer — is the appropriate application, in its own field, of the new insight which has found an intensified meaning in existence. Strain, an increasing strain, must have been present: balance must have become increasingly conscious. All the long-range activities which now were undertaken: agriculture, building, wheel-transport, weaving, pottery, these all by inevitably stressing the end (and making consciousness ever more clearly to envisage that end, in order that the protracted strain of the means might be endured) shattered the eternal present. In the palaeolithic period, before there was abstraction and analysis, the work could be itself the pleasure. You could enjoy knapping the flint unhurried from the present pleasure of your skill by any fever of expectation of the use to which you would put it when complete. That belonged to another 'Universe of discourse', another life. So use and means were not yet distinguished from beauty, enjoyment and ends.

Nevertheless there is no evidence that the proto-civilization was at its start unstable or that the balance necessary to keep it poised and productive was lacking.

5. WHY THE PROTO-CIVILIZATION SURVIVED THE STRAIN OF CHANGE

The economic and utilitarian advances were certainly not without psychological complementary extensions. Just as men had with increasing consciousness to follow the more elaborate crafts, so with equal increasing consciousness they had to make explicit in ritual, maybe mythic dogma and, most important, psychological exercises in addressing themselves to spiritual powers, the sense of their unseen relationship with forces which sanctioned their values, gave their individual lives purpose, saved them from futility and preserved their community.

We need not then as yet postulate violence as the sanction of morality and values. For man, though he is now pushing forward along two lines which will diverge, is still pursuing them both equally and so his growth is balanced, sane, whole. He is therefore still developing as an unfissured psycho-physical organism. He is still a being which not only needs and knows he needs psychical as well as physical goods, but also knows that those psychical goods are to be obtained through morality, through freely-yielded social services which are not altruistic because they are not done to another, an outsider but to his own larger self, the community and through the community he is joined to Life. He still is possessed of the intuition, essential both to his sanity and to civilization, that he is more than an individual.

He is undoubtedly at this time, when he enters the first stage of civilization, undergoing a rapid and dangerous transition. He still remains largely what he has always been throughout his, the only truly successful evolution, a peaceful, co-operative, suggestible, affectionate animal.

6. THE PRE-CONDITIONS OF WAR

At what epoch then did violence intervene and become endemic, because men could no longer see how morality could be enforced without it? How and where was this thing, which is the denial of co-operation and compassion and so the denial of the basis of morality, fasten itself on humanity, like a deadly parasite which drains the life of its host so that he has not the vitality to rid himself of it and finally succumbs to the growth he has fed?

It is clear if this thing is not present in man as an animal, nor in his first social order, we must find it breaking out later and, with our present archaeological knowledge, we ought to be able to indicate the time and place of this supreme tragedy.

Yet again it is still such a shock to the protective prejudices (with which we try and make ourselves insensitive to our present peril, disgrace and pain) that it is necessary to repeat here that War is being recognized increasingly by all Naturalists, whether their study is man or Life, as unnatural. Organized mass murder of your fellow species by the systematic use of the utmost intelligence and discipline, Napoleon called a 'fine game', but everyone who has studied it dispassionately knows that it is a deadly form of group insanity which does very rarely attack social creatures, a social disease only to be compared among the diseases of the body with that ghastly anarchy of its cells — cancer. Yet, like cancer, it is not a bolt from the blue. It is preceded by degenerative processes, pre-cancerous conditions. The community gets ready to wage war against its neighbours by distinct morbid changes in its own constitution. It is when social justice, the relationship between man and man has become so strained that the sword is drawn to 'keep order', when men are already so divided from their fellows that they allow an armed master to keep and enforce division and inequality, that the community is soon organized as an offensive instrument and becomes ready in the hand of the chief executioner to become a weapon to divide, shatter and spoil other communities.

It only remains, when this is said, to guard against the possible misrepresentation of the above argument which might maintain that it is obvious man can and must always have been capable of *quarrelling* and so is naturally warlike. All social animals can 'scrap', and though man is by far the most affectionate and co-operative, he can of course, through accidents of health or circumstance, snarl and squabble. What he will not do in a community which values him and he it, is make a real breach of the peace. He will not let his passion become homicidal and all his friends will aid him in his effort at control and insist on reconciliation. Sexual fighting is undoubtedly his chief danger and this is essentially a one-to-one antagonism. Hence the immense elaboration and fertility of the arrangements which have been made to secure by marriage taboos, etc., that everyone shall have some satisfaction and that there shall be no starvation which may drive to poaching. Man, then, naturally loses his temper off and on but the rest of the community as naturally damps him down. What is not natural is for the whole community not merely to lose its temper but in cold blood and with infinite arrangement to get ready to destroy another community.

CHAPTER VII

THE FISSURE OF HUMANITY (I)

I. WAR, THE DECADENCE OF MAN

IN this chapter we must then see whether archaeology has found any trace of an answer to the social question which of all questions it is most vital for us to solve — when, where and why did man take to war? To-day that aberrant specialization has like all unco-ordinated growths reached a stage of malignant independence that it is obvious to common sense at last that prophetic foresight was diagnostically correct. The growth will kill the patient. Unfortunately what might have been easily removed at its first diagnosis, but which common sense then neglected, claiming such opinion to be alarmist, now, its gravity is realized, may be incurable. We have seen also that behind that question about war lies the deeper question — as prophetic insight also diagnosed — when, where and why did man take to using or permitting unlimited physical violence because he held it to be the sole possible sanction of values, sustainer of order and preserver of peace? If archaeology could throw any light on that, then it would be not the study of the desiccated past but of our living and tortured nerves.

Indeed no science could serve us better than this one, for it might answer for us our most pressing riddle of the Sphinx and extricate us from our most acute dilemma. History, then, would suddenly take on meaning and the charge 'History is bunk' made by that great symptom of our age, Henry Ford — (master both of the over-riding motor and the futile Peace Ship) — would be answered. For till now we must realize *that* charge, crude, inelegant but pointed, has not been answered by anyone.

The thesis of this book is that archaeology can give meaning to History and give an explanation of why we are where we are. It is here advanced that archaeology links up our human history with our animal evolution and that as we have a new view of evolution, of Life advancing by preserving and intensifying an original sensitiveness into an ever-growing awareness, so too through archaeology we have evidence of this same process and same selection being carried on. As among all animals, as again among all mammals when at last they dominated, so now when man of all animals and of all mammals alone dominates, the same process of selection is at work among his races and stocks. The vast majority, we must expect, will specialize, play for safety and security, defend themselves — even more than against their fellows — against the intolerable strain of persisting in sensitiveness, in awareness, in sympathy and understanding. They will shut down, and from being defensive become offensive and finally parasitic and so extinct. One strain will find the more excellent way and seeming to be set on losing its life will alone gain it.

2. WHERE HUMANITY CONTINUED TO PROGRESS

Now the latest archaeological evidence it seems not only shows where, when and how man in the main began to fail but also where, when and how one strain at least felt its way to a method whereby progress might yet be continued, the long process of upward evolution be sustained and the hope of Life not be frustrated when the goal is almost in sight.

We must here survey that evidence. We have seen that the picture we have up to this point of the proto-civilization is of a complex of culture psycho-physically balanced — that is to say a society which has made equal advances in social invention and practical psychological method to balance its new unsettling economic advances and the psychic disturbance which the discovery (quite as much as the practice) of such physical inventions must cause. We have seen that culture-complex has already spread in a widening ring so far afield that it is already in danger of dislocation, and intercourse is intermittent and slight. It is already spreading widely on its three new sites and in lower Egypt, in lower Mesopotamia and on the Indus the few colonists have succeeded in rooting and branching.

As Dr. Childe has pointed out in his *New Light on the Most Ancient East*, page 206, Sumer is already an association of cities bound by a common civilization. The Egyptian 'colony' has already covered an area twice as large. But the real success is the Indus 'colony'.[1] This covered an area at least twice that of

---

[1] This hypothesis that the Egyptian, Sumerian and the Indus proto-civilizations were all truly colonies must of course not be attributed to Dr. Childe. His own present opinion may perhaps be made clear by a later quotation from the same valuable book (pp. 293-4) where he says that if the primary diffusion of, for example, metal knowledge must be traced either from the Indus or from the Nile then with our evidence to-day the Indus basin must be looked on as the only likely centre, but more probably this knowledge arose in some other way or place.

the Nile centre and four times that won over in Sumeria. Why this disproportionate success? The further we inquire into it the stranger it begins to look. In fact it becomes increasingly difficult to dismiss the suspicion that here in the Indus civilization we may have the most important clue to history and sociology which has ever been disclosed.

Once again we must recall to ourselves the new outlook on evolution and in anthropology or we shall dismiss the evidence, as once was dismissed the evidence of hypnotism, on the Humian method with miracles: that it is more likely the particular evidence is wrong than that a 'natural law' has been broken. The 'natural law' no longer says man is a ferocious animal but a highly suggestible and sensitive creature. We have then to explain how and why war arose, not to explain why it is absent. Anthropology also has begun to point out that quite apart from the evolutionary evidence, the study of man as he actually is to-day is seen increasingly to throw doubt on his inherent fierceness and pugnacity. As the anthropologist Mr. Gregory Bateson remarked in a letter to *The Times* in December 1934 it is 'time that psychologists and anthropologists carefully examined the oft repeated statement that man is innately savage and born with a tendency to warfare'. He asks for the supporting facts to be considered and says that the study of 'primitive man' — he means surviving examples of backward cultures — makes the position perfectly plain: 'Some primitive communities (for example the Arapesh studied by Dr. Fortune in New Guinea, the Sulka whom I have myself studied, the Zuni in Mexico and many others) are almost entirely non-aggressive.

Others — and here we find the majority of primitive peoples — have fitted this business of fighting and aggression into their culture; they have built up round it a series of rules and conventions with the result that in many cases the fighting is more closely allied to a sport or spectacle than to warfare as we know it. Lastly, there is a very small minority of primitive peoples who have developed something resembling the warfare of Europe. As examples of this last category we may take the Zulus under Chaka.'[1]

This is striking testimony, yet far more striking is it that though, as Mr. Bateson says, these facts are known to all the experts, and psychology, anthropology and physiology dare speak with considerable certainty against the current prejudice, the current prejudice still thinks it has scientific backing and in fact that it is based on 'Natural Law'. The onus of proof, that man is a fighter and violence the one way of preserving peace, rests then in reality with the militarist. However, because man is so highly sensitive and suggestible, he can be made believe anything about his nature and because he is so malleable, violent types can beat him, especially when he is alarmed, into almost any shape they require. So it has happened; so it is happening to-day. Wishing for peace he is told by a few aberrants, dominating men of violence and

[1] Mr. Bateson probably knew that Chaka was a Zulu infected by European contacts, already an aberrant type, for he had had to flee his country after an unsuccessful attempt to assassinate his overlord. He watches, fascinated, at the Cape, the European society depending wholly for its sanctions on violence and is naturally immensely receptive of these ideas. He especially studies the Europeans' drilling of trained troops. He returns: reorganizes Zulu society wholly on a basis of violence: but cannot save himself from the inevitable denouement, for when he becomes elderly, in spite of the fact that he asked instead of guns for hair dye from a visiting European to hide his grey hairs, he is, 'unarmoured by his dread prestige', assassinated in his own kraal.

greedy interests that he can only have it if he fights for
it. He accepts to-day because those, whom he thought
informed and impartial — told him so — those nineteenth-century evolutionists who, we now see, were
making a case to their conscience and squaring it with
their comfort. We have then to make the full case
against war, first, as we have seen, by showing it is
biologically unnatural, then by showing historically
how it arose and finally by showing, even more important, that there is also historical evidence of a way
of carrying on social life without the constant threat
of war abroad and the constant use of violence to
maintain peace at home.

To return then to the evidence from the Indus
civilization. It is startling enough to need the above
preparation. We must recall that this particular
civilization or extended sector of the proto-civilization,
is the most successful of the three colonizations — that
of Indus, Egypt and Sumer. It not only extends over
twice the area of Egypt's first civilization and four
times that of the proto-Sumerian: we have also seen
that its knowledge of metal working was the most advanced. In seal-cutting and building with burnt
brick, in drainage and water supply it seems ahead of
its two variants on the Nile and on the Two Rivers.
At the lowest levels, in the earliest deposits there is
found this complete, competent, sophisticated culture.
It can, then, be traced developing in wealth and extent. It shows, however, one amazing deficiency. As
Sir John Marshall, who excavated it, has said, it is
highly curious and remarkable that in the lowest
levels, though tools are abundant, weapons are still
to seek. In the upper levels of later ages weapons do

appear.[1] Nevertheless the cities continue to lack defensive walls, and no armour has been found.

3. HOW THE TWO OTHER 'ARCS' BECAME DECADENT

Before we inquire more closely into this which seems to us, in our topical confusion, such a strange condition, but which biologically speaking may not be so strange, we must look at the parallel development of Sumer,[2] and Egypt. Here we find the distinct steps of an evolution that leads straight to those modern conditions which we understand so well that we take for granted our protests against them must be ineffective. As these cultures begin to settle down on their own sites they develop two striking features. One is the large temple of the central God and the other is the large companion building, the palace-fortress of the king, the citadel. Once that internal growth has developed, external activity becomes evident. Rapidly the league of townships is found to be dominated by a king. He surrounds himself with a specialized privileged caste of retainers. The citadel dominates the townships and makes them maintain it. Finally

[1] Two dirks, the longer eighteen inches, have now been found, p. 127. The knives are nearly all obviously work knives. A few highly inefficient spear-points have come to light. They look more decorative than practical, p. 128. Mace heads are found (but these are thunder symbols), p. 132. *The Indus Civilization*, E. MACKAY.

[2] In one of the earliest Sumerian writings, the Gilgamesh epic, Gilgamesh tries to find out the secret of eternal life. He seeks out the primal Noah-Uta-Napishtim who has become immortal. All he can tell Gilgamesh is 'while houses are built, while brothers quarrel, while rivers go to the sea, while there is hatred in the land, man shall fear death and fail to find immortality'. Is there here an echo of remembrance that once there was a time when men neither fought each other nor feared death because they realized their common eternal life?

when the war-machine (we know by an early Sumerian scrap of carving how soon the phalanx of drilled spear-men was invented) is framed, the cities and the people have to keep it supplied and munitioned while, tired of the small resources this leaves over for those who consume and never produce, the machine is turned on to full-scale war. Raids are organized to despoil less formidable peoples whose lands may contain copper, bitumen, precious woods, gold, lapis, gems or pearls.[1] It appears increasingly likely that the archaeological evidence will compel us here, as in so many other parts of the story of man, to reverse the traditional picture of the relationship of civilization and savagery. That picture showed an unaggressive innocent towns-folk, accumulating wealth by honest toil and then fallen upon by nomads — an unprovoked assault. A useful story for authority, for the moral was 'You must keep up a large army'. It already looks as though the first organization for distant attack was made by the rulers of the townsfolk, coveting peculiar forms of wealth — which lay on the grazing grounds of the simpler people of the uplands.

The need of these peculiar stuffs was due not merely to the demand for luxury and display but also for magical objects (such as pearls, gold and lapis) which in the elaborate fear- and guilt-complex which now increasingly dominated men's minds were essential to save the individual soul. The use of violence had destroyed the old unquestioned sanctions for good social living. You cannot really trust in God if you

---

[1] W. J. Perry, in his *Primordial Ocean*, in the chapter on 'Violence' suggests war is due to the civilized war-specialists raiding the uncivilized to get victims for their human sacrifices. The peaceable simple learn then to be 'the dangerous animals which defend themselves'.

are spending your time keeping your powder tinder-dry. Where your powder is there will your trust be also. The inevitably increasing use of violence inevitably decreases mutual confidence. Violence, whether employed or latent, in use or in threat, is the most emphatic assertion of the community's belief that it itself is composed of nothing but individuals whose only corporate tie is fear or greed. Every individual feels that he and his neighbours are nothing but individuals; each feels that he will be attacked by all the others, if the state — Leviathan — did not hold then all in awe, keeping them from each other's throats as a huntsman leashes and lashes back his hounds. More, each feels that it is only natural, 'biologically moral', for him to wish to attack his neighbour and for his neighbour to be prepared to spring on him.

When individualism has been inflamed to this degree by violence, and all sense of true corporate living, of the fact that each has something in him more than his individuality and which ties him to his fellows, has been lost, then individualism itself adds fuel to violence. Self-consciousness, hypertrophied until it shuts out the last intuitions of any other sort and quality of consciousness, makes the individual insatiable. He needs more and more physical goods to assuage his sense that somehow life has lost a supreme richness of worth and purpose. Physical goods, themselves useless to cure psychological derangement, become, when they are obtained by violence, aggravations of the morbid psychic condition. To mal-ease and loss of sense of worth is added the loss of peace of mind. The acutely guilty conscience begins to appear. It is the retaliation or the response of the whole nature, the complete

164

psyche, to this disbalanced partial development. It is the soul's answer to individualism. The eroding anxiety, which becomes conscious as fear of ill luck, drives its victims, though they possess weapons and should be physically safe, to ever fresh exertions to obtain lucky objects which ward away envious fate. Raids and more raids are therefore necessary to obtain these things. The growing mutual suspicion in the community gives rise to the dread of witchcraft, and in attempting to frighten and torture people into good-will toward their neighbours, the general tension and distress increases rapidly. The priesthood, retained to counter-plot these machinations against the sword-bearing, despotic authority, first of all, like every secret police plays on its employer's nerves to prove what good grounds he has to retain its services, and then demands for its deity materials of luxury and magic which the soldier must raid to obtain.[1]

Hence we see a perfectly natural degenerative process. The city communities which first organized violence to sanction civil order, find themselves next conscripts of an insatiable conqueror. Then finally, when — as did Chaka, Khyan the Hyksos, Attila, Ghenghis and Timur — the simple grazier has learnt — from civilization using it on him — how to handle the scourge of war, we have the nomad conqueror beating down civilization into the dust. This, of course, is what befell both Sumer and Egypt. They both rapidly swelled up under war-king rule into Empires. The

[1] The Kingship and the Godship cannot be kept combined. The realism of the sword disturbs and disproves the very magic it would use. Hence the great war dynasty in Mesopotamia which combines the country into a single military power, the dynasty of Hammurabi gives up being Gods – the sword is a whole-time job. An individualist knows that there is really no God and cannot waste time playing that game.

huge raids, like floods, for a short time spread an area of devastation, the desolation which conquerors call peace. The sword, however, is not government. It has no prescriptive rights: on the contrary it is the denial of that essential of order. It is clear, he rules most securely who uses it least, for its presence deranges that field in which is built up the divinity which is the only hedge and sure cover of a king. Hence the history of Mesopotamia and Egypt is this continual explosive expansion and collapse. At last exhaustion sets in. Dread of the barbarian becomes less than dread of the home-grown oppressor. The centre of self-interest shifts — the native government cannot defend itself and the country which had at its disposal all the resources of civilization, its munitions and its organization, numbers, discipline and skill, falls captive to a savage. The new specialization, like a growth in the body, is draining the general will-to-live out of the body politic as a whole.

The periodic collapse of empires is perhaps the most striking fact throughout history. There is hardly an historian who has not realized that here is a fact which of all the phenomena he studies is not only the most striking but the most mysterious. Many have felt that if the periodic collapse of authority at the height of its power could be understood we should have an explanation of the forces which make civilization and even perhaps a philosophy of history. Hence biological, physiological and genetic theories of history have been frequent. Some are based on assumptions as to human instincts, which instincts have not been established. Others depend on even less well-founded assumptions about purity of race and race endowments. Still others depend on assumptions about stock-exhaustion, that societies grow old as the human individual grows old. Most of them are based on a discarded biology — that man survives because all life survives through incessant struggle and when — the theory of course goes back behind Gibbon to the heroic saga made to justify aggressive violence — 'martial virtue', the love of violence, declines, man degenerates and his kingdom passes. It is, of course, difficult to explain why then violence should fail at the moment of success. The militarist argument, as has often been shown, really runs, that the only way to preserve martial virtues is always to be fighting and always losing.

Impartial opinion might decide that there is something inherently unstable in violence, and its resultant huge empires. They and it can no more be permanent than man can live in a continuous fit of passion or an explosion be made a structure. We do not, however, have to depend only on the certain evidence that empires of violence are as brief in time as they are extensive in area and that therefore they may be based on something which of its very nature is really not a constructive but a degenerative process. There is evidence that empires are the inevitable end-process, the dissolutive crisis of a maladjusted and malignant condition in the body-politic.

Empires are essentially sterile: they do not invent, they exploit: they cannot produce but must squander. They release and waste the accumulated energy and understanding of a completely other form of society, true civilization. How fertile that original way of life is we may judge by the time it takes to bring about complete collapse and degeneration, to exterminate the will to co-operate and the creative forces it commands. Dr. Childe draws attention to the highly significant fact that though what may be called the first imperial phase of the Mesopotamia culture lasts 2000 years (until at last by increasing extravagance of violence the whole native social resources are exploited and reduced and the country no longer produces empires to plague its neighbours but they produce empires to plague it), throughout that long period there is no progress in culture except in two particulars, the use of Iron (essentially a militarist specialization) and perhaps the full development of an alphabet.[1]

For all the rest of its resources, which it fatally squandered, the militarist society, having increasingly to depend on violence, drew on the original productivity, invention and discovery of the primal civilization. It itself was incapable of replacing in any real manner its gigantic wastage. Like a raging star it radiated away all the energy stored in it until even its material form collapsed and only the sterile desert and a few slag heaps marked the site of the degenerative catastrophe.

The degenerative process, as we have seen, can be a slow one but it is one from which there is no recovery. Conditions become steadily worse for the ordinary man. His inventive power is at a standstill, paralysed. His relationships with his fellows grow unremittingly more acute — we see this by the steady growth of codes with steadily increasing penalties, with torture added to death and (as in the famous code of the conqueror Hammurabi who hopes by defining violence

[1] *New Light on the Most Ancient East*, pp. 290-4.

and the surety of punishment to stay 'the degeneration of manners') the deadly *Lex Talionis* 'an eye for an eye' — the principle of the fully exacted debt though its exaction be socially ruinous, of no benefit to the original loser and forgiveness and remission are common sense.

Relations with the outer world are equally degenerative, for empire can have no frontiers. The whole world must submit or be conquered. Hence war becomes endemic, the 'Natural State' until Nature will stand it no longer, and rather than this travesty of civilization, prefers savagery. It will return whence it came to that primal condition before there were these inventions which give men of violence power to plague to extinction all their fellows, powers which not even the most plagued (as we see whenever they seize power) can imagine how to employ without bringing on the same ruin. The dilemma seems absolute: Savagery and comparative peace: civilization and certain destruction. There is no way of keeping society together without violence: the more civilization, the more violence, until the inevitable anarchy and desolation.

This then is the anatomy of the Mesopotamian and Egyptian degenerative social process. Repeatedly thus it befalls Sumer and the later empires in Mesopotamia. Sargon the first[1] and Narim Sin built up short-lived empires. The hordes of 'the men of Gutium who had no kings' flooded the land. The Kassite deluge also overran it. The recoveries are like the up-grades on a switchback, only preludes to a still lower swoop.

---

[1] Sargon seems to be Mesopotamia's first Emperor and Empire-builder and he was assassinated by his soldiers. So short was this imperial effort.

Finally Persia sweeps away the last vestige of independence and the land is ruled no longer even from
its ancient thrones but from the distant palaces of
Persepolis and Susa. Persia crumbles, and after the
Macedonian raid, Rome reaches out for the border-
land prize. Persia recovers and the rich no-man's-land
is again torn between the world's two great armies
each compelled to exhaust the other.

From the desert then comes again the Nomad,
having learnt the only lesson civilization cared to
teach him, war. Khaled strikes down Persia. Omar
cuts off the hand of Rome. Mesopotamia again
becomes a centre of power. For some five centuries
there continues an uneasy mixture, in which fanatical
war-making is increasingly displaced by war-making
for loot and pure love of violence. No discovery is
made of any other alternative way of carrying on,
though, as we shall see, such a way could have been
discovered. At last the latest of the Nomads, Hulagu,
grandson of Ghenghis, in the fourteenth century
sweeps down on this centre of civilization's earliest
and most tragic error. The Tatars were highly
specialized peoples — they had no culture, literally
worshipped the sword itself and devoted the whole of
their great abilities to becoming supremely expert at
destruction. They are a late alternative development
of man — all his inventiveness turned into denial, all
his receptivity made serve defiance.

Their victims attempted to make out that they were
blind primitive hordes who by sheer numbers and
uncomprehending courage overwhelmed, as rats may
overrun and tear in pieces a man. Their numbers
were few, their discipline high, their inventiveness in

strategy and in weapons (they were among the first to use artillery) fertile. Later we shall have to consider again this extraordinary but inevitable development of specialization, a specialization which not only, like all biological specialization, marked the end of its own development but also nearly ended civilization at the same time.

Hulagu, like his master, believed in destruction and violence as itself being satisfying. Certainly nothing will assuage the acute individual's desire for power more than the immolation of all he can lay his hands on. This is far more satisfying than stupid nominal possession. To destroy is to make sure no other, servant or rival, shall ever possess. Both Ghenghis, Timur and their generals often attempted complete extermination, feeding the need for power on the sight of large cities levelled in the dust and pyramids made solely of human heads. Timur expressed this obsession with destruction by declaring he 'the small lame man' was sent especially by God to scourge and plague the human race — a brief but tolerably truthful auto-biography.

That these people, supreme practitioners of war, who reduce it to its insane absurdity, were really no savages but specialists — the logical conclusion of the appeal to violence as the only ultimate relationship between human beings — can be seen by their works not merely of war but also on those rare occasions when even these monomaniacs, through some other strong emotion, had a moment's relief from their insanity and could attend to the other needs of their submerged nature. Timur's tomb is still one of the world's distinctive works of art and even more instructive — because showing a moment's lucidity not merely at the close of life — when a maniac even will often recover his balance — is the lovely memorial tower Hulagu raised to his daughter. He set it up on the confines of Mesopotamia. He left that land, however, an even more lasting, far more impressive and completely characteristic memorial. It was he who not only destroyed its cities but destroyed the whole country. With a supreme strategist's eye he saw how he might not only crush but exterminate. He ordered the smashing of the irrigation system on which the fertility of the land depended. So in a few years there disappeared a population which must have numbered millions. Here was a stroke of destruction worthy of the most advanced type of that specialized mind which, wholly cut off from creativeness by its 'strangulated' individualism, can only show its wish for power by annihilating life. Haunted with its own futility and transitoriness, it eases the sense of its own helplessness by trying to take the side ˆof death, which it so actively, if unconsciously, fears. Realizing that itself, with its acute individualism, is a blind alley and doomed to extinction, it would send down before it to the same doom all life. Like a blind Samson it would drag down the universe on those who still can see.

So till our day Mesopotamia lay desolate. This place, once a source of civilization, became an empty land across which trekked the nomad, himself hardly able to sustain his flocks on its barrenness. It gives a secular illustration of the degenerative process whereby civilization, having taken the fatal decision of depending for its sanction of peace and order on violence, must

slowly decline, first losing its own inherent resource-
fulness, then provoking retaliation by raiding simpler
peoples and, having taught them war and they
having become complete specialists in this degenerative process, civilization (which thought to save itself
by the sword) is extirpated. Only the aimless nomad,
incapable of rebuilding it, or even of keeping up his
now frantically destructive energy, haunts its tomb.
Thy hand great anarch lets the curtain fall and universal entropy paralyses all.

CHAPTER VIII

THE FISSURE OF HUMANITY (II)

I. HOW THE TWO OTHER 'ARCS' BECAME DECADENT

THE degenerative process which we have now seen working out its inevitable development in Mesopotamia, from the first crescent nucleus in Sumer to the desolation of the Turkish Empire, we can also trace in Egypt. There, too, the original colony goes through the same decadent specialization. There, too, after the first colonial development of those co-ordinated arts, crafts and social laws, we have evidence of the rise of the king and his armed household, his guards, and beside Pharaoh's citidel is its companion hypertrophy, the house of the dominating God whose manifestation he is. It is considered a rule of physiology that hypertrophy means decadence. The same law seems to rule in sociology. It is, it would seem, only a variant of the profounder principle, which we have noted now throughout life and human society, throughout natural history and history: all specialization means loss of general sensibility and the loss of that must mean decline and in the end death.

In Egypt first the people are oppressed by their new masters and have to toil increasingly to supply the vast overplus which may keep these unproductive, heavily-consuming orders supplied. Probably no society taxed more heavily its constituents if one is to judge by the size of the works it has left behind. It may however be that works and acts, precipitations and destructive energy bear some inverse relationship. Sumer and the Mesopotamian war cultures may have expended more in martial energy and in incessant conquests: While Egypt may have put the greater part of its expenditure into religious display. The two methods seem alternative ways of controlling the people who produce the means to keep the social structure in being. Neither Egypt nor Sumer specialized wholly in one of them. Sumer had huge temples, and if it had commanded the resources of stone which Egypt had, instead of having to build with mud, it might have built as hugely and hieratically: though why with clay it did not bake sufficient hard brick and build enduringly with that, remains a problem if we are to explain all varieties of cultures by the differences of their environments. Egypt also under Thetmosis III and on other occasions made empires which expanded far beyond Egypt proper and collided with those expanding from Mesopotamian centres.

On the whole however Egypt seems to have made more use of spiritual violence, 'mental cruelty', the threats of tortures which can be provoked by fear of the unknown and impalpable — pains which, owing to man's imaginative power and his social suggestibility, can be as severe and more coercive than physical torture. Its imperialistic raids up the Levantine coast were, we know, to get the cedars of Lebanon and the other materials necessary to keep going the huge hieratic threat and bribe by which the producers might be controlled. How conscious this process became, how clearly the priesthood understood what they were doing and that their task was to dupe the ignorant and unprovided in order to make them submit, we have proofs from the earliest steam-engine known. This is a device whereby steam pressure will make a pot placed under the floor turn on its axis, so wind a rope round itself and this rope, running up through a god's statue standing above causes the image's arm to wave a Hitler salute to the people. So fraud and threat could take the place of open violence. It would not however stay the degenerative process. Values would still be without any sanction and those most concerned with the cohesion of society and most capable of running it, its custodians would most fully realize this. Using such fraud would, of course, increasingly make the priesthood, and any who were shrewd enough to discover the simple trickery, assume that there was in reality no objective basis for Society. 'The Gods are our own invention' — they must increasingly have been forced to believe, 'otherwise they would interfere'. Once reach that stage of thought and the 'God business' becomes the priesthood's property to be used ever more consciously and cynically for its own private advantage. So here again, as in the increasing planned use of physical violence, the use of a method to which man thinks he is driven by his inescapable individualism — the use of evil means because they are held to be the only means that exist to attain the essential end-ordered peaceful productive society — only aggravates the condition. For, using these methods, man is giving himself the final and fatal assurance that there can be no other way, and he is wholly and only an individual. He

176

turns away from the one path out of his deadly problem — the examination of himself and the discovery that he is more than an individual and in that extension of his nature lies the true link with his fellows and the true cement of society and civilization. Turning away he must then go steadily downwards. Because he thought he was only an individual — but still regretted the fact — he sought at first with doubt and used or permitted to be used, with repugnance, the method of violence as the only way to preserve his values, those of his fellows and their common society. As he uses violence he becomes *ipso facto* more assured that his individuality is all there is, that his fellows are indeed alien, that they all hate each other and violence or fraud alone unites them. The inevitable last state of the man is when he realizes that the values which he took violence to protect, are themselves only the shadowy superstitions of the ignorant. The individual and his individual physical appetites and passions are the only reality, and society and all human relationships can only be a struggle between individuals to gain each for himself the fullest expression and satisfaction. This can be an uneasy balance of power each submitting to as little restriction as he must pay in order to be secured proportionate leave and protection to satisfy himself. Such an inherent instability will not endure however for long. Soon the more active, ruthless and degenerate, feeling, as they must, their individualism most acutely, spurred therefore by unbalanced appetite, unrestrained by the last vestiges of compunction, will combine to deprive the remainder of as much as is possible and to give themselves a position of increasing privilege and irresponsibility. The last vestige of the pretence that violence is the guarantee of values, disappears. Morality which began with intuition, and degenerated into those customs which the majority approved and fought for, finally decomposes into whatever the few enforce for their own convenience and profit. If these few suffer from any atavistic twinges of conscience they prove to themselves that as clear-sighted individuals facing up to Reality they are so superior to the superstitious masses (which still cling to morality and think values may somehow still have their own inherent sanctions), that they, the realist few, have a right to exploit the ignorant and stupid many. If they, the few, are brave enough to live without the opium of illusion surely they have a right to pleasures the rest cowardly shun? The brave deserve the fair and as there are no fouls in this game which has no rules they naturally take everything as their rightful share. Later they will find those who will prove for their further satisfaction that such conduct is biologically moral. So Life has intended they should live. They, by recognizing the fact, show themselves the higher type and to that belongs by natural law all the goods.

This is the theme of power in Egypt as in Sumer, a theme to which the theocratic tone in the Nile civilization gives a certain diplomatic polish without affecting the harsh reality of the individualistic selfishness on which Egypt, as much as Sumer, was as fast struck as a ship holed on a rock. It is of course necessary to recall however that neither of these societies rested wholly on violence. Those at the head might naturally imagine this was so and must be so. Where else was there any other force — what else could sustain society? Can a ship float? However dangerous and painful, are not rocks the only possible place for ships, if they are not to sink, and all they carry be drowned? Individualistic selfishness existed in sufficiently high degree so that the Ship of State was no longer seaworthy and its masters, certainly at the beginning of their mastery, were able to run the ship on the rocks of violence largely because this seemed to the majority the only way to save anything. The step was fatal, but the Ship of State, in spite of the way it was handled, took so long to go to pieces on the rocks because, as it happened, it only gradually came to rest its whole weight on them. Then it was utterly shattered. Till then, although it was doomed to sink further until the rocks holed it completely, it continued for long to float partially. It hung together because it was still possessed of much of its original natural buoyancy. What that buoyancy was and how it was retained will be discussed later. Here we must complete the brief sketch of Egypt's decline, a decline which parallels that of Mesopotamia. Indeed they are close alternative variants of the same infection and disease. The symptom that individualism has appeared, that society is in consequence resting increasingly on violence and values have increasing need of physical coercive methods, is we have seen, the appearance of the king's palace and the god's temple. This twin hypertrophy is produced by the social organism's failure to function healthily and to have direct intuitional knowledge of the sense of morality, the reality of value, a knowledge which belongs to those who realize the partial and superficial nature of their individuality. The twin hypertrophy represents and covers the two sides of man's nature — his physical fear of material violence and his psychological or moral fear - of spiritual terrors. The fact that there is this division, this twinning, is evidence of the dichotomy which has taken place in man himself, a division between body and mind and life and after-life.

2. EGYPT USES MAGIC MIXED WITH FORCE

In this twin development in Sumer the Kingship seems to have been preponderant in the alliance, the temple was an annexe of the palace. As we have seen, Hammurabi found being a god more trouble than it was worth. In Egypt the converse seems to have been true. Often the Pharaoh broke away (as on the other hand often in Mesopotamia the priesthood must have trammelled the crown) but the predominance of the priesthood and its centre the temple is shown by the fact that almost throughout Egyptian history the Pharaoh, though he may be captain-general has also to submit to be treated as a mascot, his connubial congresses, his diet, his hair-cutting and nail-paring all being strictly regulated for him. The tragic failure of Aknaton — last of a successful dynasty and inheriting immense wealth and prestige from his ancestors — to break away from the power of the priesthood, is well known. At the end, the final effort made by Egypt to re-establish her own independence is made by Psamtek, who, founding the Saite dynasty, is himself of priestly stock.

The predominant balance of church against state

did not — it never does — arrest the decay, and it is doubtful whether in itself it does even anything to delay dissolution. It may however, as we shall see later, make a slightly more favourable atmosphere, than does naked militarism, for the survival and sporadic outbreak of that atavistic attitude toward life and fellow man which belongs to the saint, the naturally good, the primitive endowment which permits its happy possessor, even in an individualistic society and age, to know he is more than this, that his ideals and reality, himself, his fellows and all Life are profoundly, fundamentally one. These are the Salt of the Earth and decay is arrested in their presence. The decaying body however tends to strive to eliminate — to liquidate such. It expels them or exterminates them.[1] Hence the association of sainthood and martyrdom.

The Nile civilization may however owe its persistence to the fact that an organized religion was its principal characteristic. That religion, though inadequate to balance the reciprocating advance in material invention and self-centredness, was nevertheless an effort on the part of human intelligence to think about the sanctions of conduct and the cohesive influences required for social continuance. Men — the best minds of the time — were concerned with this supreme problem. That the vast hierarchical organization shows, beside those compilations of moral stories and aphorisms which go back to the old kingdom and which try to show morality pays. They were feeling for some power, other than naked

---

[1] For reference to the further isolated development of psychological exploration in Egypt, see p. 263.

violence, to sustain society. They did not, however, as far as we know find such a power, make the psychological discovery of the existence of the subconscious side of the mind and the invention of a technique whereby men of their degree of self-consciousness could make contact with this submerged aspect of consciousness and through it have access to the common life of all. So, instead, we have self-consciousness increasing until the religion of Egypt becomes itself individualized, an affair of magic gods. Then it must seem to priests and all administrators (as we have seen) nothing but magic and is frankly used as such. This is fatal, is as deadly as violence. It destroys the soul's power to escape and grow, for it encloses it in a prison of delusion where it is held blinded, because it is certain that it itself has proved there is nothing beyond. Hence religion becomes, not the counterbalance of materialistic advance but aggravates it. It grows to be the ally and not as it might have been the alternative to militarism.

Egypt then follows without any striking difference the decline we have traced in Mesopotamia. Indeed the resemblance is remarkably close.

In Egypt we have the forcible union of the Upper and Lower Kingdoms — a union thereafter symbolized in the double crown — as in Mesopotamia we have the union of the lower Kingdom of Sumer with the upper Kingdom of Akkad. Next we have the raids to despoil alien peoples and as Sargon and Narim Sin, having mastered the land of the Two Rivers, went into Persia and Syria, so Pharaohs raid the Levant and Nubia. As the men of Gutium and the Kassites deluge Mesopotamia, so from the two similar simpler districts they have despoiled, the Egyptians are in turn conquered and the Hyksos from the North and the Nubians from the South both succeed in vanquishing the aggressive civilization and found on the Nile their own dynasties.

Here too is shown the instability of the savage who has learnt hardly anything from civilization except militarism. These invaders attempt to become naturalized and to absorb the Egyptian way of life. The amalgam fails, the foreigner is expelled and Egypt reverts to its own inherent tempo of decline. Finally the same Persian power which took away from Mesopotamia even the right to be governed from its own capital, sweeps away the last vestige of independence also from Egypt and the land is ruled no longer from its ancient thrones but from the distant palaces of Persepolis and Susa. The epilogue is also closely similar. After the Macedonian raid Egypt suffers the same fate as Mesopotamia, becoming part of the spoil to be divided among the anarchic generals. Ptolemy settles on the Nile, as Seleucis on the Euphrates. Thereafter Egypt like Mesopotamia is acquired by Rome — though held more securely than revived Persia permitted Rome to hold the Euphrates. Egypt falls as instantaneously as did Mesopotamia under the Arab. Thence it sinks until it reaches the final Turkish paralysis.

So the two western examples of the proto-civilization steadily declined through the social degenerative changes of the armed judgeship, tyranny, or dictatorship, the military kingship, the piratical assault on neighbours, the retaliation, defeat and conquest, the common captivity with other nations under transitory adventurers from further *terra incognita*. In the end both places are completely exhausted. The indigenous people are reduced once again to a subsistence farming and herding, little if anything above the original neolithic datum-level from which the proto-civilization arose. The land becomes desolate, a place filled with ruins of which the present occupants do not even know who built them or for what.

3. THE TRUE CAUSE OF CIVILIZATION'S DECLINES AND FALLS

Such is history. Such is the Grand Cycle. All historians from the earliest chroniclers have recognized this is the degenerative process. From the Etruscans who spoke of the Great Year to Sir William Flinders Petrie with his *Revolutions of Civilization* and Spengler with his *Downfall of the West,* all men who have reflected on the past rhythm of culture have recognized this fact of decline. It is inescapable. Vico the first of modern historians writing in Naples, in the seventeenth century, even at that date, with the slight materials at his disposal could demonstrate that this belief was no pessimistic fancy but a fact as obvious as that all men die. Gibbon could remark, as an unanswerable generalization that 'history is in the main a catalogue of the crimes, the follies and the misfortunes of mankind', and he summed up the vast review he had made of part of that degenerative process: 'I have shown the triumph of barbarism and religion', of violence, and of fraud aiding violence, as violence destroys understanding. And to-day such a realization was never more acute. Spengler therefore applied the principle of inherent decay to Western civilization and reaped a lustrum of applause from that civilization for having told it with considerable learning that it was on the brink of dissolution.

Such is history and, what is more, such was, until the present generation, considered to be not only our history but all history and the only possible history. Did it not fit in with Natural History, a fitting epilogue to evolution? Did we not see here illustrated in our own species the working out of that principle which from the first appearance of Life had constantly been in play — the unwise creature continually producing attic graces, culture, values, ideals and such fancy stuff only to be cut down and out by the ruthless biology-obeying spartan type, brutal may be, but essentially the healthy progressive type, Life's chosen standard-bearer, its prize animal?

That view of evolution is however now seen to be a view in which the evidence has been inverted by prejudice. Civilization may and does collapse but that it collapses because it is not tough enough and because Life only cares for toughness, that is biological nonsense. The evidence of evolution, as was shown in the first chapters of this book, points to exactly the opposite conclusion. Man may be doomed to extirpate himself. This present squalid, paranoic way in which he behaves toward his fellows may be the only way he can bring himself to behave, but then the biological answer to that is not that he is perishing because he is too tender and Life eliminates the tender but because he who long lived, who lived from the beginning, the alive, aware, sensitive and initiative way, is now at last failing and has slipped into that specialized defensiveness into which all the other temporary successes in that process — from the giant Sea Scorpion of the Archaeozoic and the giant Saurians of the Mesozoic, to the carnivores of our day — have declined and are extinct, or wait helplessly for extinction.

But not only does Biology now suggest that civilization may not necessarily be a mistake. Anthropology shows an even more striking change in informed opinion — that this our variant of civilization is not necessarily the only one. There are, still widely scattered throughout the world, other cultures than ours. At first we despised them for not being as rich and powerful as ours. As, however, we increasingly realize how poor we are at distributing riches and how helpless we are to prevent our civilization being smashed by the power which we have generated in it, we study these others more carefully. We are discovering that, though they are without much material we consider necessary to life, they nevertheless often succeed in making an art of living out of their materials. We, with more, make a less complete way of living. With their restricted means many of them attain 'the Kingdom of ends', the sense that the individual life is not merely worth living but that all the constituent individuals together are taking part in a process of super-personal significance.

It is not then because we are biologically decadent, nor because human societies can only be what ours has been, that to-day we are in danger of destroying ourselves. Neither Life in general (some 'instinct' or physiological process, which we have inherited from our sub-human past) nor human nature (some sociological law) compels us to go to pieces and, in a frantic effort to protect civilization, destroy itself and us.

4. IF WE FAIL NO BACKWARD RACE WILL TAKE THE LEAD

It may be said, however, that as our species may after all be decadent and about to become extinct, because it can no longer preserve the courageous sensitiveness and openness which Life demands and which until to-day our stock since the dawn of life succeeded in sustaining, so anthropology may also discover that our society is doomed and with us the race. Other societies may exist but these others are, to use Moret's phrase, anchylosed. Some of them may be peaceful but they have ceased to progress. All are infected to some degree with violence. The disease is not absent but only latent. As long as they remain passive it does not appear in acute form. As soon as they should progress — as is shown as soon as our culture touches them — the latent disease is at once active and they become as squalid and as hag-ridden as ourselves.

The proof that Life does not compel us so to live — that it is no biological dilemma: values or survival? — and the proof that many cultures still live with much satisfaction yet using a minimum of force: these proofs do not get us out of our difficulty. Life has failed in most of its forms: indeed it has nearly failed in nearly all. One strain alone has survived with its power of progress still intact. It may be that that strain at last is failing and man will follow all Archaeozoic, all Mesozoic life and all his fellow mammals into defensive specialization, arrest, decadence and death. The other human cultures are also decaying. Their rate of decomposition may be — undoubtedly it is — much slower than ours, but they, too, have in them the degenerative process of violence and individualistic selfishness. They have evolved no psychological discovery, no conscious technique for resolving individuality, whereby each may resolve his socially fatal isolation. They seize upon the economic material inventions, products of our acutely individualized minds, and their brittle culture is shattered. Either, then, they will follow our civilization down to the same level of social entropy or (what appears now more probable) they will be reinfected from our more virulent strain (as Chaka infected Zulu society), become as acutely paranoic and militarized as ourselves and so touch the datum level of social dissolution, at the same time as we. Then the human race, having destroyed its civilization and reduced itself to animal level, will be a feral species.

It will hang about in dwindling numbers gazing with uncomprehending eyes at the choked ruins of its forgotten ancestors or fiddling with puzzled numbed fingers at complicated fragments of their works. There is no more reason why we should re-invent civilization if we destroy it than that an order of animals having given rise to a completely new order should ever do so again. Of all irrevocable processes Life seems the most. The one process that never repeats itself is the process we call history. And so our stock, retiring to animal level, would return quite another animal, as the rocket stick which comes down is different from that which went up. We passed up through the

animal stage with our inherent capacity of awareness
and sensitiveness still unspent, our creative power still
unspecialized. If we pass down again to that stage
we shall pass down already advanced in specialization,
already having chosen the way of callousness, loss of all
general interest, all spontaneous affection, ·all sympathy, outside the ever more rigid and narrow bound
of instinct. Every generation that narrowing capacity
will grow still narrower until we are creatures only of
instinct — only able to feel an emotion in so far as it
serves an ever narrower, more rigid action, irretriev-
ably specialized to one engrooved way of life, to one
diet.

Then any change in our environment — failure of
the special grubs on which *homo ferus* exclusively feeds,
failure of power to scratch them out of their tunnels
in the hardening earth, attack by a new infection or a
new parasite, indeed any slight change will prove fatal
to this living fossil. The bones of the final specimen
will settle in the mud of its drinking pool and the
entire geological series be at length complete.

CHAPTER IX

THE SELF-SANCTIONING CIVILIZATION (I)

1. THE INTACT ARC

WE must then, to find any sure hope for man, advance not merely the proofs that Life is not driving him to suicide and that some of his societies have been far slower than has been our particular civilization in reaching a deadlock. We must find positive evidence that there is for civilized man an alternative way of preserving his values, law, order, and peace, other than by violence. Is there any evidence of this?

That question brings us back to that historical evidence we were discussing at the beginning of Chapter VII. There it was said that there would have to be found historical evidence of a way of carrying on social life without the constant threat of war abroad and the constant use of violence to maintain peace at home. It was further suggested then that in the Indus civilization — that part of the three sectors or arcs of the proto-civilization — only lately discovered — another way of social relationships may have existed. Until the discovery of this third part we had drawn all our notions as to what civilization could be and was *au fond*, on what it rested and what were its native capacities, from Egypt and Sumer. They had developed the fatal specialization of warfare and we not only inherited this method from them, we took for granted that civilization and indeed any social life were impossible without them. They were original civilization and there was no other. Now we know, on the contrary, they were variants: there was another variant: all three drew from some common source: the two variants we have always known (and assumed to be normal) may be aberrants and the newly discovered third may be much closer to the original, balanced and steadily progressive social pattern. Moreover we know that whether the Sumerian and Egyptian war specialization was or was not inevitable, it was a specialization, an invention, a departure. It was not part of man's biological inheritance, his natural behaviour, nor was it, as far as we can see, any more necessary to a state of civilization than it was necessary to the earlier state of nature, for the first step and perhaps the most difficult in civilization, the proto-civilization seems to have been taken without war breaking out or gaining any part in man's social life.

That the Indus variant of the proto-civilization may be a less corrupt off-shoot is also confirmed by the fact that this Eastern development was more successful than the other two variants. As we have seen it spread further: it covered in its original form at least some 600 miles while the primal civilization in Egypt did not spread beyond 300 miles and that in lower Mesopotamia was confined to an area of about 150 miles. It was highly efficient and skilled. Its houses and streets of baked brick, its drains, culverts, reservoirs and baths of brick bedded in bitumen, its carved seals and pottery, its statuary and its metallurgy all show a society if anything more competent than its brother cultures on the Euphrates and the Nile. In quality as well as in size it may have been their superior. Yet this Indus culture is lacking just that grim reinforcement which we have taken for granted, from our knowledge of Egypt and Sumer and the way of life we have inherited from them, is the harsh necessity and brutal backing which the graceful façade of culture requires. We have then to ask, if this civilization and all its highly developed way of life was not supported by organized violence on what could it have rested?

Archaeologists and anthropologists, formerly, had they been faced with this lack of evidence of warfare would have filled in the gap from the sociological assumptions accepted from biology. Man was always a fighter, therefore lack of evidence did not and could not prove that in this case you were presented with an exception. Now, however, as we can no longer make that assumption neither can we dismiss the gap in our evidence as being without significance. It may, on the contrary, be of the highest possible significance. Here may be evidence of an authentic alternative way of life and process of civilization and one which therefore might if followed deliver civilization from what other- what seems to-day its inescapable dilemma. Still the task remains to find on what, if not on violence, this society rested and to answer the question, how it preserved values if it had no physically coercive forces at its disposal?

As was stated at the beginning of this book, there are three possible answers to this question. The first is group-suggestibility (a better term than the gregarious instinct, for man has no instincts and it is doubtful whether gregariousness among mammals ever reaches the distinctiveness to deserve the definition Instinct). Group-suggestibility may have lasted on among peoples who were naturally peaceable and so did not inflame individuality by quarrelling, private possessiveness, disputes, awards, punishments and retaliations. Such suggestibility must have been high in the human stock. It is hard however to see how that suggestibility could have responded to anything but unquestioned habit and custom. 'Who suggests the suggestion?' is the complementary question to 'Who guards the guardian?' Custom is the suggester and in a changing society that voice becomes confused. It is the break-up of that (the whole of the tribal ways no longer fitting in with the new methods of living caused by invention) that provokes immorality and renders both the social suggestion weak and also the minds of the individuals who are to take the impress of that social suggestion less impressionable. Personal quarrels among individuals add to the social confusion. They are however more symptoms than causes of society's dislocation. The primal cause of all change and invention is a change, a narrowing and partializing of consciousness which must be specifically corrected (by exercises which recover for the individual his sense of the whole) if social breakdown is not to take place. Social suggestibility could therefore only have kept society together provided that society made no changes and so the unquestioned, and indeed untaught, monition of custom could mould each individual without his being conscious he was being moulded, because, throughout his life, he and all had been subject to this one current and he and all could conceive of no other: this was the only possible way of living: law and nature were one.

As was said, then, when discussing the rise of the proto-civilization, that step itself, could not have been possible (society must have broken down through 'shell-breaking shock') unless the economic inventions, the new physical ways of life, agriculture, etc., had not been balanced by proportionately conscious advances in psychological inventions.

What then it is clear we must look for in the Indus variant of that proto-civilization is just some such further definite advances in practices whereby men with increasing method and deliberateness strengthen their morality so that it may be as definite, objective and part of their newly-defined consciousness as any of their new economic and 'scientific' processes. It is at this point that the other two 'arcs' in Sumer and Egypt failed.

2. RELIGION NOT THE SANCTION

That prevents the obvious answer 'Religion'. If the answer to the question, how do men hold together without being coerced, is not suggestibility we cannot with the experience of Sumer and Egypt before us allow religion, as known from such sources, to be adequate. It has been allowed that it undoubtedly may and indeed must have played a part in holding all societies together — a part also which it plays all the better the more it repudiates any alliance with the sword. Even in the other primal societies which had depended increasingly on war we find that religion had not wholly lost this power. No example of this could be more striking than the case of one of those Nubian Pharaohs who, driven from the throne of Egypt by a native who raised the country against him, reconquered the land and actually captured the temporarily successful patriot. The Pharaoh, we must remind ourselves, was what Europeans and Americans would call a nigger. His revolted subjects had they caught him (instead of he their leader) would no doubt have dealt with him as a crowd in the Southern United States occasionally deals with his race. Nevertheless the Negro spared his rebel rival. Such clemency — as dangerous as it was noble — could only have been made possible by the foreign Pharaoh having studied his adopted country's Book of the Dead and having realized the truth hidden in its symbolic language that in the end every human soul answers before Osiris for his acts towards his fellows. Somehow he and they are inextricably bound together in the Bundle of Life and he who acts nobly to another is extending his life in commonness with that which he spares, for does not Egyptian theology also teach that in the end each and all must themselves become Osiris.

Nevertheless religion, as it developed as consciousness developed, does not seem the power which could (and did in the Indus culture) take the sword's place as the sanction of morality and values.

The reasons for this view are obvious. In the first place, as all its critics have pointed out, it depended nearly always on a close and still closer alliance with the sword, until it became no more than the sword's abettor — extending the king's threats of violence beyond death whither his weapon could not reach.

In the second place, religion, mainly because of the growing individuality civilization provoked, became increasingly anthropomorphic in form and magical in method. The Numinous, the general sense of the Holy and of the sanctions that hedge altruistic and moral conduct, becomes separated off from man himself and the Gods are people outside, who may or may not care for his morality but who certainly can be bought and even, if you have the word of power, coerced. This process is evidence of a gradual deepening of the fissure in man's originally single consciousness. It shows the rise of a limen between the conscious mind which he uses increasingly in his life of action, invention and economic work and the subconscious mind in which still resides the true sanction of his morality and values; because it is through his subconsciousness that he is in real touch with his fellows, then life is indeed his and he and they share a life beyond and greater than any of their individualities. Hence religion, as it is actually present in the civilizations we have so far studied, inflames man's individuality perhaps more than it helps him to transcend it. Thus instead of reinforcing morality and giving a sanction to values and showing how the ideal is real, it may actually make for man more sheer and wide the separation between what religion allows him to be and to remain — an individual — and what he knows he wishes to be — consciously part of a greater life.

In short to summarize the diagnosis given of the Egyptian decline: Religion is only a phase or stage of that social balance and counterpoise which has to be continually shifted, strengthened and made more consciously and intentionally psychological as man's physico-economic power and his concentration on the analytic self-conscious methods which increase that power, grow. Each stage of man's growth in self-consciousness must have its appropriate, clearer-cut for more lengthy, approach-shaft to the subconscious. The simple religious methods of an intuitive unreflective age are no more use to men separated farther from their own buried common-life than would be the neolithic flint-miner's galleries and his crude technique of tunnelling, to give access to deep coal-beds or safety in winning them. Religion, the simple rites and prayers, sacrifices, rituals, vows, that pattern of behaviour cannot give men at a certain level — though it gave it to those before — the essential access to life. Therefore this religion, this stage of life-spirit knowledge, can no more balance and keep poised a civilization which has reached craft level (keep it from losing social cohesion and degenerating into war) than could simple gregariousness prevent Stone-Age man from falling into the same destructive anarchy. Living religion is the second stage of a psychological progress (which must parallel the material progress) the three stages of which are gregariousness, religion, psychology. If religion is kept on when it should already have been transformed into psychology then it becomes only magic. Like the Manna it cannot be kept. It is a bread which man must eat at a certain stage of his journey through the Wilderness on to his promised land. Nor by going back to the Wilderness can man hope to find again that bread. He must go on in faith that at each stage and for each stage of his growth an appropriate

197

'bread of the day' and of the coming day awaits him. A full and real psychology — not a wish to explain away the soul but to understand and to permit it to grow — it is in that and in that alone that the future of man as a separate soul and as a society, which in its essential nature is spiritual, resides.

These reasons however may be dismissed as purely speculative. The third reason is then decisive, not merely because it is theoretically sound, but because it is factual. The Indus civilization, we have seen, is the only one which does not show clear — and increasingly clear — dependence on violence. It has no weapons in its original form. It has no city walls. It has no great palace of the king and citadel of his overawing bodyguard. But neither has it any great temple of the God. Neither side of the old alliance exists. The State does not rest on the king's sword nor on the priests' curse — but neither does it seem to rest on organized religion which may promise blessing instead of cursing.

Here then is a culture, too complicated, too full of fertile inventions, too progressive to be held together by nothing but group suggestibility. Yet this culture shows no sign of being held together either by force or fraud, by coercive physical violence or by threats and promises of magical benefits here and hereafter. The mystery remains: each effort to solve it has only made it appear more profound. These cities[1] in their general equipment, their fine streets and fine houses with none outstandingly dominant give — as Dr. Childe has said — the impression of the homes of

[1] They are the first cities known to have been planned. All the streets are set north-south, east-west; one street runs straight for half a mile and is 33 feet wide. *The Indus Civilization*, pp. 22-5.

comfortable, equalitarian burghers. Here is a people living at peace and ease; with an increasing culture which spreads increasingly without conquest: unafraid of the stranger and strange ideas (a Mongolian has been found buried among them, and several other races; no such strangers have been found in the early Sumerian or Egyptian burials)[1] — without anxiety for this world or the next; with sufficiency and good consciences; well off in body and in mind; enjoying what they have and understand and apparently having come to terms with what is beyond them.

3. NATURAL GOODNESS NOT THE REASON

It is essential then that we should discover all we can about these terms they made. This people had no great and dominating deity, but is there any trace that they had any defined way of behaving to the unknown, the unknown that linked them and their neighbour and linked them both to Life and its purposes? The old Liberalism, the Rousseau standpoint which, having said man is good, expects him to attain complete self-consciousness and yet preserve his primal social unity, that faith we have seen is as groundless as the despair of the Realist. Man is not a war-maker, but if he grows in individual self-consciousness, through it experiences that sense of sunderment from his fellows, and through it makes those inventions which destroy custom, then his society will start disintegrating, and physical coercion and violence will

[1] The Indus civilization traded we know because a large series of weights have been found. As is pointed out, so few are false weights that a high standard of morality must have existed. *The Indus Civilization*, pp. 134-5

appear as the only way to prevent anarchy. Self-consciousness must be consciously corrected and re-balanced. A creature who makes deliberate inventions and discoveries in the outer world can no longer leave the growth and development of its inner world — its consciousness — to 'nature', to chance. That illusion has been the great, fundamental mistake of Liberalism and explains its failure.

It is here, then, in a deliberate scientific knowledge of themselves, in a technique of access to what was becoming their subconscious, that we should suspect the men of the Indus culture made discoveries and established new practices. In this sense is there any trace of evidence that this civilization had a religion? There is ample archaeological evidence that they had the usual apparatus of devotion — amulet objects, cult objects. From these it seems clear that many animals were sacred — they realized the mystery of their own life which under other forms flowed also in these strange beings with whom they were related but which were not human. The sun also was seen as sacred — the radiating centre of all being. But even if we read these objects right still they cannot have been more than reminders or even rationalizations. They are not religion but only comments on religion. They are not methods of keeping in touch with Life and preventing the individual from becoming cut off. At best they are symptoms of that achievement; at worst they are the dried bones, the skeleton once precipitated by a living but now vanished thing. We have then still to ask, Did such a thing ever live and if so how? What was its nature and its way of life? Is there any evidence of this? Undoubtedly there is and these evidences are fortunately now not indecipherable by us.

Earlier evidences of what may be called the religious attitude to Life, human behaviour not based on economics but on a psychological need, does, it seems increasingly clear, exist. In this book the Azilean painted pebbles have been referred to as such and the interpretation of similar stones by a Tasmanian aborigine has been quoted as giving confirmation of that supposition. It is clear that man must need increasingly some methods whereby to remedy the growing mental myopia which, as his individualism increases, makes him lose sight of all general purpose in living.

4. THE RITUAL UNION WITH LIFE

The symbols whereby this is done are however indecipherable, unless such have lasted down, still employed, to the present time. It was only by a last and rare chance that the significance of the Azilean pebbles was made tolerably sure and a glimpse obtained of religion in the Stone Age and of the psychology of pre-agricultural man. The religious symbols of the Indus culture are still in use in modern India. In the Indus culture are found the Lingam and the Yoni, the symbols of the Life and Fertility religion. This religion, together with its complementary economic culture, has lasted down to the present day. Mohenjo-Daro, Harappa and the other cities of this culture have for millennia been deserted mounds, so long abandoned that not even a wisp of legend haunts them. The climate changed[1] and man abandoned these sites.

---

[1] The climate to-day is evidently far more arid. *The Indus Civilization.*

SELF-SANCTIONING CIVILIZATION (I)

The culture spread and it is the basis of that of the greater part of India to-day. Osiris is only a name, Ishtar and Nilgal are still fainter names. On the Nile and on the Euphrates the spiritual being most reverenced and besought is a camel driver who lived only some thirteen centuries ago in Arabia, whose new religion replaced that of a Palestinian carpenter who was also born only six centuries earlier. In India the religion of the proto-civilization still continues. Conquest has swept down on it repeatedly but, though the superstructure has often been wrecked, the foundation has always been too firm for the hoofs of the invaders to break through and ruin that platform. That fact is undeniable. Buddhism becomes increasingly re-merged in the elder more vitalistic faith. Mohammedanism still remains, in spite of centuries of energetic predominance and persecution, a protesting minority — to-day its epoch of dominance over, terrified of becoming swamped and its stock becoming assimulated in the autochthonous cult.

Nevertheless Western civilization still looks down on India and mainly because of this thing, its religion. To the West, suffering from acute conflict owing to its unsuccessful attempt to repress sex, India's frank use of sex awakes the invariable reaction of such strugglers when faced with another method of dealing with this primal force. Horror, disgust, contempt are honestly felt. The Indian has degraded religion, is the frank opinion of the pre-anthropological stranger viewing Hindu practices. The anthropological approach however is not so precipitate.

It aims at understanding before passing judgment. It asks, in the first place, can a people which has behaved so differently toward life as we have behaved, understand without patient restraint a culture which differs from ours on such a point? It is clear that on the question of religion or sex, whether we be right or wrong and whether or no we succeed in doing what we say we believe and do, we are not so sure of ourselves as to be able to be calm.

On the contrary do we not show that complete gamut of emotional excitement, horror, disgust, contempt, startled interest and violent hostility which makes the anthropologist suspect that here we have not a supreme culture studying a lower but one which has been specialized and localized, which has now spread outside its natural limits and which is subconsciously fearful lest it should go to pieces?

The anthropological temper further asks can a social pattern which has lasted on so long and survived such violent handling by intruders be so fatal to human society as its startled opponents assume?

Indeed it would seem it is the 'repressed' cultures of which Western Civilization is one hypertrophied variant, that have shown most often instability and the weakness which collapses into complete ruin. India has often been devastated but it seems hard to find any period there during which an area with the cultural cohesion and geographic extent of Western Europe lay producing no cultural works, as Western Europe lay during the Dark Ages.

5. THE LIFE RELIGION NOT ESSENTIALLY LICENTIOUS

We are bound then to ask is this religion of Life so debauched and enervating as we have assumed. Here again the anthroplogical approach can help us toward solving the difficulty.

When we come across the evidences of the Fertility Religion we imagine that its present practice in all its emphasis and accent must always have existed. If however, as seems certain, individual self-consciousness has steadily increased as civilization has continued and has become acute when different cultural variants — such as the puritan 'repressed' type and the orgiastic expressive type, the Apollonian and the Dionysian — have come into contact, then the Fertility Religion will tend to have what we call its specifically sexual aspect defined and enlarged. The main psychological value of the Fertility Religion, which later is rationalized as magic for growing crops and making man and beast fecund, is that it rouses the individual from his growing preoccupation with his calculated personal economic concerns. It throws him back into the stream of life and chokes, at least for a moment, the growing anxiety rising from his sense of isolation from his fellows and his narrow concern as to what is going to happen to this precious perishable self, which is all that now is fully real to each. The orgiastic ecstasy floods the individual once again with the tides of life, which obliterate the silt-banks of the defining self and make the small stagnant pool of each for a moment part of the inexhaustible eternal sea. Long before men discovered by the wine of Dionysus[1] how to tide themselves over the bar which the limen had now become, and gain again the creative deep, the orgiastic force inherent in them

[1] The Dionysiac religion when centred round the Orphic tradition seems also sometimes to have used procreative ecstasy to give the initiate experience of deliverance from his individuality.

through sex had served this one of its truly natural purposes.

Nevertheless, though the Fertility Religion for long served man, by helping prevent his individuality from becoming absolute, it could evidently not wholly check that process. As therefore it failed to create in men a full sense of their pre-individual state of mind it itself became individualized. Then, of necessity, practices and rites, which till then had been general, became particular, and objects and actions which had been symbolic of the individual's union with all life and his loss of self-consciousness and private anxiety for his own satisfaction, became no longer symbol but ends in themselves, activities to heighten individual pleasure. Hence disappointed man feels first a reaction of depression and finally disgust. That is the course which, it has been suggested in *The Social Substance of Religion*, led inevitably to asceticism.

Whether that be so or not it is clear that the primal religion, probably the religion of the proto-civilization and the psychological balance which kept those first economic inventions from deranging man and society, undoubtedly declined. Religion does not necessarily evolve upwards, any more than any other of Life's manifestations. The later accent and emphasis of the Fertility Religion is probably as useless, if not as deadly and repulsive, as the puritan maintains. The purpose of religion is to give the individual true sense of his larger life which he shares with others, and thus to make all social life and all co-operative values able to be maintained through that sanction and without the sanction of violence. It is doubtful whether the Fertility Religion succeeded in this during historic times to any considerable degree, though we must remember that its influence must be indirect and so may be underrated and completely overlooked. For it does not teach morality. What it does, when it works, is profounder, more unconscious but probably more efficacious. It gives the individual direct experience of his larger extra-individual life which he shares with his fellows and so makes it harder for him to think of himself as a completely insulated consciousness which has no natural ties with those with whom he shares the resources of the community.

Yet even when Religion effects so much it hardly ever has been known to do so save over a strictly limited and inadequate area. The sense of kinship which it gives may tend to be confined to those forms of life — his fellows and his totem animals — which man knows. He may fail to feel kinship for strangers and to recognize they also are part of Life's whole.

All, then, that we can say of the Fertility or Life Religion, as it remained on in India and came down from the Indus sector of the proto-civilization, is that it may have been sufficient to account for the fact that the Indian civilization, in spite of many assaults and inundations, has lasted continuously on to the present day, while the Mesopotamian and Egyptian sectors repressed that religion, denied the orgiastic, 'Dionysian', release into the subconscious to their peoples, had to depend increasingly on coercive violence for social cohesion and finally vanished completely from off the face of the earth.

We have to allow that the Indus culture may have succeeded in extracting from a process, which as it declined became immoral (i.e. enervating and self-centred), something which nevertheless had social value and which the other variants of the common culture cut off and extirpated — extirpated perhaps because they had first prematurely degraded it.

India may, with greater intuition as to Life's needs, have kept on the Religion of Life because it felt that the alternative to some such intense way of realizing kinship with Life, as individualism grows, can only be through increased use of coercion, through physical violence. Religion in the other 'arcs' became respectable and anthropomorphic and ineffective and so had to ally itself with the sword, for it itself was sanctionless. In India it remained below the self-conscious and shamefaced level, so it remained frankly sexual and not ineffective. India may have preserved a dangerous technique of bridging the gap between conscious and subconscious, as Life has preserved in Man the dangerous capacity of general sensitiveness, whereby he can use his feelings for many different purposes — for some which are more highly purposive than instinct can be, for others which are more pointless and debased. The Religion of Life could be, and often has been, degraded to futile sensualism. It could be and has often been the way whereby men preserved their realization of their psycho-physical and psycho-social unity.

It is necessary to draw attention to this psychological factor in the Indus civilization. Its evidences, the Yoni and the Lingam, have been unearthed[1], and looking for the psychological element which held together this the only sector of the proto-civilization

---

[1] See Report of SIR JOHN MARSHALL, *Indian Survey*, and E. MACKAY'S *The Indus Civilization*.

which lacked coercive methods, we are compelled to ask, Is this the clue, is it here the explanation lies? Here is a religion which exalts Life, and gives the individual a direct experience of his kinship with it, a religion we find present in a society which seems to have no other sanction to hold it together, a religion which continues in that society while that society, assaulted and inundated, survives, when those who defended themselves (and suppressed the Life Religion) became extinct.

It is hard then not to attach some value to it and to allow that it may account in part for the defenceless appearance of the primal Indus culture and the pertinacity of its pattern down to the present day.

6. THE LIFE RELIGION NOT ENOUGH

Nevertheless the discovery, however interesting historically, is insignificant, as far as we ourselves are actually concerned, and as any contribution to the solution of the secular problem which in this our day has come to a crisis, threatening our world-wide civilization. If the Indus culture maintained itself by keeping alive the Life Religion, when the other arcs of the dissolving circle of the proto-civilization abandoned that religion and so had to depend increasingly on violence, that can be no message of hope to us.

We cannot, even if we would, go back to such a religion. Nor has it power to continue even in its own country. It has lost the battle with self-consciousness. Its vitalism has become sexuality and must degenerate further into sensualism. Instead of the

Life emotions making the individual transcend his individuality, the individual has made these emotions shrink into that individuality's limits.

The Life Religion survives then only in a dying form. It is in an advanced state of decay. It has delayed, no doubt, but it cannot arrest the ultimate contraction of the human spirit into the fatal division of individualism. We of the West cannot accept it; rather it is the East which is accepting the praxis, the technique, the frame of mind, the standards, the respectability and the possessive materialism of the West. India is now about to follow us on the same path of dissolution. Nor is this to be marvelled at, for, when we review the history of India, we see that this Life Religion never succeeded in mastering the invaders who overran the country. It made the conquered endure and when in turn, each conqueror, because of this endurance of the conquered, became himself assimilated, when, in his turn he became a fresh invader's victim, he had learnt this power of persistence, which is more enduring than victory. However at length machines have achieved what arms could not do and the wish to make and protect industrial wealth has made the people themselves accept what alien rulers could never wholly impose. Making money can become a religion and possessiveness grow into such a passion that (as our Puritans showed) it may supplant physical passion and appetite. Daily attention to business has often become a discipline which substitutes for religious devotions and services. Against this attack the Life Religion, already moribund, has no power and rapidly ceases to be even sensual. It may hang on as an archaeological curiosity — last foothold of romance in a world which efficiency has made dull. When it is thought of as not even disgusting but simply ridiculous a breath of laughter makes it vanish.

To-day then we see disappear the last ripple of that one arc of primal culture which preserved the primitive form. To-day the Indus variant of the proto-civilization descends at last to that level to which the other two variant arcs of that common culture descended far more rapidly. The world is one, and, out-voted by a two-to-one majority, the dissentient third now comes into line with the rest.

CHAPTER X

THE SELF-SANCTIONING
CIVILIZATION (II)

I. OUR LINE OF ADVANCE MUST BE
CHANGED, OR CIVILIZATION ENDS

IT would look then as though we were back where we
started. Man may be derived from a stock which
persisted and won its way to the top by retaining a
primal sensitiveness and general awareness. He may,
for some time after he was fully man, have succeeded
in retaining that condition of primal innocency and
interest by (the principle of foetalization) continually
sloughing off too rigid an efficiency, continually
casting the skin of custom, and becoming freshly,
rawly aware of all he could feel but could not master,
all he could see but not yet understand. He may have
surmounted the first great step and have attained
the proto-civilization with all its dangerously satisfying
physical efficiencies and specializations, without losing
his general sense of his extra-individual life. In the
end however he, the torch-bearer, has fallen. Specialization, realism, the sense of the absoluteness of his
individuality has overcome him. He, too, as all forms
of life before him, has at last chosen efficiency. He has
no other fellow animal to act as an adequate rival
against which he may use the destructive powers
efficiency gives him. He turns therefore the armoury

(which he has chosen in place of awareness) against his own species.

2. AND WITH US ENDS LIFE'S PURPOSE

Is not this inevitable, natural — all too natural? Did not the forms of Life which ruled the last great phase of Life the Mesozoic, did not those giant Dinosaurs do the same? They armed until they bristled with bayonets of bone and their skins became as thorny as the desert briar. Next, the more acute became carnivores and with sabre teeth and dagger claws preyed on their clumsier fellows. Life then turned to the little soft rat-like creature, too insignificant for these first class powers even to notice; if they had noticed too small to corner; and if they had cornered too immaterial to repay the labour of catching and eating.

But, to-day, where is to be sought again the minute David, out on the hillsides, for whom the prophetic Life Force (a demiurgic Samuel) calls, that on him it may pour the oil of Kingship? We can review the whole field of Life more carefully than any Saul, Herod or Sultan could search his territories for the young child which might grow to supplant him. And, whether we take the report of our searchers as the respite of our dynasty or the knell of all Life, the answer to our question seems clear. If our line fail then no one can take the throne-vital. Life will fail with us.

For a time, as Fabre has said, the insects will dance in the cooling sunbeam, the fish glitter in the shrinking sea, the birds sweep in their majestic migrations to die in vaster numbers on 'false impossible shores', shores which the frost of outer nature has bound; while the frost, of their inner nature — their even more rigid instinct — binds them ever closer to their fatal habit. At last only the mosses and the lichens will cling to the sunward side of the bare stones. Life, long having ceased to think and feel and move, will exist at a last sufferance, because it is so little different from death. The curve of its descent will be so near that final dead-sea-level that it will creep on almost imperceptibly to the ultimate extinction. Yet in the end the last spore will remain, still, changeless, its last capacity to build up chemicals into reproductive form, gone from it. Life which rose in its majestic curve, like some vast interplanetary rocket, casting more and more of its mass from it, but still with fiery head mounting the sky, reaches its climax, turns back to the place from which it sprang, still casting from it its substance and at last, a crumbling cinder, drifts soundlessly on to earth again.

Is this then the end? Do we now see, however slow the descent — the whole declining path down to that dead level where all must rest endlessly? It grows increasingly clear, no animal can take our place if we fail. All the apes, the monkeys, the lemurs and the lorises have already chosen and are more deeply committed to the ever deepening specialization which is the first but fatal step to death. Below them the birds and the fish — they chose even earlier the paths they must pursue until the dark comes down. The insects — the creatures among which alone has been built a social life comparable to humanity's — not only are they individually highly specialized, with a body which with its hard chitinous surfaces renders any sensitiveness impossible and makes instinct unquestionable, there is actual evidence that their social life is fossilized. Palaeontological evidence seems to show that since the Oligocene period — some twenty-five million years ago — the termites, ants and bees — the three supremely social insects, have not altered their present social organization.

The choice before us is then not whether a particular species shall perish when we perish or a particular Genus, Order, or Family of Life, be doomed, but whether all Life will not have failed if we fail.

The gigantic experiment whereby some power learnt how to combine chemicals into reproductive bodies, reproductive bodies into organisms increasingly aware; some such an organism into a creature which became conscious; fully conscious; conscious of still wider ranges of existence around it; conscious of life in other forms around it; self-conscious; conscious that its consciousness somehow permitted it to understand how it had arisen and what the universe around it might mean — that experiment which had gone so far until it seemed it must transcend the physical limitations which still bound it, is then to fail and to have been wholly in vain.

That seems the choice before us. Moreover on the present evidence does it not seem that the choice is already taken? Have we not already decided to specialize, to treat our individualism with its specialized, partial, expert outlook, its increasing knowledge of means, its decreasing apprehension of ends, as absolute, final, complete? Have we not decided that our values are indeed unreal because they need, if they are not to vanish, always to be supported upon the violence which disproves them? Have we not chosen, so that the only reality is our individual physical satisfaction, so that in the end our only real value must and can only be the assuagement of appetite and bodily pleasure? Are not all other values only vestigial remnants of social instincts or disappearing taboos which we have still to defend until we can switch ourselves wholly over to reality, to the realization that to live wholly as a healthy animal is Life's only meaning, reward and purpose? He lives most according to nature who breaks most quickly these adhesions from dead superstitions (these superstitious restraints which were imposed because they were thought to benefit life) and who therefore plunges without delay into those passions which, if entered upon early and persisted in until physical satiety intervenes, will leave the organism so exhausted that it will ask neither for meaning nor for continuance.

Such a 'natural development', of course, disposes of values. For these values having to be defended by their opposites are so eliminated. The means having to justify the ends — the means prove the hollowness of the ends and remain as the only reality. As Nietzschean realism pointed out — what begins under the pretence, 'a good peace justifies war' ends with a good war justifies itself. Whatever is, is Right.

This simple and straightforward line of thought is the thought of 'every sensible man' to-day. As, however, Hobbes was attacked by the bishops for saying those very things about government which they acted upon and Mandeville, Hobbes' successor in realism, for telling the age what it actually thought and what was the basis of its action, was called 'the man-devil', so to-day the conclusions which everyone is drawing must not be spoken. This is not unnatural or contemptible. When humanity fears excessively anything and yet cannot devise any objective way of dealing with the peril, its way is to use euphemisms about the horror. The deadly Black Sea, the intelligent Greeks called the Euxine, the peaceful one. The nightmare horror of the early Chinese, the Siberian tiger, they called 'the insect', so its original name is unknown. We, in turn, faced with launching a destruction of unprecedented ghastliness on ourselves, and yet not seeing how we can stop ourselves, call planning such treasons to life 'eventualities', call bombing villages from the air pacifying a restless countryside and the mass destruction of helpless unarmed fellow-beings in a vast capital, self-defence. The paranoia of the Turkish Sultan Abdul, the massacrist, did not go further. To him, as to us, the choice seemed 'Thy life or mine'. Yet our situation is in fact even more ghastly than his. His victims were mostly unarmed. In our case both sides are paranoiic and both sides are so armed as to inflict at a moment's notice and without possibility of parry, deadly damage on the other. This is realized by all thinking people. What is not realized is how fatally natural the whole development has been and is. The man of common sense cannot do other and so as this consequence of his past acts disgusts and horrifies him but he sees no escape from it, he refuses any more to foresee the moment when he must act as he has prepared himself to act. He will no more think of that inevitable Zero hour than he will think of that other inevitable hour when he must himself die.

Give him any possibility of escape, show him any path out and he will then put on the brake in preparation to swinging the engine on to the other track which is open. Otherwise he will let the trains run to their collision.

An elephant, in however great danger, cannot be made escape unless it can be let first assure itself that the track it is to take will bear its weight. Let it be convinced of that and it goes quietly: unconvinced it will remain trumpeting with agony but immovable.

Our crisis is, then, upon us and quite clear. We can destroy civilization and all our power of progress and when we have done so and sink as we then must to even greater savagery, to even more violence, with us will perish not merely the hope of man (we have drawn in all other cultures under the dome we shall pull on our heads) but the hope of life itself.

No other age had to take so great a choice or could see how much is at stake, and as the results will be such, surely it is worth exploring carefully our customary thought to see whether if it lead us to such an insane pass, there may not have been some slip in its argument and some other way of ordering the facts and drawing the conclusion?

We have seen we are not a savage beast but a highly impressionable, highly suggestible animal. We have seen we once found a way of balancing our conscious economic advance with our psychological subconscious development — individuality need not be fatal if psychological knowledge grows fast enough to discover techniques whereby we may have a method of

keeping open our vital communications with our
fellows and with life, our direct experience of our
living part with all others and all being. This is
the one sure natural sanction of values and all
ethics.

We have seen that one of the three projected arcs of
the primal culture did retain in high degree that
essential sense, and must, as self-consciousness grew,
have had a conscious method of recovering and retaining that sense. Retaining that, it had no need to
resort to that degenerative process, organized violence
whereby man hopes at first to avoid social anarchy
and ends by making (as has happened to-day) that
anarchy so efficient that it can threaten the complete
destruction of culture.

Nevertheless, though it retained a method, that
method (the Life Religion) was in the end not strong
enough. It has itself degenerated and now even the
culture descended from the most resistant arc of the
primal circle, is rapidly dissolving and cannot hope
to survive if the culture descended from the other two
arcs should — as seems increasingly likely — exercise
its power of destruction.

Yet that description, though to most social thinkers
it seems to inventory all our resources, and to show our
assets are insufficient to meet our liabilities, does, the
writer believes, overlook essential facts which may yet
save us.

3. THE OTHER LINE

In brief there is evidence which shows that two vital
facts have been overlooked: the first is that beside the

Life Religion, the orgiastic of ritual recovery by the individual of his sense of oneness with Life, the Indus culture had another method, which may be called a conscious and deliberate technique, a method which could be taught, tested and measured, whereby the individual could attain consciousness of his extra-individuality, his real nexus with his fellows and his unity with Life. So values and morality attained their only possible sanction.

The second is that that method has never wholly been lacking even in the cultures descended from the Nilotic and Mesopotamian civilizations. It has been the salt which has prevented social decomposition even when the sword has been acclaimed as the sole bulwark of peace. The method was more successful in the East because it was more consciously worked out and when the personal technique was mastered, further social thought planned a structure whereby this power might most efficiently be available to benefit, preserve and advance the whole society.

It seems that the East made this psychological progress because it was proportionately backward in economic progress. The West advanced economically — in its exploration and conquest of the outer world — because it neglected its exploration and conquest of the inner world. Nevertheless the West was never wholly without this psychological insight any more than the East was without economic power. To-day these one-sided developments may perhaps come together and so the East be given control of its circumstances and the West of its own nature.

4. THIS SECRET SOURCE TO-DAY NEAR THE SURFACE

The method worked out in the Indus culture may now be made fully objective by the West's new scientific technique and the West's new realization of the supreme importance of the latest of its sciences — Psychology. What has been an orally committed mystery — as we must remember once in our own culture were all the crafts, masonry, glass-making, metal-working, etc. — will now, we may hope, be made an open method. It may need much careful personal teaching, application and advice before it can be imparted and it will certainly require discipline, devotion and a finished technique of self-control before it can be fully acquired. But it may become as defined a practice, with specific acts leading to specific results, as any learning, such as draughtsmanship or the memorizing of languages. And not only may the West make generally current and demonstrable what has so far been esoteric and obscure, it may hope to advance still further these explorations of the human mind and its extra-individuality until, with a world united economically may be matched a world united psychologically.

Such, however, may seem too wild a hope, seen as it must be to-day under the shadow of imminent destruction. What evidence is there of such a possibility? True our civilization is turning to psychology but with such flustered and uncertain movements that the chances of our finding the clue to our peril seem little better than are the chances of a man desperately reaching out for the light because he has been woken by the hiss of a snake on his pillow.

We must then trace the evidence we now have of this method of reaching the extra-individuality and how this method can account for the proto-Indus-civilization existing without 'sanction of organized violence' and the pertinacity of that civilization's descent although continually assaulted and in the end wholly infected by organized violence.

It is clear that the discovery that the Indus civilization possessed and practised the Life Religion is not enough. That religion, that way of recovering the sense of being one with Life and of being able to live in natural peacefulness with one's own species and all life, is obviously quite inadequate for men to-day. It cannot heal the fissure of their individuality which sunders them from Life. But, further, religion of that stage does not seem sufficient to account for a civilized society, such as the Indus culture, being able to persist peaceably. Their economic, materially inventive, analytic advance was so high that it seems clear that only a ritual, a technique, which was already specifically, consciously psychological could balance and counterpoise the individualized self-consciousness which an economic advance of this height indicates and symptomatizes.

5. THE SELF-SANCTIONING SOCIETY

The Indus civilization, explored in Sind and the Punjab, has brought many remarkable facts to light. We have seen the unsuspected material equipment of this people: its houses and hydraulic craftsmanship, its knowledge of the wheel, ceramics and metallurgy.[1] Its worship of Life as an organized religion in the forms still preserved in India to-day: the lingam, the yoni: the sacred peepul tree and pillar: the sacred bull—is clearly evident. These latter signs have come to light on the highly distinctive and beautifully carved seals or small square tablets found in the deep levels of the excavations.

A great number of these has been found. Many species of animals, so perfectly carved as to be recognized without any ambiguity, appear on them. The bull, the humped-bull, elephant, tiger and deer are all commonly shown. Across the top runs, deeply incised, a script which till now no one has deciphered — though, as evidence of the diffusion of this culture, it has been pointed out that the script seems to bear affinities to another still indecipherable writing, that of the now extinct builders of the great statues on Easter Island in the East Pacific. The design on one of these seals is, however, unique.[2] It needs no decipherment of its inscription to explain its purport to an Indian. Its significance is so great that beside it all the others become only of casual interest. It shows a human form seated in what is called the Asana Attitude — the attitude, for example, of Buddha in contemplation. He is three-faced. Drawn around him, facing toward him, as by an orphic attraction, are the

[1] Not only were these people ahead of Sumer and Egypt in town planning but also in mechanical inventions. A saw has been found with an edge 'set' by making the teeth undulated. The 'set' saw (so that it will not jamb in its cut) is an invention lost till Roman times. If such a useful material invention could be lost, how much easier psychological inventions. *The Indus Civilization*, p. 126.

[2] Two other seals showing this design have now been found. *The Indus Civilization*, p. 71.

goat, the buffalo, the tiger and the rhinoceros, only the elephant faces away.

Shown to a descendant of that culture the description is given as definitely as a text: 'This is Siva, Pasupati, Lord of Beasts, Prince of Yogis.'[1] The archaeological interest of this find would be of vivid importance did it not pale beside its psychological value. For it throws light on many problems of Indian pre-history long debated. Siva then is Pre-Aryan, for this Indus civilization is Pre-Aryan. Those horsemen come in later. Their graves lie atop of all this buried record and, queer thrust from the deep earth at rash passing prejudice, the Swastika is found also deep below, centuries before the Aryan.[2]

More important, the Yogi psychology, it seems, goes back to the proto-culture. There, too, had been much speculation. When did this mental method, so elaborate in its immense variety of practices and claiming such a vast antiquity, really begin? The Aryan stocks have wished to claim this as their discovery. The Tamil speaking Dravidians, the Aryan's predecessors, have always asserted the wild horsemen learnt it from them. They, the indigenous people, had this and all other corresponding economic culture in their hands when the raiders came and they taught and tamed these ignorant violent creatures. They claim Siva is their God and he taught their fathers nigh on two hundred various Yoga practices. It looks as

[1] PROFESSOR CHILDE, *New Light on the Most Ancient East*, p. 222. A resemblance to Siva is found in other statues from the same site. See also Sir J. MARSHALL, *Mohenjo Daro* and *The Indus Civilization*, 1931. 'The peculiar half-shut eyes of the best preserved statue have been thought by one authority to represent a state of Yoga'. MACKAY'S *Indus Civilization*, p. 66.

[2] PROFESSOR CHILDE, *New Light on the Most Ancient East*, p. 223.

though the judgment of archaeology inclines in favour of the ancient race.

However interesting these issues may be they must yield before the psychological question which this seal presents and which it may answer.[1] Here may be the real clue to the strange defencelessness and success of the Indus culture and following that clue we ourselves may find our escape out of the deadly labyrinth in which our present progress seems involved and lost. We may with this strange talisman solve the strangest mystery which has come to light about the rise of civilization and also escape the dilemma which to-day seems to bar its future continuance.

To make such a vast issue plain it is, however, necessary first to discuss somewhat more fully what is the Yogi culture, its relationship with Indian civilization and its connection with civilization as a whole and the world to-day.

Our problem and that of every sociologist and historian — who accepts the new conceptions of evolution and rejects the old notion (which coloured all modern historical thought since Hobbes) — is to see now at what stage of his development man lost his inherent power of co-operation and had to seek for some conscious way of preserving a complicated and elaborating society. It is clear that stage corresponds to the period in his psychic evolution when he attained self-consciousness. After that he must do deliberately

[1] *The Indus Civilization*, p. 96. 'The most important contribution to the data amassed at present is Sir J. Marshall's identification of the male figure on certain seal-amulets as Shiva or his ancient prototype; for using this theory as a basis it has been possible to assume that many of the features of modern Indian cults are derived from very primitive sources; they may perhaps date back even to a period before that in which the peoples of Mohenjo Daro and Harappa built their cities.'

what till then he had done without thought. As American Indians still can be found saying, 'In the old days there were no fights about hunting grounds or fishing territories. There was no law then, so everybody did what was right'. As Dr. Ruth Benedict says, who quotes the above saying, 'The phrasing makes it clear that in their old life they did not think of themselves as submitting to a social control imposed on them from without'.[1]

We have seen, however, this did not lead at once to martial law. The first step up into a purposely directed world, a consciously mastered environment, was successfully surmounted and the proto-civilization attained a balanced way of life between technics and tradition, between new powers and means and old ends and values.

This change, however, was not the attainment of a new stability but only the retention of balance — a balance which would have to be continually maintained by more and more rapid, deft and far-sighted adjustments as change accelerated. The Life Religion we may then look upon as the half-conscious adaptation, the wholly artistic intuition of certain people, perhaps very few, to a rapid sharpening of the focus of consciousness. It is hard to believe that these people could have described in abstract terms how they planned and effected the transition from Animism — the sense of their kinship with all life and the whole of their experiences — to Anthropomorphism — the objectivizing of the life around them and the forces that shaped them as in animal and human forms.

This Life Religion was of course far more important

[1] DR. RUTH BENEDICT, *Patterns of Culture*, pp. 252-3.

in its practices than in its opinions, theories, dogmas. Its centring round the fact of reproduction and sex, made fully self-conscious people imagine that it must either be specifically sensual or specifically magical. This was a false rationalization. As the Life Religion was mainly concerned with practice, it did not stress conscious purpose — as we should. When asked for a reason — 'When the children shall say unto the parents what mean ye by this thing?' — then a reason has to be made. The practice, however, was framed by psychological intuition and its value and power of persistence resided in the fact that it gave its practicers deliverance, catharsis, direct sense of kinship with life which their growing self-consciousness was in danger of losing them. This Life Religion continues then in India when it disappeared elsewhere. It could not (we have seen) arrest the growth of self-consciousness but for simple people it could delay it. The danger was that, the more self-conscious certain people became the more power they commanded and so the more could they interfere with the still satisfying Life Religion of the simple. So these simple were not only economically tyrannized over and exploited but made shamefaced about their religion and their psychological comfort taken from them by persecution.

Hence we have a diagnosis of Indian History: a people, which suffers, endures, but finally capitulates and to-day abandons the Life Religion which has finally become disintegrated by self-consciousness, has become what the first self-conscious pugnacious Puritans said it could only be (because it was so to themselves) sensual debauchery.

Yet even on this showing, even if we had no direct

evidence, we should have to ask — did psychological discovery stop here? If the first step was taken successfully, so that economic and environmental advance was balanced by an equal advance in knowledge of self and of the true nature of consciousness, did complete collapse then ensue? Since then, has economic advance been the only advance and has psychological knowledge been at a standstill, only represented by 'the futile, superstitious and grotesque mistakes' which religion has made? The question has only to be stated to be answered. Civilization would never have lasted till the present day and so persistently recovered from disaster and general discouragement, had there not existed some psychological knowledge, not adequate, generally far behind economic knowledge, but still able to prevent complete capsize of humanity's vessel. Often that ship has seemed to have 'turned turtle', through its grotesquely unbalanced loading, but after a time it has swung back again. It has certainly not been a comfortable or even a safe voyage, but that we are still afloat after such rollings shows the vessel has more natural balance than superficial reason perceives.

Further, in a generation such as this, which has lately discovered the supreme importance of psychology, we hardly need to be told that psychological advances do not describe themselves in the language which textbooks favour. We are learning to look on religion not for what it says but what it does; in all its successful practices to see if we can recognize the psychological factor and translate the function, ritual or theory, in terms of a psychological equivalent.

So when we trace the steady declension of the Life

Religion in its failure to retain for man his direct sense of his extra-individuality; and the steady increase of his self-conscious individuality, leading to ever more success in interpreting that partial experience in terms of means, but loss of ends; we should also search for explorations made by man to retain, ever more deliberately, access to his extra-individuality, his social being, his realm of ends. Such explorations must have been made. They must have begun to have been made as soon as the proto-civilization began to elaborate and expand. We ought to hope to find traces of such explorations in that arc of the expanding circle which has been found on the Indus. Because of its lack of evidence of violence it needs some psychological explanation. The Siva seal provides the answer.

There seems now considerable evidence to establish the following relevant and highly significant points.

6. THE PSYCHOLOGICAL TECHNIQUE

Yoga practices (whether they are derived direct from those of the Life Religion as some authorities believe or whether they are an alternative development) are of great age and probably go back to the proto-civilization. They are essentially attempts to use consciousness as it is used on the outer world but so as to explore the inner world of consciousness itself. They are therefore precisely those parallel psychological advances which are essential to balance the economic advances which enrich but upset society. On this 'parallel dating' we should then estimate their discovery to be contemporaneous with that mature economic stage of the proto-civilization of which the

228

Indus culture is now giving us proof. The practices
are aimed at answering two questions: What is the
individual and his consciousness, and what is the
world around him? To-day they are commonly
accused of being 'escape mechanisms', the flight of the
individual from his harsh social responsibilities and
from the world which he now has to recognize will not
shape to his fantasies. Further knowledge has, however, shown that the moment the method is studied it
is clear that this is a libel. The analytic scientist who
shuts himself away to research purely into a problem
may be accused of cowardly flight. In certain cases
men have taken to highly detailed research because
they wanted to sink deep below the rough sea-level of
life-scale issues. Yet no one who has studied science
could say that to describe pure scientists as men who
flee the world and whose explorations therefore are
all tainted with defeatism would either be giving a
true account of the workers or their work. They have
cared for truth and that truth has transformed the
world. That the transformation has been one-sided is
because the truth has been partial. Truth it, nevertheless, has been.

So, too, with the Yoga method. Undoubtedly many
men found in it a way of flight, as men in cloister or
laboratory have hidden themselves. But as the
scientist who only wishes to escape will probably find
his work sterile and his retreat becoming impossible,
so the Yogi, who escapes into other degrees of consciousness, because he would abandon this one as
insoluble, is, on such an authority as Patanjali, said to
be like a man who should go upstairs in a house, find
his way blocked and the staircase on fire behind him.

He must round the cape, cross the isthmus or perish: no retreat, no staying where he is, in defensive, suspended animation is possible.

There is actual evidence that these Yoga practices are not intended to be anti-social or a-social but an essential psychological contribution to the further balanced development of social life and civilization. They are not ascetic. The ascetic is essentially the man who flees life. Detesting the declining Life Religion in which he sees only sensualism, which he dreads, and also frightened by the social anarchy, in which power grows ever more violent and cruel, he flees civilization and by doing the worst to himself would render himself immune to all that his fellow man and accident can do him. The Yoga practices are the reverse of this. They are to produce a mind more balanced and more open than that any man of the world can attain. The Yogi aims at attaining so direct and clear an apprehension of his extra-individuality that the whole social unit, the whole of humanity and the whole of life is realized as keenly as his self-hood. Further his method of attaining that, is not by emphasizing and aggravating the other grave fissure, that between body and soul, but by psycho-physical exercises to bring body and soul together, to close the fissure between the vast unconscious life which directs the body and the little intense conscious life of the individual self, and so — the only way — bring together again the individual self with its society and with all Life.

The aim is obviously necessary: the method as obviously sensible. No society is safe as long as its members do not feel it is their life. Yet if they are only individuals, how are they to feel this? And that they should feel they are members of a common society that alone is not enough. For then they will begin to feel hostility toward other societies. If then society is to be safe, individuals must have direct sense of their kinship, not merely with all their group but with all humanity. Once, however, they have reached as far as this, they must go further. Science has shown, through the intellect, that every human being is part of all Life. It is this intellectual discovery of science which Yoga succeeds in making actual, in convincing the will and the imagination so that the individual henceforward naturally feels and behaves as he knows.

7. WHY THIS COULD NOT BE RECOGNIZED TILL NOW

It was not possible, until we in Europe became interested in psychology and realized the critical importance of the subconscious, for Yoga even to be inquired into seriously. We were sure we knew reality, and even if some thinkers doubted whether our apprehension embraced all of it, we were nevertheless sure that we saw all that mattered. Look at our civilization! Had not our 'power over the environment' (the pragmatic definition of Truth) become almost absolute and so superior to any other culture that they all must crowd to copy ours? We were the first men to be raised for ever above the waves of circumstance. Such naïf self-ignorance could not last however. The most unanalytical began to realize that even if we of the West might have killed off all visible animal life that could threaten ours, and, in our temperate zone, had sheltered ourselves against the vast forces of inorganic

Nature, yet we were in increasing peril from each other. Then came the war as a practical demonstration. Ever since, all but the crudest have realized that our self-knowledge, our science of consciousness, must catch up with our knowledge of the outer world, our Physics, or our Physics will be used by our deranged passions to inflict self-injury which no animal or savage would attempt and no barbarian possess the means to work.

At the same time pure science with its most advanced front, which is also Physics, is realizing that the seen under its analysis grows to look so strange and self-contradictory that it is necessary to pause and look at the seer, to study the instrument which takes in, as, should an observer begin to notice that his lens was giving a distorted image, he would turn to examine it. Already we realize that we do not see reality as it actually is. Our boasted objectivity is a mixture — a construction made out of impressions and prejudices; yet it gives remarkable results of a sort. This late advance in analytic humility permits us to entertain the possibility that other constructions need not be pure moonshine. Indeed they may contain just that other half of experience which our civilization must add, if it is to be not merely powerful but self-controlled, if it is to be able to master instead of being destroyed by its outer discoveries.

To-day then we can study this complementary exploration made by the Indus thought, which may balance — not a moment too soon — the unbalanced opposite exploration made by our Western thought.

Even our present preliminary knowledge of this subject seems to show that this Yogic study — conscious

mind-control to counteract individualism now becoming anarchic — started in the Indus 'arc' at the
very time that the primal culture divided, and those
other two arcs (the Nilotic and Mesopotamian) developed the fatal specialization of war which to-day
drives us to the brink. This confirms our hopeful
suspicion that here may lie the counterpoise, the anti-
dote to our derangement. For even if the Indus discoveries had not been made we should presume that,
when the proto-civilization, on its two Western arcs,
degenerated into organized violence (in its fatal
attempt to compensate for the loss of its own inherent
cohesive power), then the Eastern arc would have, if
it was not to have degenerated as fast as the other two,
to make discovery of a psychological invention, to
check that dissolution. We know the Eastern arc did
not degenerate so fast: we know it somehow retarded
that descent. We know its religion, the Fertility cult,
the exoteric religion was not enough to arrest decline.
That religion failed in the other 'arcs'. But we know
the East had an esoteric teaching and discipline; we
know that it made the Yogic discovery.

The problem, then as now, was the growing fissure
between self-consciousness and the subconscious. No
doubt then it only affected those at the top: to-day the
whole of society is torn by it. Nevertheless even then
the problem was acute. If those at the top did not
succeed in solving their crisis and curing their division
then they, with the great 'menial', applied powers
self-consciousness confers, would seize power to
assuage their now aimless will-to-live, and tyranny
and war — as happened in Sumer and Egypt — must
result.

8. THE PSYCHOLOGICAL DIAGNOSIS

The method and solution were as scientific as the exploration and mastering of the outer world. The first step was to study how the impulses, the passions which increasingly were making the individual act against his social interest and his own peace of mind, came upon him. Detached observation showed that these rushed up from the subconscious and swept the conscious will before them. It was therefore useless to attempt to control the mind directly through the conscious will. The next step in analysis found that these passions were excited by anything which seemed to threaten the needs of the individual as an animal. It looked then as though such convulsions were akin to the violent nervous contractions with which, for example, the muscles of the leg, if the thigh bone is shattered, will continue to drag the split ends together. The organism is blindly trying to close a breach which has been made and, the original balance and interplay of complementary effort having been broken down, the energy of the emotion becomes purely wasteful, explosive, destructive. The individual must act as nothing but an individual and ruin himself and society until he can be given a technique of experiencing his larger being which expresses itself in his neighbour and all Life.

In short man's passions were violent, futile and fatal because their natural and constant release had been deranged.

What should have been the cylinder of an internal-combustion engine, 'turning over' smoothly with its fellows, became a gun, a bomb. The task then was so to direct these forces and so plan again the social structure that they passed round once more in their natural cycle, running and not wrecking society.

In short the task was one of 'setting' again the dislocated and shattered articulation of the group, when once again natural growth would be possible. Society is the macrocosm, the projection of its constituent psyches. When they are fissured, society is chaotic, anarchic. When the inner psychological conflict is resolved then outer order, social justice, economic health, result. That this was the discovery — that outer union depended on inner union — is shown by all these practices, but first and foremost by their name itself, Yoga. This, there is no doubt, is from the same root as our word yoke and implied that the whole process was one of re-establishing a strained or broken union. Some experts have discussed as to whether by union is meant the outer union with all Life or the inner union of the refused Psyche. The distinction is immaterial for the one union entails the other.

Indeed the discovery was of such vital importance because it solved three problems with one fundamental solution, as Einstein in his single Greater Principle of Relativity brought together in one formula gravitation, space and time. So Yoga solves the problem of the self-divided individual, that of the individual and society and that of consciousness and Life and indeed the universe, through the single solution of making the individual learn how to achieve knowledge of his extra-individuality.

With our present psychological and biological

knowledge we can see how the solving of the individual into a 'free psyche' and of this free psyche into an integrated constituent of the social organism and the social organism into the focus of Life, is to follow the steps which our present scientific knowledge shows to be the way Life should go and evolution should culminate, if only we could make our wills obey our intelligence. How life itself would be worked in with the vast extent of inorganic nature is not at present clear to us with our current science.[1] That is a final step, to become clear when we have taken the others.

9. THE METHOD

The naturalness of this scientific exploration and mastery of the inner world of consciousness is also shown by the fact that it is a psycho-physical method of advance. It is no attempt to break away from the body and its evolution and to increase the fissure between body and mind, soul and flesh, any more than it aims at anti-social desertion of its fellow men and their common civilization. The method is not only one of scientific introspective analysis but it is also one which attempts this analysis, and the consequent reintegration, of consciousness by psycho-physical methods. Body and mind must co-operate if the complete form of consciousness, which once existed before their dichotomy, is to be recovered. Soul and flesh must again become a unit as they were once, when the evolutionary creature (though under strain) was not dislocated in itself and was still in full communion

[1] We can however see the promise of further unifying development in the fact that an increasing number of researchers now wish to abandon the division of 'organic' and 'inorganic'.

with its fellows. These exercises therefore recognize a re-union of body and mind to be one of the necessary ends and an essential means of reintegration, individual and social. The mind and body must advance together, otherwise it is impossible for the mind to shift the focus of consciousness, surmount the risen threshold that cuts off the individual from his extra-individuality, which is now subconscious, and so see directly its connection with its fellows and all life. Yoga in its essence is then a practical, empirical psycho-physical technique. It is a method of mind-training so as to render human beings psychologically equal to their present physical powers, instead of being creatures who attempt to achieve a world civilization with a psychology inadequate to preserve a tribe.

Though its aim is to give the individual once again direct access to his general, racial life, it avoids the imaginative symbolism (which will become dogmatism) of the Life Religion and therefore it is far less likely to become specifically sexual. It uses the *libido* of the body but it taps it at so deep a level that it draws on it before that basic energy has become specifically sexual, before it reaches the self-conscious, representational definition where it has to picture the general creative force of Life as being expressed by the particular localized organs and centres of reproduction, by procreation and birth.

On the other hand it avoids the alternative dogma of the ascetic religion, which, because the Life Religion has become self-consciously condensed and 'fixated' on the end processes of the reproductive cycle (because physical feeling has, in its turn, concentrated these)[1] rejects the body as vile and seeks its assumption in some state when this flesh will bè discarded.

Such a method of widening consciousness from the individual self-conscious level — (which makes and can only make the individuo-economic interpretation of society and the world) to the level at which the individual has access to that extra-individuality, which he shares with his fellows and all Life, can undoubtedly be effected and when effected gives the individual exactly that sanction for 'altruistic' conduct which both he and civilization equally desperately need. Unfamiliar as the subject still is to the Western mind, difficult and even dangerous as the technique of the manipulation and dilation of the field of consciousness may be, no one who has made even a cursory study of the method can doubt that it works.

It is naturally not easy to shift the focus of consciousness and make the telescope of the mind open to another aperture. We are unaccustomed to paying any conscious or protracted attention to our minds. The standard focus we use has seemed to show a common-sense, manageable world. Only quite lately have we begun to suspect that there was more to see and, what was more, we should need to see it. The screws are therefore stiff and we, in this

---

[1] It is important to realize that we have evidence of this shrinkage and localization of sex feeling and indeed of all sensuousness. Throughout the life of the individual the senses are narrowing. Freud himself has shown how what he will call at every stage the sex feeling begins by being diffused over the whole body and contracts as life continues into specific centres. The same original diffusion and later contraction has however been found to take place with the other senses. The infant it has been found tastes to the edge of its lips. Through life the taste buds will draw in. (KIESOW, *Philosophische Studien*, Leipzig.) The power to perceive ultra-violet light also seems to contract throughout life.

matter, as clumsily inexpert as a mystic asked to compound a chemical prescription. When we succeed in throwing the present construction — our present vision of the world — out of focus, we still find it almost insuperably difficult to bring any other field into focus. We are alarmed at this unsettling experience and as, in matters of pure psychology, we are as easily frightened as a savage dealing with a dynamo — and the shocks we may get can be quite as serious — we generally give up. Nevertheless there the method is and its power of damage if mishandled is at least some evidence that we are dealing with a real force. Naturally, too, it is not pleasant. When a man's lungs have ceased to work and artificial respiration is employed he suffers acutely as his breathing is compulsorily restarted. So we have to recover this respiration of the mind deliberately and it cannot be comfortable.

This however is not the place to discuss further that aspect of the problem.[1] The objection to making an exploration which will balance our dangerously disproportionate advance in physical knowledge and power over means — that objection will not come mainly from those who are frightened at the perils of the way. All advance has been dangerous: even if this were more perilous than any other we could not shrink from it to-day. The ship of our civilization goes now with so great and so growing a list that we are compelled to throw any ballast we can on the other side.

The most serious objection to giving full value to this discovery, both as a causative factor in history

[1] Later discussion of this point will be found on p. 354 and p. 406.

239

and also as a possible way out of our present urgent peril, is that, though such a method may work personally — in so far as it may make an individual able to endure and perhaps, within his individual range, influence for sanity our paranoiic society — it can do no more than that insignificant amount for society as a whole. That objection however is not really valid. Should an individual gain in this way direct access to the extra-individual consciousness, his example undoubtedly is disproportionately effective. The sense of reliance which the average sensual man feels in the presence of another who is not 'passion's slave' is immediate and lasting. All indulgents, addicts and unstable types, all people who are domin- ated by fear, greed or malice — the three natural reactions of 'the self-regarding emotions' which define individualism — are always looking out for completely independent stable types, 'free psyches' in whom they may trust. A handful of men who both know their own minds, how they work, and how to make them part of a larger consciousness, are able to control a large mass of less aware, more addicted people, who, nevertheless, have, and cannot help having a subconscious desire to attain to the free life the superior type enjoys.

Certainly we have evidence that not only did such minds appear, that their power resided in some such extension of consciousness — control of their own impulses through apprehension of the unity of their life and that of all their fellows in a general life — but that they did also succeed in persuading the community that their experience was valid.

10. THE SOCIAL ORGANIZATION WHICH
THE METHOD PRECIPITATES

For the Yogic practice is the individual side of
what on the social side appears as the corporate
recognition of the seer as the eyes of the community.
Caste has an ugly creaking sound to democratic ears.
Caste, when it has died is as offensive as any other
decaying body, perhaps more than 'the decaying body
of Liberty'. If it means privilege, exclusiveness,
indulgence, it is the doom, not the salvation of the
State. Caste however can be the channel, the normal
irrigation system whereby the whole community is
refreshed from the top by the vision, the assurance and
the selfless courage of those who can see directly that
constituents and community are a living nexus, a real
organization.

Whether or no reincarnation is simply a rationalization, an attempt to account justly for inequality, it
recognizes the fact of inequality. Some men are born
with insight and power of will to hold impulse and
egotism at bay and so develop further their vision.
Such men command respect because men recognize
the authenticity of what they report. 'They see what
the lower type only smells.' They can teach others to
see. But to see takes time. To be involved in life is to
have far vision clouded. The seers, the outlook-men,
must therefore be kept free while the men who entrust
the star-watching steersmanship to them, 'serve tables'.
Nor does the social problem, the task of making the seer's
insight the community's sanction, end there. Good
practical men may trust the Seer. Cruder, more im-.

Q 241

pulsive, more greedy, may not be able to do that. They may only be able to respect the good practical man. As Trotter has remarked in his *Instincts of the Herd*, men can only understand and follow those who are a step beyond themselves. Two steps above them are out of sight. The caste system of some four or five ranks may then be psychologically valid; each rank standing at and marking the upper limit of the moral vision and comprehension of the class below.

Hence we should get a class of routineers, people of very short time sense, content to repeat an unvaried round of duties with a similar round of rewards and satisfactions. Next would come a class of technicians, men who repair and keep the machinery running — in a pre-industrialized society they are the craftsmen. Thirdly are the supply and distribution experts who allot products, plan expansion and foresee consumption — they are merchants in a simple state: managing directors, master distributors, balancers of supply and demand, in a more complex society. Above them are the state officials, the civil servants, the community's chief executives. In a state which has become militarized, as befell India under her Aryan conquerors these are soldiers — the warrior caste. But in any state which is to have any stability, this class must have above it, even if it itself is not militarized — and so might itself not be debarred from vision by use of violence — a final caste. For this final caste must never be executive.[1] It is the supreme moral judicature. It gives moral guidance. It does not apply the law. It replies to those who would have it act 'who made me

---

[1] 'The Brahman renounces, by self-denying ordinance, all pretensions to authority.' H. A. ROSE, *Caste*.

a judge and ruler over you?' It is a bridge which links the social order with the natural order and man with Life. It shows; it does not drive. Indeed it must never touch practical administration. It must be absolutely clear of the taint of power and the pressure of immediate need or particular topical difficulty of administration. The seer, just as much in order that he may see as that he may be trusted, must be free of all practical authority, all contriving of application. He is like the compass needle. He is guarded so that he may point. He shows where the north lies: he does not tell men how to get there. That is their task. He shows them that their life has meaning. It is for them so to arrange their lives as to live up to that meaning. Yet he does not merely advise. He inspires and influences the whole tenor of the community's life while to any who would know directly the source of power he will show and teach. He shows them within wide limits what helps and what hinders their advance. He will instruct any, who wish to know why, and how they themselves may know.

This then is the essence of the caste system which seems the way a human society naturally organizes itself when it is possessed of men who can see and so can guide it. .

As the eyes are at the top of the head and the head at the top of the body so a fully functioning balanced social life rears itself. The Yogic way is not for all. Whether this is due to the fact that this life is only part of a huge scheme of development or no, it is clear that these few are advanced types. If they are to serve with their advanced gift the whole of their society and not leave it, blind and headless, behind, they must transmit their vision. The general executive can understand their insight and his need of it, as he would plan for the whole community and foresee its development. His word, that such a vision is necessary (and such a life must be lived to obtain that vision), can be taken by the rank beneath and so on till all the community is bonded together.

It is worth remarking in this context that armies, which are bodies compelled by their way of life to a certain efficiency, cannot remain simply organized in two orders — commanders and commanded — but have also to have five ranks: the private, who respects the N.C.O. for being able to knock him down: the N.C.O., who respects the Commissioned Officer for being able to resist without effort the temptation to get drink and 'borrow' from the canteen and mess funds (at this level moral strength is first valued): the Commissioned Officer who respects the Commanding Officer for being a man of brains, who understands tactics and strategy and knows the rules of war (at this level intellect is first valued): and the Commanding Officer who respects the Chief of Staff who despises the rule of war and is an original thinker, probably insignificant in appearance and shocking in opinions, perhaps not even 'sound' on patriotism, property or breeding. None of these ranks could appreciate the rank two above his own. The range of normal humanity is so wide that it takes five piers to bridge the whole span. Caste, then, may be the natural way in which, when a community has produced men of vision, men who can think originally, men who can plumb their own minds and get access to the subconscious, that community organizes itself to avail itself of these organs of vision, to keep them free to see and to keep them at their task of seeing.

The more we study the origins of the Indus Culture, the more we attempt to discover why this part of the arc of the proto-civilization remained so long at peace and resisted so long the disintegration, which overcame the other parts of the arc that rapidly became militarized, the more we are driven to the conclusion that this, the Indian arc, through making these two psychological discoveries — of Yoga and caste — balanced the economic discoveries and so kept the society stable. The Yogic discovery of how the individual may recover and retain his knowledge of his extra-individuality, and the recognition by the community that those who make this discovery and master its technique are the community's guarantors, the valid sanctioners of its morality and values, its guiding class, these two discoveries were a social invention of incalculable value, and as they allow the continuation of the true path of evolution, adapted and enlarged to the play of conscious intelligence, they may yet save our society and set it safely on the path of continued progress.

We must now trace this influence working not only in the Indian culture but also spreading into the other areas into which, later, civilization had first been introduced under the militarist urge of the two Western decadent arcs. In passing it may be wise to stress the fact that caste in India seems to have degenerated from social service to hereditary privilege and this descent is certainly of great age. Caste was not at one time a series of bars but of rungs.[1]

[1] 'In Buddha's time we fail to discover many premonitions of the individual's inability to win social promotion.' H. A. ROSE, *Caste*.

CHAPTER XI

THE IMPERIAL EXPLOSIONS – RETARDING FACTORS

I . THE SWORD NEVER GIVES PEACE

THE natural reaction (if not answer) to the argument developed so far must be, India may have had a more advanced psychological technique than the Western cultures which have derived from the Nilotic and Sumerian 'war-arcs', but India is weak and squalid, and the West, though to-day the sword is proving a suicidal weapon, did with organized violence set up justice, prevent corruption and give peace and order. The sword therefore need not and cannot be banished. It only requires to have its sweep restricted. This argument is specious but unsound. The development of the sword until it over-shadows civilization, as a hawk a hen-run, is an inevitable development, and creative peace no more grows under its point than Damocles could dine. The sword as we have seen has to approach nearer and nearer the scales until they are overset, for, once you threaten a man, he loses the power to co-operate with you and he and you become the antagonists you believe him to be and he sees you are. Justice then disappears: for what is called justice is no more than what the sword-wielder says.

Where the militarist argument is invalid is in that assumption, that the sword has ever won peace. It is of course a natural assumption as long as everyone believes man to be a dangerous beast which has won its way to the top by ruthless exercise of violence and cunning. The moment, however, that unfounded belief is discarded we see that the sword cannot make peace any more than death can make life. The profoundest and most sincere thinkers have always pointed this out — evil cannot produce good: violence and hatred, peace and concord. It is some force profoundly opposed to violence that 'makes men to be of one mind in an house'. It is grotesquely ridiculous to say ordinary human beings do not murder and wrong one another because of the policeman at the corner. They remain at peace, for peace and concord were their original state and if no 'unnatural' strain is put upon them they relapse into the kindliness normal to their species. The policeman, in so far as he is not a pointsman and arbiter, is simply an indication of the degree of injustice in the community which we shrink from putting right by generosity and trustful courage:[1] he is not the criterion of the degree of justice. Still to-day we are dominated by our belief in our animal past and it is therefore of decisive importance that it is natural history which is establishing, both through anthropology and through biology, that we are not a violent but a sensible species. Man as a race may have gone through a stage when he could be described, to use the Linnaean classification, as *homo ferus* but never as *homo ferox*.

We are therefore free without prejudice to examine

---

[1] This of course is not to say the policeman has only to be removed and all men would love each other. That Rousseau romance arose from failure to recognize that natures deformed by violence do not straighten and right themselves as soon as violence is removed. They may indeed remain deformed and distraught until a force of goodwill equal to the force of the old deforming violence has been brought to play on them and remelt their adhesions.

247

on what evidence the argument that the sword has given peace really rests. We shall find it is as groundless as the argument, on which it so largely depended, that man is so fierce that only a man, or a few men, of exceptional fierceness are able by the unstinted exercise of their fierceness to keep a few meek from being molested by the common fierce.

'You can do everything with bayonets save sit on them' — let us begin by repeating that realist wisdom. What then is the history of the sword as we can trace its exercise out from the Nile and the Euphrates?

2. THE MIND OF THE SWORDSMAN

Its first move is, with the kingship, to assert, in the community, a principle of injustice. It sets up over the people a master who keeps his autocratic position by giving privileges to his guards who hold down the community for him. Society is then split into producers and consumers — the consumers usually frank enough not to excuse themselves by saying they are peace-keepers. The sword only begins to talk of its duty to the scales when it is becoming uncertain of its own point. The scales are the shield. How a soldier king was regarded — his natural behaviour — is shown in one of the earliest historical documents which has come down to us. In the book of Samuel we have a picture of a king whom before he is elected is known to be about to be a tyrant, and who is chosen simply because he may head the war machine and with no notion that he will do anything but pervert justice to his private immoral ends. Here is no nonsense about the father of his people, the wise guardian of the laws they cannot keep, but so badly need. They are his natural prey. He and his warrior class intend to be kept. The sword is the instrument with which kings and all tyrants screw goods and services out of the unarmed people.

The alternative argument, that though they take away liberty at home they do this out of sad necessity of Defence of the Realm, the safety of the State being the supreme law; that too breaks down under examination. The first warrior kings, having made themselves masters of their particular peoples, launch raids on 'less advanced' communities whose territories and resources they wish to 'develop'. Finally they come into contact with each other and an armament race develops in which both states exhaust the other or, as we have seen, the barbarian learns civilization's most offensive trick, becomes a specialized expert and smashes civilization. The sword, then, initiates a rapid degenerative process. The state which takes to it finds it has steadily to be given a wider sweep until nothing can stand against it. It is insatiable: there are no rights against it in the community and, outside, it can have no frontiers. 'World power or downfall' is its only possible motto.

Hence once the state has become militarized it has to expand, with increasing instability, through nationhood to empire and through empire to attempt world dominion. Hence the larger the state the shorter its life. Small communities may last millennia. Nations may continue for centuries, empires are lucky if they last for a generation.

We can watch this rapid expansion and collapse, this explosive process, taking place in Egypt and even more catastrophically in Mesopotamia. As has already been noted, the Mesopotamian empires of Narim Sin, Sargon, Hammurabi, etc., never succeeded in adding anything to the economic, intellectual equipment which had already been achieved by the city-state culture they superseded, the Sumerian arc of the proto-civilization. They simply exploited and exhausted that mental energy and technical equipment which the first, free, creative period had discovered and invented. We shall see throughout history this is all that the militarist power with its hypocritical claim to foster and spread civilization ever does. It burns up the creative thought which went before and the form of government prevents creative thought continuing. Only when free, can man be creative, because originality depends on absolute liberty to postulate anything. Also, if man loses faith in his fellows (as violence makes him lose) then society is doomed. Freedom is not a luxury or an indulgence. It is an absolute necessity for progress and to avoid decadence. For, as the Stoics saw, you must choose one route or the other. Life never permits stability. 'He that is not getting better, is getting worse.'

In these first empires however though we can watch and time the explosion and the collapse — though we can see a small delta-state on the Persian Gulf rapidly extend till it touches the Levantine coast and then in a moment disappear in chaos — though we can see the other small delta-state on the Nile's mouths similarly extend, till it, too, spreads up the Levantine coast, breaks over into Mesopotamia and with equal suddenness subsides — we cannot watch in detail the disintegrative forces at work. We are like astronomers watching a Nova. We see the small state suddenly blaze into a power of the first magnitude and as suddenly decline. We can only estimate the catastrophic discharge of all its resources in an explosion.

When, however, we approach the time at which men began to reflect on this violence, we begin to get detailed accounts of the personalities and motives, of the psychological causative factors which worked this collapse. We see that they are, what the first explosions made us postulate, the frantic degenerative actions of men who, having lost all direct sense of their extra-individuality, their real kinship with each other, are rapidly driven to throw away any pretence of sanctions — that violence guarantees peace and justice — and to take to increasing realism. The violence and cunning increase rapidly. For a short time the first exploiter of the situation makes what seems a spectacular success. He cannot however stabilize his gains but has to push on to still further conquests. Meanwhile his own character undergoes rapid degenerative changes. What had been sure cunning and focused violence becomes megalomania. He collapses and his empire does not outlast his life.

This is the psychological analysis which Plutarch has been able to leave us. He gives the classic description of the first empire in which we have the leading characters and their motives put before us — the Alexandric adventure.

Before however considering that extreme development we must see how the empire which preceded the Macedonian and succeeded the Nilotic and Mesopotamian empires, developed, as it is the link beween those two first empires, sprung from the arcs of the proto-civilization, and the fully individualized state.

3. THE PERSIAN EMPIRE

The Persian empire was unstable but not as unstable and as rapidly degenerative as some. For the genius of Cyrus intuitively perceived three things: (*a*) The Zoroastrianism, which he inherited and controlled, was at that stage prepared to offer tolerance to other religions. Hence for example the return of the Jews to Palestine and their encouragement to build up again a theocracy, a state held together by a new morality claiming sanction of traditional authority and so without obvious dependence on violence.

(*b*) The Satrap system, which he invented, allowed the subject nations to run themselves by their traditions and with the sword taken out of their hands. All they had to do was to pay tribute, send levies and for the rest manage their lives by tradition with the sword taken away to far off Susa or Persepolis. So in the provinces the degenerative process of violence was arrested and the process itself was confined to the central power and its pressure directed upon its frontiers. There the empire had to continue to press forward, because of its inherent instability, to its inevitable doom. (*c*) The Third intuition was more due to accident than insight. Persia exploited the accident of having acquired the sub-empire of Croesus. The conquest of Lydia, where money had first been invented, gave Persia a new form of force, less rapidly degenerative than the sword. Lydia, by the accident that it was the place where the caravans coming up from the western coasts of Ionia met those coming down from Asia, was also the place where electrum (a mixture of gold and silver) was found and further, that it was the place where some genius lived who saw the advantage of coinage — Lydia gave a new instrument of 'indirect government' to Cyrus. Therefore the Persian empire, though unstable — though it cannot stop expanding without — hence the fatal clash with Greece — and degenerating within — hence the megalomania of Cambyses and a Xerxes which was of the true imperial sort — nevertheless degenerates with comparative slowness. The sword will destroy it; but meanwhile other forces: financial credit (which is a low morality but a true one, for it is based not on violence but on mutual convenience): the Persians own new religion of Light (an intellectual, not a psychological belief in abstract righteousness, and so lacking foundation): the subject peoples also having reformed 'religions of righteousness', religions which claimed God rewarded here or in another life good social action: these factors although none of them really sound — would all delay collapse. In the end however they would all pass on the thrust they could not hold, to the ultimate physical power, violence. Bad debts would lead to punitive expeditions — Zoroastrianism would begin to persecute when it found that God did not avenge himself as expected — the other religions of righteousness would turn to despair when they too made this discovery and were denied the sword-power to fulfil their own threats and promises. Finally as we shall see with the Diadochi money itself would allow a rapid and complete degeneration, which without that method of draining resources, the earlier empires could not effect.

The Persian empire is, then, a turning point. The

empire of Alexander showed the turn effected and decline in headlong career. The sword alone is in play and makes short work. Before seeing how the rapid degeneration takes place in the Macedonian stage it is however necessary to see whether the preceding Persian period is sufficiently well lit for us to be able to. trace, if not the detailed psychological factors which made for collapse (the degenerative changes in character and action in the men who controlled Persia, as they realized that justice was what they chose to call it), at least some of those main psychological elements which made for the retardation of that collapse. We must look for these in the religion of that time.

4. GOOD-INTENTIONAL RELIGION POSTPONES COLLAPSE

The Religion which stood behind the Persian power as it rose to dominance was, we now recognize, one of that belt and order of individualized religions which between the seventh and eighth centuries B.C. began to sprout from the old stock of the 'sacrificial-auguristic religions' or what are better defined as the ritualized religions of Life. It and its kindred — such as the prophetic ethical religion which Amos initiates in North Palestine in the early eighth century; to some extent at least on its Pali side, the Buddhist reform, and later in date but similar in spirit, the Confucian teaching — are a confession that man has become self-conscious, that he recognizes a dilemma in himself in that he feels no longer a spontaneous loyalty to the community and yet feels guilty for that lack, perceives the community is thus endangered and would find some new sanction for social conduct, which without sanction is too painful and perilous to perform.

This conviction and these religions, in all cases we know of, arise after an age of brigandage and anarchy — a 'Heroic Age' — in which all the ancient traditional moralities have been swept away and social life has become a horror. The ethical reform is due to a desperate feeling that unless men can control themselves no human society — let alone a civilization — will survive. It is then at this stage that we get prophets declaring what ought to be the relationship of man to man — if there is ever to be any real humanity. But though all these prophets — e.g. the Hebrew prophets of the eighth and seventh centuries B.C. — declare how men should behave, and by their denunciations of the material and economic advances and complexities, show they are aware that somehow it is this disproportionate change and development which has upset man's balance, there is no sign that any of them were either able to realize that this change was due to man working and inventing with an insulated aspect of his consciousness, or were able to devise any method, any technique whereby man might again bring into action that side of his nature which had become buried. That they knew nothing of such a possible discovery seems clear. For lacking it they sought, and had to seek for external sanction.

That sanction they maintain is to be found either in a personal God — a reflection of the now personalized self-conscious individual — or (a more philosophically respectable but not more real notion) in a principle, a natural law that rewards the individual for social conduct and punishes him for conduct which is a-social. Each man is to pray to such a deity and the deity will then do two things. He will answer his supplicant by giving him a new heart — 'I will write my commandments in their hearts' — so man will himself be socially guiltless. And God will also make possible the social action the new heart dictates. If the converted so act they will not perish. The order of nature, as well as the minds of men, will be bent by an outer power which will miraculously make practical, actions otherwise suicidal.

It is clear that such a new theory is evidence of a new rationalism. Man sees the need of sanctions for morality. He still wishes to be moral, i.e. intuitively loyal to Life. He is subconsciously aware he is not an individual. But he is unaware of the subconscious. He does not recognize its existence and that there lies the path to his extra-individuality and to his union with his fellows and with Life. Hence he projects his need of inner assurance and experience, that social action is good and possible, into the belief that there is in the world without 'a magnified non-natural man', an anthropomorphic deity, an isolated centre of self-consciousness similar to the isolated self-consciousness he now feels himself to be. His faith — that justice and mercy, truth, beauty and goodness, are valid in themselves, are real — is so strong that he is quite sure there must be this deity who incorporates these qualities and who makes them work in the actual, material world.

His faith springs from the strong subconscious apprehension that Life has advanced by sensitiveness which in his stage of consciousness becomes mercy,[1] and by awareness which at his stage becomes justice. It is not until repeated disappointments, repeated failures on the part of nature and of his fellow man to honour his faith, have shaken that faith, that he begins to relapse again into the use of violence. He felt God must openly justify the man who acted righteously. Here was the moral law in his own heart, there were the men — yes, and all the blind forces of nature who would not keep that law — and there above and beyond, was the personal God who, like himself, was sworn to uphold that law. Hence, if he the righteous man acted righteously, the righteous God must on his side work miracles so that, as the creature trustingly stepped straight across the stream of wild nature and the current of lawless man, Jordan would be divided by divine power, the creator would reverse the course of creation for the sake of the just.

Time after time, as this did not happen, good men were increasingly puzzled and disheartened. The scrupulous searched themselves for sin. Their God had failed them because they were impure. Every action on their own part became suspect. Food, drink and sex were all in turn given up to see whether in any of these pleasures might be an indulgence which thwarted the divine power and prevented it giving open sanction to their faith.

Extreme asceticism did not make social miracles — the reign of mercy and love — any more evident. On the contrary, under ascetic rule life became more filled with friction. In this strain the Hebrew prophets

[1] In an even more violent and heroic age the primal sensitiveness can still be found present under the forms in the Greek Heroic Age of Aidos and in the medieval heroic age as Chivalry.

declared the Chosen People were being destroyed by the Gentiles because Israel had not purged itself of the Life Religion which had become licentious. It was clear, however, after the purgings of a Hezekiah and Jehoshaphat, the nation was no more free from foreign molestation or more successful in resisting it. Indeed as far as the puritan reforms and ultimate fate of the latter king are concerned his failure was so striking that it brought the ethical religion to a crisis among the Hebrews. He was defeated and slain at the great battle of Megiddo. The meaning of such a reversal of faithful expectation was too plain to be excused. This verdict of fact could only mean one thing: the personal God, which men had postulated because of their moral feelings, did not intervene.

He did not sanction the moral conduct taught by the prophets and reformers who were founding the individualistic ethical religion.

Two courses were then open. Society might say — in a few temporary cases it did — God does not care for this new morality of righteousness. He is offended by the fertility religion, the religion of Life, being forbidden. True he is a person as we and as we lose our tempers so has he lost his. As we can be placated by heavy compensation, so can he. Hence in moments of panic not only has the fertility religion been reinstituted but its revival has been attended by violent sacrifices and persecutions which are the counter-reformational reaction to the ascetic's persecutions. The alternative course is more common and more gradual and so does not awake so much comment. But it is as mistaken and as fatal. However, men cannot go back. The fertility religion is dead. It was the reflection of an earlier state of consciousness — a state of consciousness which was already gravely fissured. It did nothing to re-fuse that fissure. At best it only checked, it did not arrest, the rate of cleavage. Asceticism therefore holds the field.

Hence if most men were to have any religion — lacking a new psychological knowledge of the nature of their consciousness — that religion must be ethical and individualistic. Ethics, justice and mercy, must be upheld. If God refused to intervene then a heavier responsibility fell upon man. Jehoshaphat was not a martyr. He was attempting with arms and with an alliance with an infidel to prevail politically. He was defeated. The lesson drawn is highly significant. His righteousness was not questioned. That side of the problem is taken as clear and settled. He had acted so that God should have intervened and given him victory. Both his puritan purgings of religion and also his use of military force and infidel alliances were morally right. The first answer to the problem is then to justify God. This is done by saying that on this spot Megiddo, Har-Megiddo, or as we render the name of the locality Armageddon, God will ultimately do what then he abstained from doing. He will bring together all the forces of the world, Right and Wrong ranged against one another, and the verdict which went against the righteous Jehoshaphat shall be reversed. God will intervene and the morality of the individualistic ethical religion will be established by miracle. The wills of wicked men and the blind forces of nature will all be bent by a superior intrusive divine violence so that the morality of the righteous man may be openly sanctioned and vindicated.

That, however, will not be till the end of the world and this picture is only made so as to allay doubt as to the bona fides of the deity. It is an essay in theodicy, not in practical morality. That had to be dealt with in answer to the more important question raised by the defeat at Megiddo — the question as to how meanwhile man was to behave. There could be only one answer, so practical that it had better not be stated too baldly.

If God did not back up the moral man, if law, order and peace had no sanction in the outer world and could hope for no creative intervention, then the moral man must back up God or God's morality. These declining steps follow one another easily to Avernus. First I fight as a reformer, as champion of the new morality. Though I fight, I fight within rules, only to impose the new morality. I am spreading religion by the sword. Gradually my defeats or the world's resistance drive in on me that I am the only channel of the Truth, it exists only if I win. If I perish, Truth perishes with me.[1] So exposed and with such a treasure solely in my charge, I am compelled to use any extremity of violence to assure victory. The next step is swift and terminates the process. Truth is what I maintain. Once at that level there is no further advance. In seeking for security and sanction for right we have touched bottom. Man has come the full cycle and in seeking for a power to make righteousness real he has come to where whatever is real is righteous.

[1] During 1914-1918 many Christians, some of them clergy, openly stated that if God let them lose the war, they could not continue to believe in Him. This frame of mind probably accounts for much of the Neo-Pagan revival in Germany. Anthropomorphic religionists often punish an unresponsive god by deserting him for a rival.

Truth being only what I maintain, what I maintain
is Truth.

Hence the ethico-individualistic religions fail to
stabilize the degenerative descent of society, as the
Life Religion was also failing to arrest that descent.
We must look on them as one more of those efforts
which man makes to recapture the original wholeness
of his nature. They retard the dissolution, but because
man does not explore his own nature, does not understand that in it and by curing its fissure he will heal
the trouble between himself and society, between his
views of objective nature and subjective morality, the
dissolution continues.

Each stage of advance in economic mastery, control
over the outer world, is due to a corresponding stage of
advance (or condensation of focus) in man's 'objective
mind', his self-conscious individuality. The advance in
control over his environment, in its turn, reciprocat-
ingly increases and intensifies self-consciousness. The
individual feels himself increasingly cut off and completely distinct from the world around him and his
fellows. He is no part of all that, because he can alter
all that, bend it all to his will if only he has the insight
and courage to break with the ignorant prejudices
men once had (and had for comfort's sake to have)
before they knew how to make the rules suit their
convenience.

This one-sided advance, however, naturally sets up
internal strain in his psyche. He increases in physical
power and loses proportionately in peace of mind: he
adds immeasurably to means and knows less of ends.
When this process has gone sufficiently far it makes
such a dichotomy in his nature that if he is tender he

cannot stand the inner strain — he grows sick of knowledge that only leads to the conclusion that there is no general meaning, no purpose or plan, no final truth. He then ceases to discover and invention dries up in him. Violent societies are therefore sterile societies. If he is tough the end is as near. Inevitably he becomes such an individualist that no one will trust him for he trusts no one and seeks only his own power. Hence society, with its invention parched and its energy dissipated into mutually suspicious individuals, must. dissolve. Many have collapsed at this stage. Those few that have gone on have done so by allying with the state one of the varieties of the new ethical religion.

This is the explanation of Persia's temporary success, and of Egypt's persistence. Both states allied themselves with reformed religion which honestly but mistakenly (because pre-psychologically) attempted to teach that moral conduct, the right the individual has to live and the obligation that he has to serve, are objectively valid.

Being pre-psychological they could not find where the real proof of this lay — in the raising again of the subconscious into consciousness and so obtaining for each man direct evidence of his extra-individuality. They attempted first to teach that a personal God intervened to deal out justice and to protect the undefended, and then, when that could not any longer be maintained, to teach that after death this personal God would exact justice from the oppressor and reward the oppressed.

We have then in the Persian Empire's temporary but considerable success an illustration of the important principle which was stated earlier, that even where the sword is active, is eroding society and claiming with each encroachment that it is sanctioning justice and protecting the meek, another force is present and it is that force which retards if it cannot arrest ultimate collapse. Man feels he is not an individual and that therefore society does not rest on force. He shrinks therefore from being a 'Realist', intuition telling him that his picture of reality is dangerously, falsely incomplete. He cannot, however, interrogate that intuition, analyse it, make it actual. He can only project it in forms which are therefore false — the form that there is a God who intervenes in the world's natural order. He cannot see that these two conceptions are both rationalizations of his partial consciousness and the partial picture it gives of reality. He has to postulate an interfering, purpose-imposing personal God because his personalized, partial consciousness has made a world without any purpose and a society without any values.

We have seen the same delaying process present in the Egyptian civilization — the effort to evolve a religion which should through its psychology teach man access to his whole nature, as through his physics man had learnt to control and shape outer nature. But such ideas, which if interpreted with their full psychological significance, would show men how to re-fuse their sundered consciousness, come through only as a picture which, without that re-fusing, are 'wish-fulfilment dreams', not a restorative recreative therapy.

Such an idea is the Egyptian Book of the Dead. As we have seen this elaborate concept of the soul is in the pictorial form of the Spirit's voyage to the after-death world for its trial, reward or punishment. The Book is an importation from some country to the far north-east. It has undoubtedly undergone change.[1] It seems, then, probable that what we have is in origin a codex of psychological exercises — or phrases which at the stage they were framed could so be used — which exercises were originally meant for constant use (for keeping contact with the extra-individuality) but with the increase of the objective mind, making the subjective mind less and less accessible or even known, these exercises became confined to the moment of death, the only state in which the individual could conceive he had another sort and quality of life. This may seem wild speculation to those who have not read the *Bardo Thodol*, the Tibetan Book of the Dead or more strictly of the *Bardo*, that is 'the intermediate state', the state between two incarnations. Here we certainly have not only strange resemblances to the Egyptian Book of the Dead, resemblances that throw some light on whence Egypt obtained its 'Bible', its alternative to the sword as a social fixative, but it also looks as though we had a rendering of ideas which, still highly pictorial and concerned with death, are far more psychological than the Egyptian. The Egyptian is concerned with the repetition of the proper texts and answers at the proper time — while the trial before Osiris on the other hand is almost purely ethical. The Tibetan is concerned with making the dying man able to discriminate between his physical symptoms and his state of mind and so to control and expand the focus

[1] 'It is now a matter of common knowledge that behind the Book of the Dead lies a long chain of development from earlier compositions.' SHORTER, *An Introduction to Egyptian Religion*, p. 3.

of his consciousness. In short the tradition which gives rise to the Tibetan book seems psychologically, and possibly historically, a transition between the Book of the Dead and the Yogic discovery, that advance in the objective mind (with its consequences, increase of means and loss of ends) may be and must be balanced by proportionate advance in the subjective mind (with its consequence, increase in clear apprehension of ends and the purpose of Life and all existence).[1]

We see then that the two Western Arcs of the primal culture had degenerated through the sword and, under the exhaustion it causes, had several times collapsed, blazing up into empires and sinking into complete anarchies quickly after.

It is clear that, had they not found some restorative conservative force, they would have gone completely to pieces. They diagnosed that the sword was fatal, that such a sanction destroyed morality and would murder the community but they were without a therapy to follow up their sound diagnosis. The psycho-therapeutic ideas they got hold of, they could not understand but projected them as a false cosmology — an interfering personal sword-armed-God — instead of a true psychology — the reunited consciousness of man. The idea worked for a little time, for it was true that the sword did never preserve any values but only destroyed, and man had hidden in him a need and power of co-operation.

But simply finding out that the sword is purely destructive and man is innately constructive did not

[1] The diffusion of ideas between Asia, Europe and Africa has lately had a peculiar confirmation as menhir avenues leading to stone circles similar to those in France, England and Ireland have been found in Tibet.

show the way to the real source of social cohesion. That has been a common impasse. To-day nearly all pacifism and liberalism find themselves stuck here. 'Force is no remedy' they have repeated. That, however has not prevented force, unlimited violence from being used. War does not pay, proved Norman Angell. That does not prevent man making war. You will not prevent war, William James showed, till you find its moral equivalent, that combination of risk, excitement and concerted aim and self-forgetfulness which war gives. Force and violence will be used (at first regretfully and as a means only justified by the goal: in the end for every private appetite and whim), unless some other sanction can be found, some other means of preserving society and its values. Pacifism must be positive. It must not merely say that war is inefficient and beastly. It must show a way which is not only noble but efficient.

Because the civilization, springing from the Western arcs of the primal culture, failed then to find how to enlarge self-consciousness and give the individual proof of his extra-individuality, it could only gain a breathing space, a short moment while men watched to see whether the wishes of idealists were real, whether 'God would act', whether justice and mercy had any sanction save violence and cunning.

Then with sadness the tender had to call for arms and the tough hailed them with delight. Only a little while of this sort of thing, they knew, and those sloppy pretences of mercy and justice could go overboard, the flag with the scales on it could be struck and the other flag, with the skull and crossbones, be run up in its stead. True enough, they saw further than the

266

idealist who thought ideals were not 'really real', values had to have a steel core under the bunting. The realists, however, no more than the idealists, saw to the end. There the pirate is hoist with his own petard. For the animal which preys on its own species is doomed to rapid extinction.

CHAPTER XII

THE IMPERIAL EXPLOSIONS — UNRESTRAINED ACTION

Now that we have accounted for the preserving power which lay behind the social forces of Egypt and Persia and neutralized to some extent the corrosive effect of the sword: now that we have traced this preservative to its source and shown why, because it was so diluted and misapprehended, it could only retard not arrest the social decay the use of violence caused: we can trace that decadence of pure violence working ever more quickly, as the misapprehended alternative sanction (man's psychological insight and penetration into his true and whole nature) is discarded as illusion.

The Persian empire and the later condition of Egyptian culture come close enough to clearly documented historic times for us to see the forces of conservation and peace working behind the façade of arms. Persia we have seen had Zoroastrianism as its new faith in man's individual responsibility and the vision that he was taking part in a gigantic struggle of Good and Evil, Light and Dark of which this life was only an episode and all life only an act. Egypt had the reformed Osirianism giving much the same ideas expression in local forms. Every soul comes before Osiris and is judged on its moral record in its past life,[1]

---

[1] The confused state in which this morality also remained is illustrated by two of the questions which, according to the Book of the Dead (the forty questions of the negative confession), Osiris asks the soul, 'Did you ever between the day you lent and the day of repayment remind a borrower of your loan?' How fine a spirit here — but it is followed by 'Did you ever frighten the ducks on the Sacred Lake?' And there we are back at magic.

and further every soul in the end will become Osiris. Here we have an idea which suggests that Yogic doctrines, if not practices, had been heard. The individuality of the person cannot be absolute if in the end he is somehow made conscious of being the deity. Unfortunately, once again we see the extension of individual consciousness is not something which can and should be won here as a final elucidation of the individual's relationship with his fellows, with all society, all humanity, and all Life, but is something to do with the future life.

Persia and Egypt we should then postulate must give way to a much more unstable outburst of imperialism, and as this period will be even closer our time we shall, as has been said, be able to trace the characters and impulses of those directing, and involved in, this rapid degenerative process. The postulate is, as we have seen, confirmed by the Macedonian empire and the psychological detail is given by a number of Greek historians much of whose work has survived.

I. THE MACEDONIAN ERUPTION

The adventure of Alexander, for that is the name it deserves rather than an empire — ten years divide the battle of Issus (333 B.C.) from the victor's death at Babylon (323 B.C.) — is meteoric. The leader only has time to raid across Eurasia and heap all the loot of the three arcs of civilization. The followers, the Diadochi, in three or four decades (323-281 B.C.) have succeeded in dissipating the treasure, smashing communications and shattering social confidence. In little more than

a generation the Near East, which had been Civilization, which had played with the sword but had kept
it from absolute mastery, which had recovered time
and again from anarchy and ages of disorder, was
sunk in ruin. It becomes the soft spiritless 'asiatic',
sunk either in sensualism or superstition, escaping the
hopeless task of social order in physical indulgence or
spiritual fantasy. Out of it will only come creatures
who know how to debauch their masters with luxury
or philosophers who teach these masters' victims how
to endure a state of society which cannot be altered.

The period and its personalities are so brilliantly lit
by contemporary writers that we can follow the rocket-
like trajectory in detail.

Alexander himself is the typical conqueror. He
inherits from his remarkable father Philip, the bomb
he is to fling at the rusty Persian safe. This bomb is
composed of the Macedonian highlanders who have
been trained in an improved form of the Theban
phalanx, that military invention with which Epami-
nondas, a generation before, had jolted war out of the
jousting rut in which Sparta had set it. The bomb is
launched on the gold of the Macedonian mines.
Here, then, we have an almost perfect picture of the
barbarian, on the fringe of culture, shown by his
clever neighbours how to use his country's strange
product of gold in a strange way, and himself specializing one of his clever neighbour's inventions, the improved war machine. Money and military tactics in
the hand of one who simply wanted to learn in order
to dominate must lead to an explosion.

Alexander himself is supposed to have intended to
have used the immense hoard of Persian gold, his

expenditure of the Macedonian gold gave him, to develop an even greater empire than Persia's and one all Greek in taste and Aristotelian in balance. It is doubtful. The man himself is not in sympathy with the Greek critical intelligence. That is clear. He is, as would be expected of a highlander, at the heroic phase of cultural development, dominated not by Aristotle, with whom he quarrels, still less by Plato or Socrates. His real taste is Homer: the Iliad he carries about in a golden box and his atrocious torture of the Governor of Gaza is given — true mark of a snobbish savage — justification because Achilles so behaved to the *dead* Hector. Brutal in action, he becomes megalomaniac on reflection. He believes himself to be a God when the priest of Amon Ra so hails him and he murders his friend Clitus when this faithful comrade-in-arms tries to mock him back into sanity. This does not look the type of mind out of which a stable society can issue. Its instability will rather throw in ruin the last walls of the order of which it has possessed itself. Whatever might have been, that which actually happened the hero by his violence richly earned. Raiding by day, rioting at night he destroys himself and dies quickly at Babylon.

His generals are left with only one thought — 'What an empire to sack!' — and only one strategy, each to tear off as much as he can carry of the carcase and drag it where he may devour it in safety. Civil war, however, broke out widely and the generals, like snakes thrown together, were unable to extricate their fangs from each other's bodies. The Wars of the Diadochi are perhaps the most illuminating illustration of how quickly the sword, if used by whole-hearted specialists, destroys them and everything. Nearly every one of the generals is either killed in action or murdered by treachery. Alexander's mother, who had herself murdered his father Philip and now began again assassination as part of policy, is herself assassinated. Her assassin Cassander shortly after rounds off this piece of policy by murdering Roxana, Alexander's widow, and her child. The battles are brilliant, the generals are as gifted at the game of killing as they are lacking in any other capacity. Even their incessant treacheries are clumsy. In consequence each particular victory brings general dissolution nearer. As a military historian of the period has said, 'the mercenary now came into his own. He was bought and sold on the battlefield'. Armies were sometimes purchased on the spot with such speed and such completeness that all the killing that remained to be done was that of the general who was outbid. Discipline in such an atmosphere became a tricky question — the sword was becoming all edge, killing everyone impartially. Bravery was nonsense if cunning could get there better. War therefore under this pressure of Natural Selection threw off its disguises and appeared ever more frankly in its true nature, large scale assassination. You are no longer fighting because you protect the weak or you love risks and wish to boast of your heroism. You are fighting to get gold and absolute power. In the end the only one of the Diadochi who dies in his bed of old age is the octogenarian Ptolemy who was cunning enough to seize Egypt which was the most isolated of all the fragments of the Macedonian Empire, to assure his succession by adopting the customs of the country — the Ptolomies though Macedonians swallowed their taboos and married their sisters in proper Egyptian incestuous manner — and even to spare his enemies, when it paid.

In short this empire sinks into passivity only when each descendant of the original freebooters is by exhaustion of forces and ruin of communications sufficiently out of reach of the rest to lie still and lick his wounds. With the central structure of the Persian empire burnt out, fragments of social building form again where there had endured, during the outburst, foundations of earlier societies. The Macedonian nation continues a feeble development in Greece. The Seleucidae build on the ancient base where the Sumerian culture had begun and made that first fatal departure into war. The Ptolomies have landed themselves on that other arc of the primal culture Egypt, Egypt which too had chosen war for riches and safety and found itself the captive of a rapacious mountaineer.

Such a solution by exhaustion could however only be temporary. The Seleucidae, set in the Euphrates valley, have a frontier out on the Indus. India is now learning to hit back and finally the Indus basin is bought back by Chandragupta from the Mesopotamian Macedonians for an armoury of elephants, the 'tank' of that day which was transforming warfare. It may be significant that one of India's most military rulers bought a rectification of frontier by selling arms instead of fighting. Certain it is that India itself never became fully militarized — that is, a country from which spread empire-making hordes. Mesopotamia was never invaded from India. While then the collapse of Alexander's empire leaves a great gap of disorganization throughout the Near East, and the field lies open (until from the West a people even more outsiders than the Macedonians, and from the East, a re-barbarian Persia, again swoop on the *disjecta membra*), we must see how India was developing.

CHAPTER XIII

PSYCHO-SOCIAL ADVANCE IN ASIA — INDIA

WE have seen that forces of conservation, psychological forces were present even in the countries dominated by the sword, though these forces were too misunderstood really to be efficacious. In India the sword, too, prised its way into the social structure but because, there, this structure was held by a much stronger cement it resisted the sword. Hence, as we have seen, caste never permitted the soldier to be the man at the top. The Brahman is the pinnacle and he is — or should be — the contemplative, the man who by psychological exercises has opened up again passage between the conscious and the subconscious, between the world of means and that of ends. The Brahman did not always fulfil this duty. Pride and indolence and even indulgence made him cease to function. He looked often enough on his position as one of easy privilege instead of supreme and arduous obligation. The office was made hereditary. Caste, by doing this, did itself a deadly injury. Any man must be free to accept the highest task if he is prepared to accept its deprivations and has the inherent capacity to develop the powers it demands. No one can say where in the community this capacity may appear. It must be watched for, selected and reared — the most precious growth and gift that Life has yet bestowed, its highest achievement.

In the hereditary system itself there is then sufficient reason for India's decline. She had the way to wisdom, to the good life and balanced progress. She has let it become dangerously contaminated. The caste system itself, lacking the strong stream of vision flowing down from it from the head — the Yogic practitioners — became, and had to become, like an irrigation system through which there only oozes a muddy trickle. It became choked, gorged, the banks broke and the organized social life became half swamp, half desert.

Nevertheless the system was always there, functioning however feebly. Further, as civilization continued and constant progress was made by the objective mind in understanding the objective world, some proportionate progress was being made in exploring the subjective mind and understanding the subjective world.

The old view of India as a place of alternative anarchy and tyranny, of savage conquests alternating with debauched despotisms — a place where there were only Rajahs who lived for lust and loot and ryots who toiled and bred at the very limit of subsistence — such a picture is now known to be hardly more accurate than the pictures Moscow up till 1935 drew of conditions in England. We now know that mathematics advanced steadily in India and that there before our era the great discovery in abstraction, the discovery of the Zero, was made, a discovery without which the decimal system and all modern mathematics would have been impossible and yet a discovery the Greeks did not make. While then such minds were making new techniques for measuring and mastering the outer world by abstraction, we should expect that they, who in their tradition, had a unique technique for exploring the inner world, should have brought this also to greater definition to match the increasing definiteness of their objective mind.

I. THE PSYCHOLOGICAL SIGNIFICANCE OF BUDDHA

Was Buddha such a genius? It is difficult to know. The official Pali position has been — one welcome to Western scholars — that he was a rationalist reformer purifying the confused exuberance and superstitious over-statement of Hinduism. He was a Protestant and taught men to be sensible about religion. That does not seem much of a gospel or a teaching which could be called the Light of Asia. His success seems rather to suggest that he was a psychological genius who discovered some way of making more clear, definite, and as we would say, psychological, those ancestral methods of enlarging consciousness which had become through age inadequate and through tradition corrupt. His success seems to compel us to postulate that he translated in terms of his own more individualized age (found again the contemporary psychological equivalent for) phrases which had ceased to be psychological and become cosmological and practices which had ceased to be psycho-physical and had become ritualistic or magical. This descent into magic is the constant degenerative process as the mind gains in objectivity, and it has to be continually corrected by compensating deliberate exploration of the subconscious. As the crocus, whose natural habitat is the Himalayan slope. where the rains wash away the soil, every year roots itself deeper and so preserves contact with nourishing earth, so man, owing to the growth of his mind and the way in which it 'sheds its skin' in that process, has continually to penetrate freshly into psychological reality or he will find (a constant sad experience in religion) that instead of having hold of a living praxis which puts him in touch with the larger Reality of which he is part, instead of a complete vital psychology, an empirical religion, he has only hold of a cosmological dogma, which is vague and inaccurate, and a few irrelevant tabus.

This very natural supposition about Buddha, which our present psychological knowledge prompts us strongly to make, gains confirmation when we learn that the Pali official, protestant and rationalist description of his life and teaching is not accepted as adequate by very many schools of Buddhists.

Throughout India there are Sects which maintain that beside the exoteric general teaching there is an esoteric particular instruction. They do not deny that in the seventh century B.C. there was in India, as in Palestine, Egypt and probably, through the Pythagorean order, in South Italy,[1] a 'Moral reform'. The

[1] That as far west as South Italy (Magna Graecia) religious influences from India probably spread at this time, is shown by the rise of the Pythagorean 'Rule of the Saints' in some of the cities of Magna Graecia. There this order of philosophers seems to have succeeded for a short time in imposing some sort of organized theocracy in accord with their peculiar theories of number and diet. They seem also to have tried to impose some rudimentary system of caste. But they appear to have been ignorant of the kind of mind training which is needed to give the Brahman his moral ascendency and also – the one fact depending on the other – not to have known that it is vitally important that the seer should rule only indirectly and advisorily, having no executive control. So they were easily disliked and as easily overthrown. More detailed evidence of the dispersion of religious influences and words from India to Italy at this time is given by the Campagno Gold Tablets, No. 5 of which runs 'I have escaped from the sorrowful wheel', leaving little doubt as to the oriental influence present here. But as Rivers pointed out, here again we probably see another example of how words and forms can travel and the essential meaning evaporate on the way.

Individualistic ethic began to replace the Life Religion, for men who thought began to realize they could no longer hope to plunge themselves into, and come back refreshed out of, the evaporating and muddying waters of the old religion. They saw that religion (owing to growth of self-consciousness) was becoming less and less able to give the essential awareness of social solidarity just at the time that this was becoming recognized as most needed. The aims of religion must then be defined and made as consciously clear as was now man's thought on all his other interests. Hence 'the sevenfold way' — the deliberate statement of what man's conduct should be — is essential Buddhism.

But it is not all. To a people crudely rational, ignorant of the subconscious, pre-psychological, such an ethical statement is enough. The Sermon on the Mount, the Sevenfold Way, you state these propositions, they obviously point to the good social life — peace of mind for the indiviual: peace and creative order for the community — and then you have done all that is necessary. That is the Gospel. You preach it and men are saved by following it.

But they do not follow it. They cannot. The whole of this outlook is so inadequate, so ignorant of actual human nature, as to be by itself almost useless. It is no more than a rationalistic fantasy, a pious hope. As we shall see, the same difficulty arises when Christianity appears with its Sermon on the Mount. The West, however, was always, we have seen, psychologically backward, for with it the unbalanced development of the objective mind (with proportionate starving of the subjective mind) had been allowed to go forward bringing it finally to an acute conflict between what was thought real and what was thought ideal — between the sword and values. The East never permitted psychological ignorance to increase to that degree. Hence it is absurd to think that Buddha and his hearers would have been content with such a crude, inadequate statement of moral platitudes.

Sometimes Westerners have said the ideal set was so sublime, so original that that itself was the stroke of creative genius which made him the Light of Asia, the Illuminated one. However unscalable they might be, here, he showed, were heavens of perfection of which man had never dreamed before. The vision was so lovely that for a moment even the most human wished, with humanity's pathetic enthusiasm, to scale the sky. And still after centuries of failure the dream remains a haunting beauty.

This explanation, however, is not valid. We have seen that the picture of men like beasts is untrue. Buddha was not telling them of a morality so unheard of that in the midst of their constant carnivorous rage they were startled into a moment's belief *quia impossibile,* by the sheer extravagance of this man's absurd faith. He was saying, in terms of that age's self-consciousness, what their religion, the religion of Life has always postulated and often indicated: That men are one life and that one life of theirs is one with all Life and with all Reality: That to live for others is not altruism but to live for one's full being: to live for one's self-conscious physical self is to mortify, decay and corrupt.

There was then nothing original in the morality — it was simply psychological common sense — a common sense apparent to a people who still had the

Life Religion about them and still were aware that their nature, though double, was not yet sundered into an active completely dominating objective mind and an entombed subjective mind.

2. HOW IDEALISM IS MADE REAL

It is clear then that the only part of Buddha's teaching which was original, his particular contribution to human evolution, could have been and must have been a technique, a method whereby men might find it possible to attain the clear awareness that the sevenfold way was not only right but possible. He is the Enlightened one, not because he stated moral 'eternal commonplaces', but because he found a new way, suitable to the stage of self-consciousness his epoch had reached, whereby men might make actual — might live up to — the eternal commonplaces. According to Buddhism you are 'saved' not by creeds but by Gnosis, by knowing the method, the technique, the way of enlightenment.

The Life Religion was no longer able to show this way to men at that stage of self-awareness. In consequence, for them to keep practising it any longer was only to make their self-consciousness more acute and its symbolism more sensual — specifically sexual. New wine must have new bottles: new self-awareness must have a new specifically psychological technique of rebalancing itself. The acuteness of conscious separateness could only be cured by acute concentration on the way to re-link the self with the whole.

Buddha therefore must have been, as all religious teachers we now see must be, a psychological genius.

Their morality is not theirs: it is the common wish of all men; the common realization that this is the way to live, the way of Life, and to live as individuals is to die to extinguish all Life and miscarry the purpose of creation. What is theirs, their contribution to evolution, is the technique — the new adaptation to modern needs of old methods whereby men may achieve the morality they desire, by living in and of the larger Life of which they are units.[1]

This view of Buddha and what his enlightenment actually was, we have seen is held by many sects both in India and without. It is indeed worth remarking, also, that it is these sects which have kept Buddhism really alive while the intellectual protestant moralists have lost increasingly to revived Hinduism. This might be expected, for ethics without a psychological technique to make them work, we now realize, are no more real than the word 'bread' written on a blackboard is itself nourishing.

We are not concerned to mark the particular successes and failures of specific religions or sects. The day is passing when religions will be called by particular men's names. As in science, such a method of classification is found clumsy and ambiguous. The essential discovery which a great reformer makes and which his disciples make the *raison d'être* for their founding a new church or religion may be, and often is, lost by them and acquired by the very religion from

[1] Our new conception of Evolution as the growth of consciousness, also allows us to solve a difficulty which seemed insuperable to earlier Western historians of Religion. The Buddhist Nirvana, is it extinction? If so, why s⸍ ⸍e so hard for the inevitable? A Buddhist saying that he who thinks Nirvana is extinction and he who thinks it personal survival are both ignorant of what it really is, appears now, not a paradox but as common sense. Nirvana is the transcendence of individuality.

which the reformer departed. He may be enlightened longest or most deeply who is enlightened last. The conservatives may, in the end, gain everything which was of real advance and advantage in the departures and excursions of the progressives.

What in this inquiry we have to note is not whether gradual modification or sudden revolution, growth in grace or convulsive conversion, Raj Yogi or Hathi Yogi, is the better way. We have to trace, spreading across Asia and percolating from time to time into Europe, psychological advances, explorations and discoveries which balanced those other advances and inventions being made in physics and economics.

Buddhism, we have seen, spread out of India into Tibet. There, we now know,[1] it succeeded, in natural psychological evolution, the Life Religion which was beginning to fail and turn into its final decadent condition of sorcery and sexualism. Here there is no doubt Buddhism was specifically psychological. It consisted of techniques whereby mind and body might help self-consciousness to be dilated into awareness of its sub-conscious linkage with all Life and Being. We have seen some of these discoveries may have been made far earlier than Buddha's date: the Tamil speaking Dravidians, claiming Yogi practices to be their discovery and pre-Aryan, are probably right. And many times, new-psychological methods, appropriate to men at that particular stage of self-consciousness (and equally inappropriate and misunderstood and misapplied by those still below that stage) may have been discovered and have spread over

[1] See Dr. EVANS WENTZ's three volumes, *The Bardo Thodol, Milarepa the Great Yogi of Tibet,* and *Tibetan Yoga* (Oxford University Press).

Asia and beyond, carried to those who needed them and could use them. The Egyptian Book of the Dead, as has been suggested earlier in this context, may be the last end-process or final degenerative inert state of such a technique.

What is clear is that in historic times the technique of expansion of the self came into Tibet under the name of Buddhism, whether it joined on to earlier similar psychological discoveries or whether it had once more to start from the ground level of the decayed Life Religion. A Tibetan king marries a Chinese and an Indian Princess and from both his wives accepts the doctrine the essentials of which every state must receive if it is not to dissolve in irreducible anarchy.

It is clear then that Buddhism must already have reached China — either having already passed through Tibet, before it returned to spread widely, or by the other route which once linked India and China through or round the Malay peninsula. We must now therefore turn to that civilization in order to see how far its stability may be due to psychological advances, its collapses may be referred to those advances failing to keep pace with the growth of individualism and materialism.

CHAPTER XIV

PSYCHO-SOCIAL PROGRESS IN ASIA—CHINA[1]

THE development of psychological balance, of an inner awareness equal to growing outer awareness, is so clearly illustrated in China that this division of human evolution must be marked by a fresh chapter.

Indeed China's experience is invaluable for us. Here is a people who, as observers have pointed out, is far more Western i.e. practical, than Eastern — speculative and imaginative. It has made perhaps the most extensive and protracted successes in corporate living of any of the human divisions and, while possessed of a profound wish that all thought should be practical, should have social consequences, it has, because of its great intelligence, realized that thought, if it is to work, must be profound. Not easily is the truth disclosed. All too easily is man misled by the simple rationalisms and realisms, which never question that reality is simple and facts are hard, clear and handy.

This of course is a discovery not made in a moment or without pain. The rationalistic realist is specious — more he is perfectly right, his argument is valid, within his terms of experience. It must be allowed he is one of those examples of J. S. Mill's rule that men are generally right in what they maintain, wrong in what they deny. For he is right in

[1] For the historical background of this chapter I am deeply indebted to Mr. ARTHUR WALEY'S remarkable work on the Tao Tê Ching, *The Way and its Power*. For further particular information acknowledgment is made later.

claiming fine words butter no parsnips, moral senti-
ments by themselves do not make men moral and you
will never get an inch off the ground or crush the
daisies an ounce less cruelly by pulling yourself up
by your own braces. He is wrong in denying there is
any other way: he is wrong in denying that some force
other than violence has held men together: he is wrong
in denying that all the sword has ever done or can do
is to devastate: it can never preserve justice.

This controversy was then argued out in China with
discussion and also with terrible practical demonstra-
tions. To and fro swayed the battle of opinions with
millions of lives and a noble way of life as the stakes.

Time and again rational realistic individualism
seemed to have won and to have first crushed into
slavery and then into chaos all social form. Time
and again psychological insight, not clear enough to
point the mistake, not clear enough to prevent its
repetition, nevertheless reasserted itself. The play,
the agony, of these two forces is the history of China.
Because these have been so balanced throughout
history, throughout history China has been time and
again the most civilized and the most brutalized of
human societies.

I. THE RISE OF ACUTE INDIVIDUALISM IN CHINA

We now know that China became individualized at
much the same time as the other ancient civilizations
which have been glanced at here.

Somewhere about that momentous seventh century
— or at most three or four generations later — the
majority of thinking folk, in the Far East limit of that

belt of diffused culture, which spreads in a thin girdle from the Mediterranean to the Yellow Sea, reformed the Life Religion. That religion, infected by an individualism it could not understand or correct, had finally ended not merely in rites specifically sexual — rites which inflamed instead of allayed individualism — but in a far grosser form of individualism, human sacrifice.[1] This had to be stopped. Tomb furniture shows us how and when this decadence was checked and turned into a harmless symbolism.

Individualism however is not so easily cured. A man may feel an intuitive intense repugnance to its manifestations, and so may check such manifestations the use of which individualism itself may question. If you have always had murdered the wives and slaves at their master's death, reason may throw doubts on whether such selfish brutality serves any purpose. Individualism prompted the murder: further individualism checks it, for it makes uncertain the future life into which you had to go and to which therefore you would drag your human property with you.

If you are nothing but an individual body, when that body dies it is much more likely that that is the final end of you.

Human sacrifice, as a useful selfishness, can be got

---

[1] This cruelty we know from Mr. Wooley's excavations was also imposed on their people by the sword-bearers in the Sumerian culture. Here also we should mention the fact that the Aryan conquerors in India seem to have imposed suttee on the Indus culture and that this sacrifice of the wife seems to have been accepted by India because, though in most ways a repulsive practice and in origin dictated by gross individualism, it could among a people who were passive, masochistic and other-worldly be interpreted as voluntary immolation on the part of the victim, a deliberate abandonment of her individuality and personal rights. See also p. 163 for reference to Mr. Perry's explanation of the spread of human sacrifice (imposed by conquerors) becoming the reason of warfare reaction among otherwise peaceable peoples.

rid of. The survivors wish to preserve your slave property. War — the killing of men not to carry off their spirits to serve you in another life but to carry off their goods to enjoy here and now or to enslave them and their children — war is intensified. Something more than rationalism is needed to check it — indeed rationalism by itself can only make it worse. True it may ruin civilization and it is all pretence that it advances justice, but my life is so short that with a sharp sword — as a late Lord Chancellor of England said — there are gleaming prizes to be won, and as civilization crashes I may loot and batten and even prosper in the general collapse. I can roast my pig in the blazing house of culture and as I shall not live till the winter anyhow, it is for those who come after to complain if they freeze.

In consequence of this line of thought, Chinese philosophers set themselves to work out a way of life which would make morality valid in itself. They were not visionary or imaginative thinkers. On the whole Chinese thought has tended to be Apollonian, to believe in orderly, conscious and deliberate methods of obtaining mastery. It shuns the Shamanistic method of Dionysic rapture, of spinning the conscious objective mind violently out of focus in the hope it will come to rest, if only temporarily, on another focus, which will give the individual that glimpse of the whole and of himself as its part, which may sanction social living.

2. PREHISTORIC KNOWLEDGE OF PSYCHOLOGY

Chinese thought of course is not ignorant of this method. The 'Shi', the medium, the sensitive who deliberately brings about mental dissociation and seeks extra-associations, extra-individuality, is an integral and important part of Chinese early religion. This mediumship presents however (as we in the West know) many difficulties. The individualized may use such a bridge — such prophets, such dervishes, to get proof of extra-individuality. The proof however is always second-hand and almost as often adulterated by the characteristics of the personality through which it has percolated. Any proof, any conviction, comes through the whole filterage, or rather infusage, of the medium's mind and must finally be expressed by her or his conscious mind, an instrument of expression nearly always woefully inadequate if not distortive.

What reformed religion, real, implemented, morality requires, is a method whereby the individual himself (the more powerful and wilful he is, the more this is required for his own sake and for society's) may experience extra-individuality, not merely hear a person he can seldom respect give proof (sometimes remarkable, sometimes not) of that extra-individuality, that collective subconsciousness or co-consciousness.

Here then we can ask the historical question, did the Chinese learn from Buddhists the technique of dilating consciousness? Does this technique come into China before — say from the original Indus culture's discovery of Yoga or even farther back from the proto-civilization — or does China make the discovery for herself? The second alternative is more probably true. Buddhism, according to some authorities, is not the source of such practices — though as we have seen Buddha may and probably did 'restate in terms of

T   289

contemporary psychology' such practices — and if as seems clear the Chinese had a conscious and organized interest in dissociation and extra-association, using mediums, in the effort to obtain extra-sensory information, as part of their reformed religion, it is hard to believe that they themselves, the directors and thinkers, would not experiment not only with mediums but with themselves.

Whatever the source, the fact is that this method begins to be evident. Men see that morality is only a paper screen against a cloudburst unless that paper screen can be impregnated with something which will make it really waterproof. The trouble, as ever, was to make that method scientific, empiric, practical. Access to the subconsciousness, clear recognition of the subconsciousness and that the world of values and ends is apprehended there (as the world of 'facts' and means is apprehended by the objective mind) is extremely difficult to attain. The discovery is only made slowly and uncertainly. It becomes confused with pictorial imaginings and so what should be knowledge of the mind turns into theories — fatally premature — about the outer world. Then, the 'outer world' remaining 'stubborn', there is a reaction. All psychological explanation is dismissed as no more than self-illusion, self-suggestion. So the uneasy 'tacking' advance has to be made until men can define exactly their aim. Meanwhile as they zigzag up the pass to fetch reinforcements, slowly winding up contours (never seeming to win a foot of ascent they do not lose at the next turn) there is the constant attack of rationalized violence on the whole social structure. The saint and the psychologist often sight the way out just at the moment that the greedy, no longer to be held off with threat or promise, break in and bring all to ruin.

Still in spite of relapses into a barbaric physical realism, an individualism which seemed to make any future of civilization impossible, in spite of 'ages of disorder' when man seemed settled for good into the hopeless degeneracy of a morbid species, recovery set in. What is more, after each collapse it is evident that the thinkers can see more clearly their problem and define more exactly their technique for solving it.

3. HOW MILITARISM COMPELLED PSYCHOLOGICAL ADVANCE

Indeed the two specific solutions to militarist realism which China produced and which became, the one her contribution to the world's progress to a balanced civilization, and the other her personal technique which gave the lasting power and the characteristic tone to her own culture, were it seems produced in reply to and as reaction from, a peculiar, ruthless and logical application of the sword. Logical thinking in one direction, the breaking free from the restraints of tradition and the appeal to reality on the one side, wakes up the other. Reformation leads to counter-Reformation. A realism which maintains food is nothing but fats, carbohydrates and protein and that with a synthetic food containing these, the old-fashioned natural foods can be discarded, such common sense, because it leads to death, leads to the discovery of vitamins.

China collapsed after the failure of her sacrificial

auguristic religion into a heroic age of appalling anarchy. Then the militaristic Realists out of such facts tried to build a state philosophy of violence. As Mr. Waley has said, 'It was the failure to inquire even in the most superficial way into the nature and functions of the things which they sought to discard that caused the Realists to build an edifice, which despite its coherence and solidity never became and could never hope to become a dwelling place for the human spirit.[1]

[1] ARTHUR WALEY, *The Way and its Power*, p. 84. Mr. Waley's whole description in this book of the rise of moral religion in China, the struggle to prevent the newer consciousness becoming a wholly unbalanced 'objective' physicism, a dependence on materialistic power, and to correct this disbalance by proportionate advances into and command over the inner world, is masterly. It is an original and invaluable contribution to the history of civilization. Where however he seems to accept an earlier but unfounded assumption is when he claims there must be an a-moral state in human history, and not far back, because moral only means customary. *Dikaios* also only means in origin that, though it came to mean 'righteous'; and *virtus*, *nobilis* and *gentilis* were also morally 'neutral' words. That such words show a pre-conscienceless condition to have belonged to man's nature is only so if we allow that the customary and what was done by the noble stock and had virtue in it was not socially valuable and not acts which bound man to his fellows and to Life. It is exactly that assumption, natural to nineteenth-century evolutionists, with their timid fancies about the savage and indeed 'the lower classes', which 'modern' anthropology does not permit us any longer to make. Early men, it is and should be allowed, did not realize and define their actions as moral any more than a bee realizes its tending of the hive's egg and honey cells is altruistic. To talk of them being either moral or immoral is to read our fully individualized mentality into less condensed minds.

Later, the division growing in their minds, they began to sacrifice deliberately, to coerce nature and life, and the step after that was to throw over sacrifice, and take to the sword to help yourself. Acts of union, or identification, these acts made into coercive spells, these acts discarded because they did not give gain and the sword taken instead, that is the degenerative process as man's unbalanced development of his objective mind continues. This finality, (as Mr. Waley in the passage quoted above, points out) itself brings about a crisis in men's minds and a counter-balancing development begins. Then morality appears as a definite thing, justice and mercy as personified abstractions forbidding lawless violence, and as they are these increasingly anthropomorphic projections of man's individualized nature they are helpless to achieve justice or mercy. It is, however, as we have seen, only when men realize the fissure in their nature, and that it is this which gives rise both to a justice which is helpless to avenge itself and a violence which cannot satisfy itself, that the process is complete and the crisis over.

China, as all the other societies we can study going through this transition, 'tacked' out of undifferentiated state-feeling, uncritical acceptance of tradition, across the sea of individualism toward the haven where again the constituent and the State should be once more a single, reciprocating process and individuals would form a symbiotic whole. The individual becomes, he has to become, conscious of himself.

This at first is not a lawless discovery. He is an advanced type who is capable of this distinction; he is an explorer, not a robber. Still he must think that, beside this vivid reality of self-consciousness, all is shadow and all other claims have been based on illusion or sham. The community can only exist to bring about such wonderful creatures who are free, creative and 'have the knowledge of good and evil'. Hence the State has no right to interfere with individuals at all. Its destiny is to be transformed, its liquid to be finally crystallized out into so many perfect distinct cubes. This is the dream of Liberalism and, as has ended Liberalism to-day, it ends with despotic tyranny far more exacting and capricious than the cramp of custom or the pressure of tradition. The first individuals feel that they have a right to fulfil themselves and a power, if they do so, to make the perfect Free State of *laissez-faire*. This is a natural but fatal ignorance of psychology. The individual by first fulfilling himself cannot fulfil the community. He may wish to live up to conscience but the fact of his existence is evidence of a fissured psyche. In a community where psychological knowledge was kept equal with physical knowledge he could be given the expert insight which would save him from becoming completely individualized. In any other society he will find that he will desire the good and do the evil.

Meanwhile individualism will continue to spread until at last men exist who feel it is nonsense to desire the good — the only good is material good and each individual is the only judge of that. He begins by believing the State can only be fulfilled by his individuality and right of private conscience being allowed the fullest responsibility and freedom. He ends by realizing that his only logical conclusion is *l'état c'est moi* — a conclusion which means a dreary fluctuation between tyranny and anarchy. Quietism, Hedonism, ruthless militarist realism, all these possible logical extremities of pure individualism were rapidly reached in China after the outbreak of the discovery of independent self-consciousness and the 'right of private conscience and judgment'.

The first stage of self-consciousness, the self-awareness of what China has called 'superior persons', found its balance in Confucianism. The superior person conquers desire in others by his own lack of desire. He sees how fatal unregulated desire is and so he restrains it and by his example others are restrained. This is of course only partially true and so the stabilization is only temporary. He himself has only rationalized his individuality, i.e. seen that it does not pay and decided to 'repress' it. He has not resolved it and it will reappear. The Roman Senators, seated like statues, overawed for a space the Gauls. But on the Gaulish soldier touching one's beard he struck the insulter and they were all massacred. An animal psychologist, whose work will be referred to again,[1]

[1] Cf. p. 416.

who has tamed many carnivores has pointed out this is possible only if you not merely show no fear but feel none. The animal can detect your fear — perhaps smelling you because your adrenalin, which fear passes into your blood may change your sweat — and it attacks because it fears attack.

The superior person who remains only a heightened individual, really delighted with his individuality, is not a person lacking desire, on the contrary he is full of the wish to demonstrate and dominate. He has no solution for individuality. Others feel this and though he may dominate them for a space they must, because they wish to be like him, revolt against him. If he knew the way out and beyond individuality he could not go alone — they would be drawn after his unconscious example. For all streams are unwilling to find themselves at a dead end: they desire the sea.

Confucius therefore is content to tell people to obey the law, keep order and preserve traditions, for that will bring a man peace in the end. Whether Confucius himself thought that was enough — a map without a motor, advice without inspiration, an aim without a method — is now being doubted. It is possible he thought something more than tradition was needed. Nevertheless he stands in China as the teacher who solved the problem of the individual by pointing him back to his ancestral duties, the laws of intimate social relationships. Probably at his date the full crisis of individualism had not arisen.

That crisis is becoming distinctly more acute when Mencius has to maintain the innate goodness of man. The ancient organic ways are ways in which man has

not to think at all acutely whether he is being good.[1]
He is moral, he serves himself and life when he goes
the way of custom and does as his nature, shaped by
tradition, dictates. Mo Ti has to maintain the need of
peace — that man is and should be pacific. Here is
another symptom that consciousness is making men
more rationistically and purposely violent. Wars had
now existed for some centuries certainly. As man
became individualized, to that degree, if he cannot
correct that aberration, he will use violence. The
efficiency of his war, the degree that it is realistic and
relies on pure violence, is an exact indication of the
degree of his individualization. Though then there
had been war, war had been all part of a magical
tradition, a rite whereby you righted a disbalanced
nature and even cannibalism is sacramentalism, the
power of assimilating another's virtue. Dr. Rivers
said, and saying it made clear a principle, 'You must
not try and explain the blood feud from vengeance
but vengeance from the blood feud'. Using this
principle we can say the war-dance is not a result of
war but war is a result of the war-dance.

4. THE DESCENT TO INDIVIDUALISM

However, growing self-consciousness, increasingly
unaware of its full nature, can think only in terms of
purpose which will satisfy its particularized nature
and to be efficient is to do that and nothing else.
Hence war becomes increasingly unmanageable and
deadly. So Mencius has to say man is really loving
and can, by recollection, recover his true nature, and

[1] Cf. quotation from BENEDICT'S *Patterns of Culture*, p. 255.

Mo Ti has to point out that war really does not pay and is somehow a hideous mistake. They cannot however stay the decline, though they may have made the descent less violent and the reaction more certain. Certainly the development is then exceedingly rapid. By the third century B.C. individualism is so intense and blinding that the doctrine is openly taught that the State rests and can rest only on punishments — to which later are added, grudgingly, bribes — and good feeling, co-operation, natural kindliness are dismissed as fabulous attributes. Good men may exist but they are so rare as to make no difference. Man in a lump is bad because obviously each man is and can be only for himself. This frame of mind, this acute terrifying individualism, produces its case, its defence. It is perfectly indicative of the morbid condition. To those who still believe that man somehow is part of a profound unity, these Realists replied that all such imaginings were only a mystification of the fact that man is the servant, slave and pawn of the State and only exists at its pleasure and for its purpose. So China in the third century, through an acute extension of individualism, arrived at the Hegelian position, a position which has in our Europe resulted in all the tyrannies from red to black, from the Marxian dictatorship drawn straight from Hegel himself to the Facist and Nazi autocracies which have the same spiritual father. Such individualism ends in individuals resolved to destroy one another. War therefore, in China two millennia ago, as now in our contemporary Europe, at this stage flings off all pretence. China produces the Realists' handbook and credo, the *Shang Tzu*. 'It is not,' says Waley, 'like previous works of the kind, a recipe for maintaining frontiers intact, with the vaguely suggested possibility of uniting several states into some sort of hegemony. It is an exaltation of War.'[1] There is no further temporizing nonsense of the sword protecting justice and being essential for mercy. The sword is to get power and loot, for there is no law save

> The good old rule, the ancient plan
> That he shall take who has the power
> And he shall keep who can.

When men could imagine that such thought was a complete and final answer to all social problems and the deeper questions of their own nature, the judge was at the door, the end upon them.

As in Greece with Macedonia (and, as we shall see, in the same situation when Rome rises) a state on the borders of civilization, a state which has specialized in crude individualism — which for instance has fallen into the practice prompted by crude individualism, human sacrifice and stuck to that brutally stupid practice — a state which like Macedon has learnt every discovery which civilization has made about war — suddenly accepts this doctrine without reservation or scruple. The Chin came down on China as Philip and his son came down on Greece and Persia. The further rapid discharge of this unbalanced energy follows in curious detail the meteoric rise and disintegration which had, a century before, marked the other effort at a realist empire, at the opposite end of Asia. In 221 B.C. the leader of these provincial savages became the first Emperor of China. In ten

---

[1] A. WALEY, *The Way and its Power.*

years, the empire was in the same state of disintegration, as ten years after his crowning victory Alexander's
empire vanished with his life. In another five years
the Chin empire was in the same ghastly chaos as that
into which the Diadochi five years after Alexander's
death had reduced his imperialistic dream.

Like causes lead to like effects. Individualism —
which cannot cure and resolve itself — first takes the
sword to save the State, next it drives the guardian to
betray what he guards and finally there can be no law,
order or peace: every man does and can only do 'what
is right in his own eyes', what is for his own interests.

Such a decline — though realists will not foresee
it — is inevitable and has been constantly repeated.
If individualism is final, if man cannot have direct
experience of his extra-individuality, society will be
destroyed and culture will perish. Man will become
lower than an animal. This descent however was fore-
seen by thinkers — though, as ever, the practical man
was sure they were alarmists in foreseeing so grave a
smash and mystical visionaries in indicating that
a psychological discovery, a complete change and
extension of consciousness, was the only way out and
up. In consequence it is somewhere about 240 B.C.
(some years before the Chin gave practical proof to
the common-sense compromiser that the sword would
prove not the guard but the death of civilization)
that the Tao Tê Ching appeared.

5. THE WAY OUT

The mysterious author we call Lao Tzu wished to
show two things: first that violence defeated its

supposed end: it would destroy those who used it: the talk of the essential guarantee of justice was merely the talk of the wolf at the door of the hen-run, promising, if let in, to protect the chickens. The Chin proved the book's case for it, up to the blood-stained hilt. The second part of the author's case was that the only way to prevent this degeneracy into violence, which finally became and must become internecine, was through resolving individualism. If men were only individuals then they 'could not other'. They must seek for sanctions against each other and the armament race must end in a collision of such violence that beside it the wars of the Kilkenny Cats were formal debates. The existence of society, the fact of their own nature, if they explored it, proved, however, men were not the individuals they assumed. Their partial blindness was due to an unbalanced development of their character, absorbed, as they had been, in exploiting the outer world and insensitive to the first prickings which should have warned them that paralysis was creeping on them, the natural circulation which kept them and their fellows in one life was becoming checked.

Was Lao Tzu right? His book undoubtedly made possible the salvage of a huge society in danger of complete disintegration. Was his argument, however, only a skilfully presented 'wish-fulfilment'. People were sick of violence. Clearly these militarist rationalists pushed their doctrine of individualism and realism too far. The common man was glad to hear that there was something beside violence in the world, something that held people together and let you get on quietly with your own business.

Was the salvaging of civilization the Tao Tê Ching suggested, and to some extent achieved, no more than this? Men were tired of practical violence and so, for some time, preferred to believe that they were tied to each other by invisible bonds and society rested on forces other than the sword — was it no more than such a reaction? Certainly China as a whole never got beyond that point. The final philosophy of life which the Celestial empire made was, not the advanced psychological method and plan which lies behind the Tao Tê Ching, but the rationalized, 'de-natured' ethicism of the Confucian tradition. Man was not to seek to explore the limits and cross the frontiers of his individualism and so have direct experience of the larger life of which he and his fellows were all parts and their society a manifestation. Man was to accept authority instead of experience, tradition instead of vision.

Hence China became the most stable and the least adaptable of societies. It could endure: it could hardly advance. We may perhaps add, it became also for the same reason a society which was immensely callous toward human suffering, for if authority is the only tie of civilization then the individual must be ruthlessly crushed if he fails to conform. It is expedient that thousands should be tortured rather than the State, civilization, be endangered. They have to be crushed because the State has lost the secret which would have resolved them. Yet, as we have seen since the disappearance of the Manchu emperors and the collapse of the traditional order, all this force has been insufficient. China has been jarred back into a state almost as bad as that endured under the Chin. Piracy on the coasts, brigandage in the countryside, torture and loot and massacre, the collapse of defences against nature, the constant oppression, treachery and treason of the rulers — this has been and is her lot. The latest weapons only make slaughters more efficient, the latest ideas such as Marxian communism only make anarchy more complete, the latest inventions such as electricity only make torture more ghastly.[1]

Hence to-day the lords of the machine guns are driven back to preaching 'the New Life'. Men must recover a moral way of living. But how? Can Confucius and the reverence for the ancestors be reinstated? Is not all this traditionalism simply rationalism, the rationalization of something which is real, but only if one can get oneself into actual touch with it? To talk about the ancestors and of one's kinship with them and reverence for them, is like talking about electric current. It will never lighten the darkness. This talk does refer to something real — the ancestors and their services do stand for the constant abiding life beyond and above one's individual life, the life that makes possible the community and civilization. But if all one actually *experiences* is one's own sharply cut-out individualism, then the ancestors and the life they symbolize, are, however pleasant, however necessary for society, only shadows.

Society, then, whether Chinese or European, is faced again by the dilemma: Either I must experience a life transcending my individuality and as vivid and as real as my individuality, or society cannot hold

---

[1] It has been discovered by the sword-holders that when a rich merchant cannot be made confess where his wealth is hid, though his nails have been torn off, his thumbs screwed and his soles branded, attaching him to the electric current and switching it on and off through him, quickly reduces him to amenability.

together. All other ways fail: they may refer back the question for a little, gain a little time, get a stay of execution, but time is against these other ways. Self-consciousness grows, individualism grows: unless some proportionate and balancing growth of the psyche can be made then the old interpretations no longer serve, the case must go forward, man must face the fact, society must smash and humanity begin its retreat into savagery, decadence, animalism, and extinction.

Lao Tzu at least was scientific enough in his diagnosis. Tradition would not serve. Believing in an ideal past would be no good if you yourself remained unchanged. That would be no better than looking at a well but being unable to drink. The change the author advises, there can be little doubt, is this psychological method of extending the personality, of directly experiencing extra-individuality.

Did he inherit this method from early Yoga practices and are they part of the slowly diffusing discoveries of the Indus civilization or, may be, of the proto-civilization? We cannot say. What we have to recognize is that here they turn up again with their offer of the one way out of civilization's impasse. Whether the route be possible or no: it is clear that across that col alone lies any path out of the corner in which to-day we find ourselves ever more narrowly hemmed.

6. CAN THE WAY CHANGE THE WORLD?

We must then again look up at that track and see whether it is as unscalable as some have thought.

Many have said it is impossible because there is no real hold for the climber: it is illusory to suppose man can change the nature of things. But the mystical outlook, that is the teaching which says, Violence is fatal, simply doing nothing is equally fatal, some force must be used, psychological forces can be generated, employed and directed to solve our difficulties: that attitude was originally rejected because men did not know either of the subjective mind and its extent or of the limits of the objective mind — how Reality was not objective but a selection of data which the objective mind built up into what it assumed to be Reality.

When men are at that stage of psychological ignorance, to speak of changing our social conditions by changing the focus of our minds is so absurd and inconceivable that any talk of this sort they imagine must be pure magic, talk of changing nature, moving mountains by spells and sorcery. Man's nature and outer nature, the organic and the inorganic, are thought of as all one, and it seems as absurd to claim you can raise a blister with a cold penny on a person's hand by simply telling him it is red-hot, as to claim you could command stones that they become bread.

What may be the limit of the mind's control over that picture of an outer world which to-day it calls objective reality we cannot say and here need not inquire. It will obviously grow and will grow by our widening power of apprehension quite as much, one might say more, by that, than by power to interfere. What we can say and need to realize is that what has passed as the mystical outlook, our present psychological knowledge divides into two parts. If that outlook claimed power by thought, by enlargement of consciousness to change the outer world (as undoubtedly some adepts seem to have claimed), then that is a side of this extension of mind of which psychology knows at present not even enough to say it is impossible. On the other hand where that outlook claimed to see the way, by enlargement of consciousness, to control of human nature, human society and indeed to get into sympathetic influential touch with all Life, there psychology can now divide off this as a separate province of power and sphere of influence, and produce evidence to show such influences do exist and are extraordinarily effective.

It is with this second division of the subjective mind, with its power over our individual will and the control of our passions which concerns us — and Lao Tzu and all the Yogic tradition, in so far as it is concerned with the balanced progress of civilization and its recovery from its capsize and imminent foundering. Whether the mystic can alter the course of the stars is not our question, for the 'fault dear Brutus is not in our stars but in ourselves' and what we have to remedy to-day is not outer-nature which is letting us alone but inner-nature which has us by the throat.

The prescription which Lao Tzu advised is not therefore impracticable. It does not propose coercive magic of the Universe. It may suggest that the Universe is changed to the Seer who has learnt to take it in more fully. That proposition modern psychology could not deny. What however is the Tao Tê Ching's message is that society can be re-made and only re-made by men recovering the direct awareness of their common Life of which they are members and their society is its expression.

This solution has been, it seems, proposed again and again. Each time as man's objective mind moved forward a step, condensed harder, focused more sharply, saw more exclusively an outer world, shapeless and purposeless for his power to shape, at each of these stages society has been shaken. Ends had proportionately to be lost sight of. Then the Seer arose and pointed out how this unbalanced advance must be balanced by a proportionate advance in self-knowledge and extension of consciousness. Unfortunately men are lazy. To advance at all is exhausting. To advance proportionately on two fronts, outer and inner, is altogether too much. When outer advance is too rapid, values disappear, sanctions fail to guard and even material progress is endangered and begins to collapse. Then it is the practical man grows alarmed. The Seer tells him that conditions are even more dangerous than he suspected. At the same time the Seer is no defeatist. 'Offences must needs come': it is disbalanced growth which threatens collapse. Things have gone as he forecast and he is ready and willing to show the practical man how to recover his balance and society's safety. The way however is too steep and narrow. The practical man is frightened and will give the Seer right to guide. What the Seer wants him to do, look for himself, that he feels is beyond his powers. Caste system might have acted as an irrigation system from head waters. China however seems to have failed to make that social invention. It avoided the dangers of the hereditary system. Mandarins were appointed by examination but it taught them the 3000 classics: not illumination. Hence after an age of disorder instead of Lao Tzu we get Confucius, instead of vision, a return to authority, talk of absolute values instead of real experience — experience as real as those partial facts which have upset the world. Men are frightened and willing to trust authority — and so, they only take at second-hand (and so it is no more than a 'wish-fulfilment', an amiable ideal) the belief that society need not rest on violence, that there is something, some power in ideals themselves. But what it is they have never known for themselves.

Soon, after a short tranquillity, in which all their attention has been on increasing power, increasing means (and so their minds have been directed away from the realm of ends, their individuality has been growing, not decreasing) crises begin inevitably again to appear. They have been living on illusion, on a diminishing wish for a better order, a wish and not an experience. Even the wish begins to fail: quite obviously it has not produced the order. The ancient authority is called a fraud. The few Seers who have vision are dismissed as self-hypnotized cranks who are afraid to face up to reality. No practical man has ever had any such experience. Man cannot but impute himself. Regretfully and slowly, then with ever less regret and more speed, men begin to arm and even to rush to the crisis.

Here then we see the slow Aeonic fluctuation of two vast forces, expressing themselves in man and shaping him under their play. The one force is the power to apprehend even more clearly the outer world, but to be in danger of so specializing in that knowledge, becoming so absorbed with that partial vision, as to cease to recognize it is partial. The other force is man's power to apprehend even more clearly himself and his own full nature. Both are aspects of the growth of consciousness.[1] If however the second does not keep up with the first, man becomes specialized, his general awareness shrinks into a narrower, more hypnotic focus, until, having first concentrated exclusively on what he imagined alone could pay, he is finally confronted with acts which are ruinous and an outlook which only reveals chaos.

7. MAN, DOUBLE-NATURED, NEEDS TWO-FOLD ADVANCE

In short man is double-natured, double-visioned, and the whole art of civilization and secret of his progress lies in keeping those two outlooks in a single focus.

The history of thought on this supreme problem in China brings out that issue with uncommon clearness. It underlies however all history. All history repeats this continual divergence of the two outlooks. This divergence grows and then, when the strain has become too great, the divergence becoming a complete contradiction — order snaps, chaos appears, the individual behaves insanely — the tender are all neurotic, they become ascetic hermits and call Life evil; the tough all criminal lunatics, they smash civilization down to ground level. Men after untold

[1] It might be objected that if this is a natural *growth* of consciousness then as man has learnt to see the outer world with ever growing clearness he will as naturally learn to see the inner world. The growth however though natural has to be acted upon and provided for. If man – as some races have indeed done – had seen the outer world with his present clearness and yet by appropriate invention, discovery and foresight failed to act on that insight he would have been wretched physically, economically. So, if he only feels that values are somehow true, but cannot see how he can act on them, apply them, he becomes psychologically wretched.

suffering, again resume society, determined again to observe, but still not to understand, the dictates of their buried nature.

History, however, though it repeats the theme does not repeat the words. Each crisis is more grave and makes a real settlement or a final irretrievable collapse more certain. For each further extension of man's partial, objective-mind knowledge of the outer world gives him increasing powers and decreasing sense of ends, and so as these powers grow and he comes nearer to the point when he can become a super-creature able to destroy itself and its environment, the inherent restraints in his nature, his sensitiveness, his good sense, his *aidos*, his compassion begin to seem increasingly to his intellect to be shadows, relics of a period of life before he knew he was the only free power and purpose in the universe. At the same time his values, crushed down into the subconscious seep through as increasingly strong emotions. Hence the highest sensibility in our age — an age of subsistence allowances, prison reforms, anti-vivisection — (General Göering, who thinks as little as Hotspur of a 'clean-up' among humans, forbids vivisection) is accompanied by conscious preparations for universal massacre.

For this reason the crisis in our present day is so grave. We are more powerful because we are more individualized than any other age, and because we are so individualized, so 'intellectualized, there is less restraint than ever before on our full use of our unprecedented powers.

Is it then to be guilty of temporal provincialism if we look upon our age and its crisis as the most momentous, perilous and acute through which man and indeed life has ever passed? Before trying briefly to estimate our chances, the hope of man in such an issue, we must however glance at how our particular tradition of culture and way of civilization, arrived here at this pass where the writhing centre of the typhoon, driving down from the blackness above, reaches out its devastating touch toward our devoted heads and homes. If this age of civilization collapses, it is most certain to collapse (the centre of the vault will cave in first) here and now — in Europe in the third decade of the twentieth century. How Europe came to this pass, how the force we have diagnosed actually arrived at the present acute disbalance, is therefore of particular interest, not merely to us but to the world at large and to history. If our doom cannot be fended, at least observation of how it drew upon us, or rather how we drew it on ourselves, may be of some value to those who may yet come after and learn from our fate.

CHAPTER XV

THE IMPERIAL COLLAPSE

WE have seen that the arc of proto-culture which, spreading from the Indus, developed a social advance which was balanced, extended over Asia as far as the eastern coast of the continent. In consequence, eastern civilizations although often deeply corrupted with violence — resultant of the disproportionate development of the objective mind — never were without an apprehension that there existed for social order and for all values a sanction which was not violence.

We have seen that the other two arcs of the proto-culture, which early developed violence as a means to cohesion and expansion, quickly entered a series of unstable alternations between anarchy and tyranny. When this condition became unbearable, short respites were won by the acceptance of religions of authority, religions which vouched that another order (which sanctioned morality) did exist, but which religions did not give their followers the power and technique to attain that experience for themselves. In consequence, as soon as the desperate need for social order was assuaged, men began to behave as the still unresolved, unrepentant individuals they were, and society was soon once again on the brink of disintegration — there was war without and panic and despair within.

Further, as individualism is not a stable state but if

unresolved, unbalanced, must grow increasingly intense and exclusive, the efforts to revive religious authority must appear increasingly disingenuous and as deliberate shifts of expedience. Hence these efforts lose in power proportionately as war-efficiency, the inventions of destructiveness, the fruits of the partial, intense, specialized activity of the partial objective mind, steadily increase. Checks fail to have any purchase, while the force driving to destruction increases.

It was at this state, this stage of decomposition, that we left Europe. The Diadochi had torn Alexander's empire to fragments and had squandered the huge wealth the Persian Peace had let accumulate. This wealth, the Lydian invention of money for storing credit, had allowed to be made realizable, releasable at any one spot at any one moment. The further inventions of the objective mind — instruments and machines — money allowed to be constructed and these were used all for war, to accelerate destruction. The siege of Rhodes which began in 307 and was raised in 302 showed means of destruction growing as in a forcing house. Larger and faster ships than had ever sailed appeared. Quick-firing engines became so efficient that decks could be swept clear without needing to board them. Yet the mechanized violence is so balanced that the siege is fruitless. The combatants fall apart exhausted. The Levant is using all its inventiveness to drain its own civilization. Soon even Macedonia will be extinct as a dead volcano. The genius of the crafty Ptolomies will smoulder in the granite groove of Egypt. From a limit beyond even Macedonia will come a heavy farming people, who, as all semi-barbarians, has learnt only the special art of war. Rome was roused by the Etruscan City States and those of South Italy — Magna Graecia — as Macedonia was roused by the City States of Greece proper. She was hammered by the skills of Greek and Carthagenian-Phoenician. She took what she could assimilate, war on land and sea, and money as the means and prize.

I . THE ULTIMATE EMPIRE

Rome later came to talk of justice. No society so continually prated of the need of guaranteeing peace by preparing for war and of the sword being the only possible prop for the scales. While she grew she never talked such nonsense. Delenda est Carthago, Etruria, Sicilia, Macedonia. Every neighbour must be destroyed. When the widening sweep of the deadly sword touched the lands the previous empire conflagration had burnt out, they passed helplessly into the new exploiters' hands. The last of the Attalids (a house which had shortly before ruled much of still wealthy Asia Minor, the cradle of money-wealth), like a bird falling into a snake's mouth, leaves his kingdom to Rome. The Mithradatic wars only serve to spur the pugnacity of generals who had sufficient loot and now must conquer for conquest's sake as a fox kills all the hens in the run from wantonness, needing to eat only one. This passion to destroy, beyond any carnivorous need, is later called glory. The legions must be flung against anything left to smash. Finally the whole of Alexander's empire up to the Indian and Persian borders, all Africa to the Sahara, all Europe to the central forests, is Rome's. The exactions are so pitiless that even Romans have to condemn them. The trial of Verus who had administered the Pax Romana in Sicily, shows how that peace worked. He had ground the people, torturing the rich to get their gold, exactly as any brigand works. The provinces lay like panic-struck sheep while the wolves devoured.

Rome itself was in complete confusion. If England acquired its empire in a fit of absence of mind (or rather by its right hand not looking too closely into the sinister activities of its fellow) Rome acquired its empire in a frenzy of unplanned pugnacity. The capital itself was as lawless as the newly-sacked provinces, and a Roman citizen had no more protection, no more public peace and order than his new subjects in Syracuse or Athens. While the Roman legions are continually smashing their way outward, their masters, the generals, are continually trampling into mud the simple political structure of the small city which had become the destructive centre of the world. Marius, who massacres the Nordic hordes which were threatening Italy, returns to proscribe his political rivals at home, is himself proscribed and his friends are massacred. Sulla, his successful rival, purges even more drastically the upper ranks of Rome. Still peace and order will not follow, crush and cut as you will. Clodius and Milo are gangsters who with their braves make life impossible in the city whose forces are conquering the world; and generals, before whom no new barbarian or ancient Asiatic power can stand, dare not in the capital which had given them a triumph, go out at night without their bodyguards. To such a pass had the peace-giving sword brought civilization.

No stability can be found because everyone in such an imperial city realizes that the control of unlimited violence is the only sanction. The small crabbed *Religio* of former Rome, no more could net and hold the new forces than a housekeeper's string bag could hold a Siberian tiger. The pretence that Rome is governed and governs by anything but martial law, the naked sword, is torn to shreds. Eloquent pretenders, such as Cicero, try with their oratory to make facts appear less brutal and, as with the denunciation of Verus, even to maintain that the state must establish an abstract of justice, but the moment they attempt to stabilize the decadence and make the appearance of stoic virtue share any reality with the sword, they are cut down. The Senate and the People of Rome had shrunk to the Senate of Rome. Now the Senate was to shrink to the single arbitrary dictator. The old compromisory order which had tried to mix violence and tradition, custom and outrage in an amalgam, had to yield to the realist who outbid it and wielded the sword without the trammel of precedent. The Senate, next, bunglingly tries to copy the new realism. The assassination of Caesar only removes an ageing man. It does not cure the conditions which drove him to become a tyrant. It leaves the throne open to a fresher brain and gives the new dictator an excuse to assassinate the last conservatives and compromisers who might have delayed the development. So Cicero himself is dispatched; and after the alliance of generals, which had disposed of all civil power, have themselves, as is inevitable, fallen on each other and the most crafty and most capable has survived, the short transitional state of triumvirate ends in the dictator who is life Princeps and in all but name Emperor.

Augustus is crafty enough neither to delay nor to hasten the inevitable descent of the social order till it rests wholly and openly on the sword. He realizes that men must have time to get used to reality. They always begin by shrinking from new weapons. They will connive at any cruelty if you can show them it is customary. This is the truth as tyrants see it. It is still truer to say that men cling to the buried feeling that social order does not rest and cannot rest on violence. As, however, their objective, partial mind cannot see what other basis social order can have, grudgingly, shrinkingly, they permit the hard necessity as the only way to preserve any peace and order at all. Augustus honours this prejudice. He takes care always to appear in civil dress in the streets of Rome. He hides the sword under the toga as a dentist puts his forceps-extractors under a demure piece of cambric until the gas has worked. This pretty pretence does not and cannot prevent the sword at the slightest pressure cutting through and coming nakedly to light, and as there is no other support for society the pressure must come and the toga fall sundered.

Quite apart from outer disturbances (revolts and conspiracies), quite apart from inner problems (the autocrat's own moods and nervous strains) — the succession itself, when the supreme power, the sword, has to be handed on, always creates a moment of acute crisis. Then some snatching will take place, blood will flow, and any stabilization will be on a lower, franker, more brutal level. So even while the Julian house reigns we see a rapid decadence. Power is forced on the Princeps to keep it centred unmistakably in one place: to prevent civil war. Tiberius becomes a melancholy dangerous recluse; Gaius openly insane and is assassinated; Claudius is only appointed because he is of the Imperial gens and descent may give a mould if only of clay to the molten flux of violence which melts all and shapes nothing. Surrounded by women who scheme for the world order as a property for their children, and Greek freed-men who know the machine and so control its titular master, he is let reign until it suits some intimate realist to poison him. His successor, Nero, repeats, if more spectacularly, the collapse which overcame young Gaius. It is clear, control of supreme violence makes a young man a megalomaniac; an old man a paranoiic.

Meanwhile a desperate effort is made to stabilize the immense conquests Rome has united into a single state. Save on the Persian front no force of an equality faces the legions. Wealth begins to accumulate when through so vast a territory there is only one unstinted consumer to be kept. People reflect how happy it would be if such a state were to become perpetual. Here surely is the perfect balance, the individual desires; a condition wherein he can pursue his own private ends and be always protected; where he can remain for ever as he is, peace being a continual preservation of the *status quo* of society and of himself as an unresolved individual in that *status quo*. Such a dream is illusory for man. Some species can stabilize. As we have mentioned, the cockroach and the shark have remained unmodified for some 200 million years. Higher forms of life, however, seem

inherently more unstable — they must go up or down.
Man must develop or degenerate. He is, as Nietzsche
recognized, a transitional animal. Stoicism's judgment has already been quoted: 'He that is not getting
better is getting worse'.

2. THE STOIC WEAKNESS

Yet it was the Stoics who most deliberately and
with most appearance of success attempted to stabilize
the Roman order and to make its Pax a real self-
preserving, self-sanctioning Peace. Stoicism, indeed,
contains in its short history the whole secret of Europe's
failure, the reason why to-day in spite of nobility
of thought, aspiration after justice and accumulation
of power, we find ourselves on the brink of chaos,
threatened by and threatening our fellows, who share
our civilization and our aspirations, with a destruction
more awful, more extensive and more complete than
even Ghenghis could inflict. The fundamental trouble
with Stoicism, is that it is a second-hand philosophy.
It accepts the common-sense view of things as real.
It does not see that the world around it is a construction made by the highly selective capacity of the
partial objective mind. For philosophy, when it gave
rise to Stoicism had already relinquished half its
kingdom. It had ceased to be a co-ordinated effort
to penetrate into the nature of things, to understand
first and foremost what the world is and how man
comes to apprehend it. It had become ethics. It
accepted the universe, that is, it ceased to question
the individualist's ignorant conviction that he saw
reality, all reality and nothing but reality. It con-

centrated on trying to show the wise man how to put up with such an outrageous construction.

Such an attempt was muddled and inconsistent. Stoic thought showed that the individual was 'to live according to nature'. But what was nature? — Surely what happened. In that case the child of darkness, the practical man was the true philosopher for he behaved naturally. The Stoic, on the other hand, was really trying to live up to some higher nature which he could not define. He felt intuitively there was such a nature, but how to get at it he could not say. Zeno, their founder, is a Levantine whose parents came to Cyprus. He must have heard of Asiatic religions which gave a new insight. He probably thought they could only be orgiastic — as had become the Life Religions in Phrygia and on the Nile.[1] He evidently knew nothing of the psycho-physical research which India had initiated and China was at that moment pursuing. Hence the muddle in thought about 'nature'. Stoic practice was of necessity as muddled. Cicero, whose tragic attempt to infuse it into real politics has been noted above, records how, early in life, he visited the great Stoic teacher in Bythinia. This man dilated on how by living according to nature and thinking of noble things the Stoic became superior to circumstance and master of his fate and of others'. Suddenly he rolled over on his couch gasping 'It is no good'. He was dying of stone and the exercises he proposed could not anaesthetize the body even as much as could competent hypnosis.

[1] In Egypt the Osirian religion had been largely replaced by the worship of Isis, and in Phrygia, the worship of the other Mother God cult, of Cybele, had also become extremely orgiastic; these religions as they penetrated to Rome were for some time prosecuted as licentious.

The Stoic then was bound to fail. He did not understand either the world around him, how it took shape, or his own nature, how his acts and feelings might be and could only be controlled by access to the complete psyche across the limen and through the subconscious.

Yet his very limitations, the fact that he seemed both common-sensible and heroic made the world, which wanted such a mixture to prove its solution and its stabilization, give him his opportunity. At least as soon as Nero is seen to be in the succession to the throne he is given Stoic teachers and trainers. The supreme sword power is to have a hilt of philosophy. Seneca, whose meditations we know, was his tutor. The verbal teaching must have been noble but quite unreal. 'Seneca called himself a Stoic but had a thousand tables of lemon wood' joked the realists. The young Nero, greedily wishing for indulgence, like all young pupils, must have sensed what his teacher really lent on, verbal philosophy or the solid and gracious comfort of those inlaid couches. Nero of course breaks loose, and with a melodramatic touch, a creature with as poor control but better taste would have spared, has his Polonius murdered.[1] Still after mopping up the blood spilt in getting rid of the Julian gens, and that of the next military dynasty, the Flavian house, the new military emperor Trajan sets about finding a frill of philosophy to put round the sword. Domitian, the last Flavian, had become para-noiic and been killed. Trajan stabilized the retreat of civilization as a frank soldier. He tries to limit the spread and sprawl of the empire. He looks for a

[1] Seneca was permitted to take his own life rather than be executed.

successor to secure the transition of power. He finds it in that super-clerk Hadrian. The Stoics are called back. There is enough talk of virtue, the noble life, of living according to nature, of men being all brothers, to hide in a steam of fine words the fact that chattel slavery is everywhere, crucifixion is a normal and frequent punishment, scourging, torture and even burning alive part of the famous Roman Law; 'the games' the people's chief amusement, a display of sadistic butchery a Greek, a Persian or an Egyptian while they ruled would have forbidden; and the divine Emperor himself, though he talks philosophy, banishes a philosopher who dared disagree with him and made another confess, when chid by a colleague for an undignified climb down, 'It is unwise to differ with the master of twenty legions'. Nevertheless though not a Stoic himself (both he and Trajan were homosexuals, an aberration which the puritan Stoic would probably think more disqualifying than capricious use of absolute power) he felt Stoicism could make the compromise he wanted made and stabilize the empire by gradually making consent take the place of coercion. Certainly he appointed as successor a fully qualified Stoic, Antoninus Pius, and this emperor and his more famous, but not more strict, heir, Marcus Aurelius, not merely employ, they are themselves philosophers.

No philosophy has then had a better, fuller and fairer trial. Its failure was due to its own inherent hollowness. Marcus, though autocrat of the world and, what is more, divinized so that a field of superstition should surround his unquestioned sword, never dares even modify the cruelly bloody games. He even

x   321

does not stay away but ostentatiously does official work while presiding. Could philosophic impotence be more extreme? He has no judgment of character, appointing Verus, a characterless self-indulgent fop as his colleague and, unbelievable act of blindness or irresponsibility, his violent dangerous son as his successor. Complete lack of any insight into men's motives and the forces which direct them is also shown by his energetically brutal persecution of the Christians.

This is a catalogue of tragic mistakes for which civilization paid. The real importance of them lies, however, in the fact that the man who committed them was not only politically all powerful, he was as wise, as noble, as self-controlled, as lofty minded as any man who has ever sat on a throne. His catalogue of the men who trained him is of a colonnade of icy monoliths of rigid, almost expressionless virtue. These men could claim with pride that they were super-human and their pupil they made desire to be like them.

If then Stoicism itself had been sound the world would have been saved. Its psychological and psycho-physical ignorance, however, was so great that it remained arrested, a 'wish-fulfilment dream'.

3. THE BANKRUPTCY OF STOICISM

Thereafter retreat is rapid. Stoicism had had its chance. It was found wanting. As the third century of our era opens 'the Stoic increasingly finds reason for withdrawal from the world'. The emperor has to be increasingly divinized, his arbitrary sword power emphasized, not disguised. Corruption spreads; the empire creaks; it fissures; huge fragments such as North Britain, will shortly become detached. Violence, still unresolved at the head, spreads out again into the provinces. Generals such as Carausius set up separate kingdoms. At headquarters the Praetorian guard, on whom the emperor must depend to hedge his divinity from assassination, itself takes to evacuating the throne it is supposed to secure and actually once succeeds in putting up the lordship of the world for sale. It is clear that the sword has produced its inevitable consequence — it has destroyed all justice.

Men had hoped much from Stoicism when it climbed to the throne. It had failed. The sensible upright rationalist world, wherein common-sense law and order would be preserved by 'a reasonable use' of violence, the Pax Romana under which individuals could continue for ever to mind their own business and pursue their private pleasures untyrannized over from above, indifferent to the sufferings of those below, whom the system crushed, the slave, the convict — this temporizing unstable scheme of things was obviously caving in.

Something which had more reality, more sanction than Stoicism, and yet less fatally destructive a force than the sword, some cement must be found to grout into the yawning cracks now running right through society.

CHAPTER XVI

THE WEST LOOKS FOR LIGHT

So men cried out in their fear and the Church answered. We are only beginning to understand Christianity's debt to the East. This 'Religion of Southern Europe' it has long been recognized, took up into itself all the psychological discoveries made by the mystery religions, those psychological out-growths of the Fertility cults, the decadent Life Religions. What it has taken longer to recognize is that this religion, the successful competitor for the post of sustainer of the empire, combined in itself something more.

We have seen that the instability of the West was caused by the unbalanced, partial development of the mind in the Nilotic and the Mesopotamian arcs of the original culture. We have also seen that the continual recovery of the West and its periods of comparative calm, short as they are, can only be accounted for by postulating a preservative factor present and working to check and counteract the appeal to unlimited violence. This factor is partly expressed by organized Religion. Organized Religion is the rationalization, the wish-expression of the profound feeling that there is some other way of holding society together and guaranteeing values besides violence. It seldom if ever gets beyond this stage. It is therefore a restraint which only works when men are sufficiently exhausted and exasperated by violence so as to believe there must be some other method, so as to eschew violence and await a new way, although there is no clear indication of what that method may be or how that way may be found. In short, religion, as the West has understood it, is hope and faith, a hope which is deferred and makes the heart sick, a faith which is held to be a belief in something which is not really there. It does not attempt analytically to explore its situation and its need; to find out what its nature is and see whether it can master that. Being committed to an unbalanced individuality it takes that for granted as insoluble. Its way is to project that individuality on to the outer world, maintain there is a person like itself using physical violence as does itself and that to this person it must appeal to smite its enemies and wrench circumstances to its advantage.

1 . *EX ORIENTE LUX*

Such a development is as natural as it is mistaken, but it is also so mistaken that it leads men to recognize the fact and make a second and more searching attempt to solve their dilemma. We now know as an historical fact that the far deeper analysis made by the East — the recognition that man must cure the fissure in his mind and then he will see how to heal society and understand the world — that psychological discovery filtered in from India to the Levant as did the knowledge of mathematics. The fact that certain protracted exercises could at last alter the aperture of consciousness and not only give you control of your will but direct insight into and influence over the wills of others, does not, however, save Europe from disasters. For this knowledge not only spreads slowly, is hard to put into practice — he who would know must do — and itself must be fully mastered before it can be conveyed. It is in short an esoteric doctrine which each person has to fit into their own frame of reference.[1] But more, the very successes, when won, are apt to postpone the time when the method can become of public benefit. It is the acutely troubled individual, already estranged from his society, who alone can be sufficiently convinced that the whole construction of things is mistaken, so that he can make the immense effort of going back on all the common assumptions and attempting a radically new way of apprehension. When at last he succeeds he may be all too content. Such is the solitary adept. The other case of fatal success is when a few like-minded people make the exploratory effort together. Their success is probably more swift but their content is apt to be even more final. Such form those groups — either of sects who encyst themselves in society, in it but not of it, giving it only the minimum economic tribute it demands — or actually leaving it and forming colonies independent economically as well as psychologically.

2. THE LIGHT UNDER A BUSHEL

It is in these two forms, that of the solitary adept and of the sundered group, that the East's experience of the deeper secret of religion (that religion was more than appeal to a personal deity for help) came into the West. We can trace two such settlements.

[1] Hence caste which, like a radiator, carries and makes sure a comparatively small amount of enlightenment over a large area and social structure is probably necessary if society is to be saved.

326

The Hermetic groups in Egypt have left their writings. In these it is clear that they came into Egypt somewhere during the Persian occupation, for the specific Persian word 'Satrap' appears in their texts. It is equally clear they came from India. They set up their coenobite life on the outer terraces of the lower Nile. Another such sect we know of by a contemporary account, though we have not their scriptures. These are the Essenes who lived in Palestine.

The psycho-physical discoveries of Asia, the basis for an empirical religion, the possibility of developing the neglected side of the mind and balancing the disproportionate development of the objective mind which had led to civilization's disasters — all this was now on the threshold of the West. Would this, the only possible news deserving the name Gospel, get disseminated? The answer is doubtful. There can be little doubt the outlook is present in primitive Christianity, and many scholars have in consequence maintained that Jesus must have known the Essenes. The Sermon on the Mount is undoubtedly the *consequence* of such an outlook. Unfortunately, though it is the consequence, the natural action, it is not itself the outlook, the transforming vision. Has, we must then ask, the Gospel an esoteric, an illuminating, a causative doctrine? As we have seen (p. 279) Buddha also taught this sublime ethic but also it is equally clear that it would have been no use his teaching it and indeed in India none would have attended to it — it would have been so pathetically platitudinous — had he not taught men how to practice it, had he not, after pointing to the old mark — which now everyone was missing — shown a new technique of hitting it.

Perhaps when we know more about Christianity's murdered half-brother, Gnosticism, we shall recognize that, under all its vanity about Gnosis, the saving knowledge, there was a real technique of the psychological approach to further reality, a method of obtaining that experience of extra-individuality, which is the only true sanction of values.

Research has at least shown that though Gnosis tended, as did Taoism, to degenerate into magic and a superstitious belief in the spell-binding efficacy of the secret word, this was degeneracy. Psychological study of Yoga has also explained very largely why such a degeneracy tends to take place. In such psychophysical exercises for the enlargement of consciousness, among other methods used to aid mental concentration few are found more helpful than sounds. Every psycho-therapeutist down to Dr. Coué, every successful teacher down to the Linguaphone has demonstrated the importance of the sounded word. This, of course, is the psychological basis of the Mantra. The spoken word is intended merely to aid the mind to hold to the task of 'changing aperture'. When this purpose is mistaken then the words themselves become not means but ends, not mantras but spells.

Gnosticism then was in origin a psychological method or a derivation of such from some form of mind-training, or Yoga. In confirmation of this we have the evidence that it was tending to organize itself on a rudimentary caste system: the enlightened, the Psychici — the religious minded who accepted at second-hand the insight of the enlightened — and the ordinary people, the Hylici. And there is also the striking fact that as has been said, 'The fundamental ideas of Gnosticism and early Christianity had a kind of magnetic attraction for each other'. It might be more exact to say that in the psycho-physical practices of early Gnosticism were found the means to the otherwise unattainable ideal behaviour preached by early Christianity. The two teachings were complementary to one another. The last great master of Gnosticism is Marcion of Sinope and in his writings the issue is perfectly plain. He is striving that Christianity shall not relapse into a religion of violence. He sees that the choice the Church must now make is to go on with Christ and the doctrine of love or desert him and it and go back to the wrathful sword-bearing Jehovah of the Old Testament. The Old Testament, he said, must be frankly repudiated. The Church refused. It could not do so, it could not wholly accept the Sermon on the Mount, unless it could find some method, some Gnosis which could take the place of violence and make real idealism possible. This it seems it could not accept.

What is clear is that without some such means of illuminating the mind and making the individual realize he is actually part of the life, which includes him, his neighbour, the stranger fallen by the wayside, the foreigner, yes, and the animal, the Sermon on the Mount remains only an aspiration. It can only be, as the Modernists have pointed out, the Interim Ethic, the morality of the meanwhile, a lofty non-interventionist code, a spiritual 'holding one's breath'. The Modernists think the matter is settled when they point out that this ethic was associated with Apocalypticism, viz. the rule of conduct was linked with the belief that the present physical order was coming to an end.

You were to be passive, non-interventionist, not because such conduct is possible in this world but
because this world is on the point of passing completely
away. This world did not pass away, and, we modernists know, could not pass away, ergo, the pacifist ethic
is impossible. That point of view is, however, pre-
psychological. We can now see that the Apocalyptic
point of view, the belief that man's actions and the
world he experiences have an obscure but intimate
and profound relationship, was an anthropomorphic
rationalized statement of a fact. We can translate its
crudity into the psychological equivalent that man
does make his world far more than the man of action
realizes. Reality is a composition and man can re-
compose it.

It looks then as though early Christianity had
received some of the East's psychological enlightenment. But as happened before when the Nilotic and
the Mesopotamian arcs of the proto-culture received
some of the East's earlier mental insight, they could
only misstate it as an anthropomorphic religion (a
God of Justice who would himself avenge the weak
and wronged), so now the same mistake of 'projection'
was made. The Kingdom of God was within them.
They insisted on looking for it to appear with Apocalyptic display in the sky. For, they thought, if it is
only within, then it is only subjective, it will make no
real difference and we shall never be able to live up to
the pacific ethic. The step that was lacking, to bridge
the gap between the fact that the Kingdom was within
them and yet must and would lead to a pacific conduct
which would bind up the world's wounds and make
the sword rust, was a technique of widening conscious-

ness and giving each man, if he would, awareness of his extra-individuality.

With or without — probably without — that essential knowledge, the real Gnosis — Christianity spread. The world was sick of violence and all too anxious to believe that violence ought not to be effective and could be safely dropped. Whether Jordan had divided, the people were determined to cross into the Promised Land; whether the flood had subsided, they were going to escape out of an ark in which they had suffocated. The wish to believe good news and the intense sense of fellowship which they experienced, in their own small groups, these feelings were strong enough for the time to produce the 'fruits of the spirit', the actions of the free, open psyche, the creative happy life of the being which feels for all, as it may and must in the full sense of its unlimited eternal Life. Without, however, a more deliberate and conscious technique, such a state could not be retained; access to the extra-individuality, the life of all, would be lost. Christians then would lose their nerve and the world would know they had lost it, and their secret. They would, like Peter, realize it was absurd for them to be walking on the sea; they would cry out and sink.

3. IS GNOSIS ENLIGHTENMENT?

This then seems the psychological history behind the early success and later failure of Christianity. Christianity has in it two strains — a salvationist, sacramental strain, which it takes over from the Mystery Religions and which the killing of its Founder permitted it to emphasize. This, when developed, can become that mixture of magical support for political authority and otherworldly comfort for the subject which Marx has called opium. But beside that strain there is the strain of enlightenment, of Gnosis which leads, if it is pursued, to psycho-physical knowledge whereby man can shift the focus of his consciousness, see the reality of his values and the completed whole of experience, when objective and subjective are united.

As the Church continued, the Gnostical element of immediate experience gives way to the sacramental element which promises revelation after death. The two factors are, however, still present when the State decides that somehow the sword must be found a scabbard, it is cutting the roots of life. Some alternative support must be found, for society, resting only on the sword's edge, is being split asunder. The State, however, was too crude to see that if it called in the Church to save it it must not pull the Church down to its level. Till the establishment under Constantine the Church had been openly pacifist. Whether it could implement the Sermon on the Mount, whether it had the secret to make it work, the teaching could not be disowned. The denunciation of violence stood out as clear as the denunciation of unbridled lust or idolatry. If you could get round Christ's pacifism you could sanction brothels and worship Jupiter and Mars along with Jehovah. Right down to Lactantius, the father who lives to see the Peace of the Church, the Edict of Toleration fully established, the Fathers had all denounced war, the use of the sword as impossible for a Christian. Justin Martyr, the fierce Tertullian, the learned Origen, the highly educated Clement of

Alexandria, the intensely orthodox and fiery Cyprian, these men who shaped the Church of the pre-established days, were all quite certain, whatever else they might differ on, that black could not be white and that Christ's words meant and could only mean that the sword must go, or Christianity — they were two mutually exclusive ways of carrying on.

4. THE PEACE OF THE CHURCH: THE VICTORY OF WAR

Constantine, like most realists, thought he knew better, and certainly knew what he intended to get. Christianity should make the sword safe for autocracy. The Church accepted the role. The descent was then swift. The Church itself is soon calling in the sword to crush heresy and paganism. The Church becomes purely a sacramental magical force. The tragic history is all too well known. We, however, can, as no earlier age, realize its inevitability. We can see how as the religion of experience dies away the religion of authority has to take its place. In China that authority could be so formalized and ritualized and words could be made to change their meaning so gradually that religious wars were rare and highly uncharacteristic. In the West, the disputes about words and their meaning, which the need for authority awoke, rapidly became violent. The exasperation that the disputants felt was further inflamed by the desperate feeling that behind these words, buried under their rationalizations, there lay some fact of experience which was vitally important and which, if only it could be grasped and brought clearly into consciousness, all would be well. 'Life and immortality' would come 'to light', the Gospel be real and a new order of love become fact.

The Church then, failed both itself and the State. The State finally disintegrates completely. The huge Roman empire, which even Tertullian had assumed would last to the world's end, was only a ghost, a name. There descends on Italy Atilla, the Hun, who with logical militarism, as the final term of the sword, wipes out all life in his track. Then it is not the legions of the sword of Justice that save the helpless decaying capital of the world but the Pope Leo advancing undefended, in a sudden extremity 'throwing back' to the Sermon on the Mount and proving once again that there is a spiritual power which can save if the sword is let fall.

Before following the further development of religion in Europe, the effort to find sanction for values which will not destroy them, we must at this point glance back over the decline of Western civilization. The sword has again completed its work and destroyed the order it was to preserve. Rome, by the sixth century, has sunk into a more complete dissolution than had Macedon at the very nadir of its empire, when rising Rome defeated, captured and killed in prison the last successor of Philip and Alexander. Rome has sunk even lower than the Persian empire collapsed, for Persia proper rapidly revived under the Parthians and then, with further energy, the original stock, the Sassanidae, reasserted itself. The original realm of Cyrus was re-established. Rome, on the other hand, had returned to the state out of which its first wars against the Etruscans and the Southern Greeks and

Carthage had raised it — a township trying to claim the suzerainty of Italy. The city which had secured itself as residual legatee of the empire, was the Greek polis, Byzantium. The decline of Rome was then slower than that of Persia and far slower than that of the Macedonian empire, but the final dissolution more complete.

5. THE STERILITY OF ROME

The slowness of the decline may be accounted for by the fact that though Rome depended, as frankly as any military power on the sword, and that in the end would pierce and kill it, the very stupidity of the Roman character made this accidental accumulation of powers and resources decompose less fast, than happened in more intelligent societies. The amazing uninventiveness of the Roman power has often been noted. Marius invents the legion a couple of centuries before the Christian era. With this instrument Rome smashes its way to power. Solid drill makes it a projectile no other force could withstand, till the Persians first lanced it with the Parthian mounted bowmen and then broke it under their heavy armed chargers, the cataphracti.

But when Rome was in the saddle it invented nothing else. Even in war, New Rome, Constantinople, is made impregnable by a Syrian's invention. It is Callinicus, who came apparently from Damascus, who

[1] The barbarians never actually met the legions with any success save at the Philipopolis disaster. Varro, when he lost five of Augustus's legions, was bogged by Herman in the Tutobergerwald. The loose fighting barbarians, each out for personal glory and to show off his physical prowess, had no more chance against a drilled mass than had the Highlanders against Butcher Cumberland in 1745.

found out the secret of explosive and flame warfare. The famous Roman Law is an invention of Stoics such as Ulpian[1] (who himself is murdered by his 'certifiable' master) who as we have seen were, like all the Hellenistic moralists, desperately seeking for some system which would sustain society and permit the sword to be withdrawn at least into the background. Roman Law tries to base itself on the Stoic assumptions of the rights of free men and the idea of equal justice. It cannot, however, rid itself of violent means and so its ends inevitably become corrupted. It is the great codifier, Ulpian, who has to defend torture not as a deterrent punishment but as the only method of obtaining justice because the one way of extracting the truth. Here, in a single example, we have vividly illustrated the reason for Stoicism's failure and the collapse of the Law it attempted to frame. When authority treats its essential co-operators, the witnesses, in such a way, we see how little hope there is of social stability. The Law becomes hateful; the State an alien monster. In attempting to make Law work these Stoics assassinated the very spirit of justice which they thought they were making actual. Even the hardly less famous Roman concrete which made possible the vast Roman Baths is also a Hellenic invention.

This Roman uninventiveness has been thought a fatal mistake. If only they had been able to discover a proper arithmetic — such as Archimedes, whom they killed at Syracuse, could have given them — then their accounts would not have fallen into such an inextric-

---

[1] Roman Law owes its completion under Justinian very largely to the Anatolian, John of Cappadocia.

able tangle, the taxation would not have become ruinous to the payers, unremunerative to the authorities, the huge unlimited liability company would not have become bankrupt. If only they had been able to invent some improvements in agriculture then they would not have had to build a costly system of roads, aqueducts, military works, legal establishments, colleges, fora and other vast public building on a substratum of food-growing, which in the north was still the ignorant inefficient Keltic tillage — giving a minute percentage of surplus — and in the south was the even more inefficient system of the *latifundia* — the most cruel and unproductive of all agricultures, slave tillage.

This view, however, is unhistorical and pre-psychological. Inventions in a state which is militarized — in any state frankly depending on the sword, destroy, they cannot conserve society. We have seen it was the intense mechanical inventiveness of the Hellenistic peoples which in the wars of the Diadochi so quickly brought Alexander's empire to ruin and exhaustion. They let the destructiveness of men, which by itself is very limited — we have no natural arms and can build so we find it hard to cast down — be wholly released. Invention in an armed state is like a forced draft to a smouldering fire. In the present state of Europe, with death-loaded wings casting crossing shadows from capital to capital, till we lie in a net of darkness and fear, there is no need to labour that point — as the less inventive nineteenth century might have required. Accumulating evidence from the Past, and our rapidly intensifying apprehension of the Future, establish the fact that invention is the greatest possible peril to the state which cannot find any sanction for order, save order's negation — violence.

Psychology explains quite clearly why that must be so. Invention, the increase of means regardless of ends, is evidence that the partial, unbalanced development of the objective mind is being accelerated. Man is becoming increasingly ignorant of ends, of his integral power, of his complete nature which he shares with his fellows. That side of his mind and apprehension becomes increasingly, proportionately forced into sub-consciousness. Every success, every practical achievement in mastering the outer world and his fellows ('as though' it were nothing but a blind machine and their bodies only and wholly to be shaped to his will by physical violence), every one of these unbalanced advances makes him increasingly incapable of entertaining the notion that this is a misshapen picture of reality and makes him dismiss the ever fainter hints rising from the subconscious, as obviously illusory. Finally invention ends, uninvents itself, for a completely ruined society makes no further discoveries even in the 'outer' world.

Rome's stupidity preserved — did not destroy — its accidental system, as inferior coal smoulders longer than coal without slag. We have seen this lack of inventiveness present in the earliest Mesopotamian empires. Indeed we may say that an empire's power of endurance is in precise ratio to its stupidity. The empire of Alexander explodes because it contains too much inventiveness. Intelligence must combust an unstable society. We shall see this illustrated in the modern world. It culminates in our day. We shall be more lucky than we deserve if we live out our lives without such a demonstration of this rule that our only remaining value will be as an awful example to the few who may survive.

6. EUROPE TO THE BARBARIANS

Rome had then to collapse. Its sword was short and clumsy. It dug down civilization not with machines but mainly by patient persistent hand-work. In the end, however, it had brought everything down to the simple subsistence level, the tribal life which men had followed since wandering hordes picked up from the genius of the proto-civilization such inventions as they could understand and carry in their minds. The Church, however, still remains. The Dark Age broods over it, almost as heavily as over the soil-scratching, superstitious peasant. Barbarian lords are to be frightened by magic. The ecclesiastics are as puzzled as anyone else. They have sacramentalism, a hierarchy, and the Sermon on the Mount. Sacramentalism holds lay-folks together. A hierarchy, claiming apostolic descent of magical powers, can hurl excommunications, interdicts and even more frankly magical curses at superstitious brutal rulers. The Sermon on the Mount remains encysted — hardly known to any lay-folk; a sore problem to any ecclesiastical thinker. Obviously it belongs to a completely different realm of thought. Puzzled, confused morality is apt to lead to highly inconsistent action. The rulers of the Church have to struggle to get hold of the magico-moral power which may defy the barbarians' violence. Where outer power is transferable there will be a scramble when it passes. Hence the gross scandals of the papal court and its elections in the seventh and eighth centuries, culminating in the pornocracy, when harlots could influence and control the choice of Peter's successor, Christ's vicar. These reach such a pitch that finally there intervenes a simple sword holder, Pepin the Frankish King, himself with hardly the first moss of divinity grown over the harsh fact that his house had dethroned the legitimate Merovings. That Europe's chief spiritual power has to be told to attend to its spirituality and eschew violence and all physical passions, by such a man, shows the depth to which it had sunk.

7 . ARABIA'S IRRUPTION

Meanwhile, as Europe lies in this hopeless muddle, springing from the ignorance of the relation of human nature and spiritual power, another explosive experiment to solve the relation of values and reality is made in the Near East. Mohammed is a typical example of the sub-civilized man who living on its frontiers hears what it is discussing and suddenly, with the conviction of the half-educated, is certain he sees the whole solution. Informed as we know by a Nestorian monk he was sure he saw with the suddenness of an inspiration where Christianity and Judaism had gone wrong and his own backward people could go forward. The new revelation that there was, under his people's fetishism, under the racial exclusiveness of the Jew, under the Hellenistic theological subdividing and defining of Christianity, one great uniting principle, Allah, the all-wise, the all-powerful, the all-compassionate, struck him as sufficient to win the world to a new order. Here was the sanction society must have.

To him it was so self-evident that he at first and consistently declared it must be pacific; it was the alternative to force and would make force unnecessary. It was to many of his people, weary of the fetish level of their own religion, psychologically ready to advance to the realization that all mankind must be united by contact with a single principle of justice and mercy, a revelation which was almost as self-evident, and after a few squabbles with the conservatives and a little persecution, many accepted it. It was, however, not only to his Arabian rivals, but to the whole of the civilized world which spread round Arabia, anything but an obvious solution, an authentic revelation. The Prophet then swings round completely. He could not do otherwise. Even had the civilized world of the orthodox Eastern empire and the Zoroastrian Persian empire accepted Islam, sooner or later the new order would have found itself depending on arms. For Allah was a typical projection of that highly individualized person who, we have seen, has specialized in war, the nomad, in this case the Sheikh. The Koran is full, not merely of the distinction between God and man — Allah is nothing but an outer interventionist as separate from the world as from man — there is no thought that man discovers God in himself and that his salvation is in realizing his own nature, which, if he would explore beyond those narrow bounds, he assumes its limit, he would find stretches out, until he is united with all. The Koran inevitably, with this psychologically mistaken assumption, can only show Allah as himself a sword-wielder gaining his ends by unlimited punishment. And as ever the means, not the asserted ends, indicate their employer's true nature. At his first battle, of Bedir, Mohammed sees angels fighting. His final revelation is of that Hell which leaves no depth of insane sadism untouched. Once more then, a religion (breaking out from the stock descended from those two arcs of the proto-culture which had specialized in war and so failed to find any other sanction for society) had been born mortally diseased.

At this point it should be asked can a religion rising so close to India learn nothing from the psycho-physical explorations and inventions made there? Mohammedanism is rigidly anthropomorphic and traditionalist, nevertheless it seems that the Sufi development in Persia and some of the Dervish developments in Asia Minor did undoubtedly come into touch with such knowledge. This must be referred to later for it throws a little more light on the problem of sanction and the sword.[1]

It is possible that beside the groups of adepts such as the Essenes and Hermetics, in the solitary figure of Apollonius of Tyana we have an adept who single-handed tried in vain to illuminate the Romanized near East (see p. 326).

---

[1] See footnote (p. 345).

CHAPTER XVII

THE WEST EXTINGUISHES THE LIGHT

I. THE CATHOLIC COMPROMISE

THE Sword of the Koran and the Sword of the Gospel disputed which should dominate Western civilization. For a short time the scimitar seems about to cut down the cross. Then at Tours Charles Martel the Carloving Catholic beats back the crescent. Its horns, however, press Christendom hard. From the Bosphorus to the Pyrénées a ring of fighting evangelists hem in the Church. Yet Mohammedanism like all false simplifications of man's problem, was bound to find its immense temporary success set off by an equally rapid decline. The Caliphate divides. Soon Islam is making, as did Haroun al Raschid with Charlemagne, alliances with the infidel and before long it will be on the defensive, first in Palestine and then in Spain.

Catholicism had really more resilience in it, for though often depending on the sword (Boniface openly tells Martel he could not have made propagandist progress among the Saxons save for his armed protection) and though setting up societies in which the sword is sanction for order (there was all too early precedent for this in the Petrine text advising obedience to the Roman magistrate 'For he beareth not the sword in vain'), the Church never depended wholly on the sword. Neither in spreading its doctrine nor in preserving civilization did it feel that nothing but violence was needed to produce results. Indeed it was always uneasy about the use of violence at all. A pope of the Dark Ages actually advises the Bulgarians against religious persecution as being not only contrary to the Gospel but also to natural morality. Such insight or aspiration became clouded as the papal power felt itself driven increasingly into politics. Yet all manner of strange shifts are employed to mitigate and disguise violence, shifts which, whether they were disingenuous or no, reveal recognition of an inconsistency in the Church using physical violence when it ought to be able to attain its purposes by spiritual power. Like the statesmen of to-day, the Churchmen then sought for any compromise that might check, if not cure, the passion for violence. This still seethed in the blood of those races which had found the easier life to be that of a feudal aristocracy that lived on its serfs and kept its hold by incessant martial exercise. Truce-days in the week, *Teruga Dei*, were promulgated — like early closing days — to give the harassed workers a little rest. If bishops fought, then they must only wield maces, not the specifically forbidden sword. Here is the spiritual father of proposed pacts to outlaw in war aeroplanes and aerial bombing.

2. THE CRUSADES BREAK THE NEAR-EAST BRIDGE

Finally there came the brilliant idea of the moral equivalent to civil war, the Crusades. The turbulent could be shipped off to clear the infidel from the

344

country of the Prince of Peace. This series of adventures, notorious in their brutality and chicanery succeeded only in one thing. It prevented the development of thought and culture which was springing up again in the Levant with Damascus as a centre. We have specimens of the incomparable glass work, the Cairene lamps, the stained glass windows in the Dome of the Rock at Jerusalem, the fine mosaics there, and the even finer in the converted church of St. John at Damascus. We know of the chemical knowledge which led to the discovery of several sorts of incendiary and explosive Greek fire. It is impossible not to suspect that such culture was backed by an equal degree of speculation and that the East was again being sought to give profounder ideas to the West. Now that we are able to link Gnosticism and Manichaeanism as phases of one development of psychological thought being worked out in 'the Fertile Crescent', in the country from the Levant to the Persian Gulf, that suspicion becomes certainty. We may also suppose that it is here that there rise the roots of thought which will feed Sufiism when in turn Persia attempts to give Islam some other sanction than the sword, as the Levant with Gnosticism had striven earlier to do a similar service to Christianity.[1] This rising bridge, the deluge of the Crusades swept away. Damascus becomes famed only for making swords. Its deadlier discovery, flame fighting, is in Saladdin's hands and the inventive skill of the Levantine, which had fourteen centuries before, permitted the Diadochi to exhaust all the Near East, now again, on the same site, allows the Saracen to keep up equally devastating

[1] See p. 329.

wars against the tides of Crusaders.[1] Neither side can assure its victory, and, when at last the European assault begins to slacken, the Saracen is exhausted, the Levant sterile and the Near East ready for the inevitable deluge of the pure militarist, the specialized destroyer, in this case the Seljuk Turk.

3. THE EAST AGAIN OFFERS ENLIGHTENMENT

Meanwhile the Church at home had not been able to correct its inevitable lapse toward complete and open dependence on violence. A rapid descent is marked by the founding of the Inquisition. The Inquisition is the Church's desperate answer to Catharism. Why the Church was so terrified of the Catharist religion has often puzzled scholars. We can, however, both judge the strength and estimate the sources of this movement better than could an earlier age. It may be that the Church resorted to unlimited violence because here was a force which had actually achieved what catholicism had felt after but missed, a force then that was both accuser and superseder.

The outline of the historical evidence is as follows: Catharism was always known to have appeared with full organization in Bulgaria whence it spread rapidly until Provence became its stronghold. Now we can trace it still further into the East. It is probably present in Armenia before it reaches Bulgaria and thence it may be suspected, passing always by hill country, into the Caucasus and Persia. The question then

[1] The one attack before which the Crusaders blenched was that of batteries of flame casters with which the Mohammedan forces were equipped by Levantine engineers.

arises, is it to be linked up with that Manichaeanism, whose founder the Sassanian King Bahram had executed in 276 at the wish of the Magi, but whose faith outlived Zoroastrianism and spread, through the very Mohammedan conquests which stamped out Magism and of course would, if they could, have exterminated this other religion also? The answer grows increasingly certain. Mani taught gnosis, enlightenment: he organized his followers into two castes, leaders called the illuminated, picked (*electi*), complete (*perfecti*), and followers called the hearers. The fully qualified had to keep completely free of the world but the hearers also had to accept the full pacific ethic. Killing was absolutely forbidden all Manichaeans.

Two things then appear from this: Manichaeanism is not only the predecessor of the Catharist faith. It is the descendant of Gnosticism. It teaches the pacific ethic. It will not make the fatal compromise with the sword. It maintains that it can attain this ethic, make all values real, by some mysterious inner knowledge and technique which it possesses. The exoteric teaching, which is outwardly a mass of cosmological speculation about the origin of Light and Darkness, of Aeons and Qualities, has always struck the student as almost incomprehensible. But even to the most pedantic and literalist of scholars this fantastic cosmological theology presents one amazing mystery. Manichaeanism maintained the pacific ethic. It was everywhere persecuted. If you were even only a hearer there was no country you could fly to where your faith would not be a capital charge. Yet it spread; spread in one direction, at length, along the very channels Mohammedanism cut with the sword, spread; earlier, in another right into the heart of the Roman empire. Gnosticism we have found also on the same site, the frontier of East and West, teaching a secret knowledge, a way of being illuminated. Next we see Mani teaching in the same place the same thing. We know his ethic — it is the pacific ethic. We know the words of his theory. They seem hopelessly uninspiring and unlikely so to illuminate the ordinary man that he will drop the sword and live up to the Sermon on the Mount. Yet this religion, which it is death to confess, spreads through the countries which persecute it. It sinks down at last. The Vandals seem to have exterminated it, with nearly everything else, in North Africa. Latest research, however, shows it is still to be traced up to the thirteenth century hanging on in north-west Asia. By then, what we now have to recognize is the third wave of the one movement, Catharism, is already passing out to its renewed campaign which will carry it to one of the most ghastly mass martyrdoms ever inflicted by one religion on another, the Albigensian Crusade.

The question then can no longer be burked. What was the force that kept this religion going and, more, kept it maintaining, faced with constant unlimited violence, that violence was not the path of life and could never lead to it? That leads to another question. This fantastic cosmology which was given out as the basis of this lofty ethic, can this be the real teaching? There is no doubt this was the official language it used. Can anyone imagine that any human being is going to attempt to live the Sermon on the Mount on such a sanction, especially when for him to avow that, as his sanction, is for him to be executed?

It is no use saying as scholars, completely ignorant of psychology, have said, when trying to explain away this vast historical mystery, that Manichaeanism and Catharism gave people an elaborate cosmology which 'explained' the world and an assurance that if they lived nobly in this life they would enjoy felicity hereafter. In every country which made the faith of enlightenment a capital charge there was offered, enforced, a religion which also 'explained' the world quite as well, indeed much the same way (for evil and good remain the two facts all religions have to explain and if possible reconcile), and these religions also promised and, generally on far less exacting terms of actual practice (quite apart from treating you as an honoured citizen instead of as a plague spot), assurance of eternal happiness. No: something other than the superior charms of one theory out of many speculations, the superior assurance of one promise out of many offers of salvation, is needed to solve this great riddle.

Indeed it seems clear that no unbiased mind could doubt that in the fantastic cosmology is disguised a psychology. Under fictitious creation and eschatological myths is concealed a psycho-physical method of obtaining just that power, just that vision of unity which will make the pacific ethic natural and possible. Nor is this conclusion arrived at merely by the failure of any other explanation to account for the movement. We have historical evidence how in India and in China these discoveries in psycho-physical advance, these methods of enlarging individual consciousness and becoming aware of the general consciousness, were guarded. Why — considering their vital importance to the community, to civilization and to Life —

we must discuss later. That they were, is an almost invariable rule. More, when these exercises begin to percolate into the western or anthropomorphic religions we find the same heavy disguise. Cosmological symbolism is here forbidden. Islam, Christianity, and Judaism have reserved cosmology for themselves. It is heresy to theorize about the order of nature. Hence the Persian Sufis when describing states of consciousness use the terminology of wine and intoxication — an example which has become notorious, notoriously misunderstood is the *Rubiyat*. The Hebrew Kabbalists — the word means the oralists, the mouth to mouth, even the whispered, doctrine — when they wrote down their discoveries and instructions late in the thirteenth century[1] disguised the terms from all but the informed by pretending these were treatises on alchemy and magic. The Christian Rosicrucians also pretended they were dealing with astrology and alchemy.[2]

It seems therefore clear that in Catharism there was an invasion of the West by the psycho-physical knowledge of the East. Here was an opportunity for the West, pierced by the sword which it dared not throw away, because it could see no other support for law and order, no other sanction for values, at last to get free of this deadly dependence. Such choices are,

[1] The Cabala was, at least partly, put into writing in 1290 and called Zohar the Book of Splendour or Illumination. It is important to note that the first teacher known is Isaac the blind who lived in Provence somewhere about 1190. We cannot doubt this psycho-physical teaching was known to the Catharists for unorthodox Christians have ever since studied the Zohar and certainly of late its association with Yoga has been recognized.

[2] The same thing is found in Taoism. The Tao Tê Ching holds according to Waley that the art of Tao is in its essence not merely unmentionable but essentially occult. The information is not merely secret. If the uninitiated — those who have not done the practices – get hold of the words they seem nonsense. Even the esoteric passages are not intended to convey information. See *The Way and its Power*, p. 99.

however, highly critical. If you fail to accept, you must then fall rapidly further. You must attempt to destroy what wishes to save you. Persecution is so ghastly because not only is the persecutor degraded but the persecuted also. Only perfect saints are undamaged by martyrdom; most martyrs only gain their saintly title because of their sufferings.

Catharism had had a success denied the two earlier advances of the psycho-physical gnosis or enlightenment. It had established itself as the philosophy of the first modern European culture. Provence had become the home of a small civilization where, though surrounded by the savage, the fanatic and the superstitious, there flowered a way of life in which poetry and lyric love were conceived as the natural expression and most perfect exercise of human intelligence and feeling. How far the heroic consistency of the pacifist ethic was modified and softened in these lovely surroundings we do not know but can suspect. Once more men naturally relapsed into the belief that all that was needed to keep life as beautiful as they found it, was to be gentle, sensible, friendly, happy, gay. They considered the lilies of the field and arrayed themselves like Solomon: the birds of the air and imitated their song, plumage and innocence. They forgot that the grass, so prettily clothed to-day, to-morrow is cut down and cast into the oven. The nightingale and the goldfinch always are shadowed by the hawk.

The *perfecti* should not only have kept open the way to a secure world, showing how all who would might gain the full illumination, which, if unattained, however gay and gifted the society, it must relapse on to violence — these teachers should have checked any use of violence, however slight, and have insisted that only a community quite clean of that infection, wholly dependent on another sanction, wholly aware of a reconciliative vision, could hope to preserve its peace and its values. We cannot doubt they failed to do this, for we know the Catharist religion began to concentrate on death. Its supreme rite, the mysterious *consolamentum* which made a Hearer a *Perfectus*, was now given the ordinary individual as a final rite. A 'Hearer' might live gaily careless and then, when life was over, be given a sudden reconciliation with the underlying reality.

We may never know exactly the nature of the *consolamentum*. That it had some curious efficiency we may judge from the fact that people who, during the persecution, passed as Catholics were found when *in extremis* to have sent for *perfecti* to give them this deliverance and at-one-ment. We can also, with our knowledge that Catharism is really a European extension of Yogic psycho-physical knowledge, construct from our new information about that technique an estimate of what the *consolamentum* may well have been. The *Bardo Thodol*, the Tibetan Book of the Dead or of the Transition state, referred to earlier, seems in its present form a manual constructed for a society in much the same unstable condition, as was Provençal civilization in the twelfth and thirteenth centuries. In this snowbound theocracy we have society in two immense classes: of *perfecti* — the monks or lamas — and of Hearers — all the lay-folk. The *Bardo Thodol* is then a set of instructions which shows how those who through life have neglected, or only partially developed their method of access to the

larger consciousness, may, at their last hour and gasp
be helped to accelerate this expansion of consciousness
and so not only be freed of death's terror but avoid the
confusing and even terrifying illusions which (so says
the self-consistent Yogic theory) must attack consciousness if it leaves the body still convinced that it is
wholly limited and referable to an individual 'persona'
which has lived solely by the 'self-regarding emotions'.

This 'compromise with the world' is not confined to
Tibet. The age-long controversy between Raj Yogi
and Hathi Yogi in India itself is at bottom a dispute
between those who say, lifelong practice and gradual
expansion by mind affecting body and body reacting
with mind is the only Royal (Raj) road to Illumination and to the world's salvation from the ruin of
violence: and those — the Hathi Yogins — who say a
sudden physical convulsion or series of convulsions can
tear open the veil, burst up the threshold and convert
a man in a moment into 'an enlightened one'.

In China the same controversy is found present
under the names of half a dozen religions. There the
real and only vital distinction in empirical[1] religion —
whether that religion called itself Confucianism,
Taoism or even Nestorian Christianity or Mohammedanism — was between these two methods — the
gradual method and the convulsive, between 'growing
in grace' and being catastrophically 'converted'.
Indeed, this, it would seem, is the profounder distinction that underlies that surface definition under which
Nietzsche classified all religions, the Apollonian,
which stands — or at least can stand — for a lifelong

[1] By empirical religion is meant the religion of psychological experience,
distinct from, though generally using the forms of, the official exoteric
religion.

practice and growth, and the Dionysian, which stands for violent, instantaneous eruption.

We find that even in societies which have been acquainted with psychical knowledge, coextensive with and complementary to physical knowledge, societies which have known of the technique of changing the aperture of consciousness so as to obtain that realization of the unity of Life in which a society may find its sanction and dispense with the sword, even in such, the Way may not be kept open, the social order may gradually relapse, take to authority instead of direct experience and finally find itself without vision.

Some such decay must have infected Catharism after its success. Some such decay would also give Catholicism reason for misunderstanding it. These psycho-physical exercises, their techniques of crossing the frontier between individual and general consciousness, are, as we have seen, always dangerous, and therefore adepts have grudged telling those unprepared, untrained, of the way across the pass. Unless you can breathe the high air you will collapse and fall. This vital point, which arose before (see page 239) (why becoming aware of the complete and full life is dangerous to those who have lived so concentrated on the partial material life, that they have thought it the whole of Reality), will be discussed at the conclusion of this essay. All that need then be said here is that to attempt such a technique without sufficient training often leads to extreme sensualism and to insanity, and a less excessive but equally damaging failure is collapse into fraud and hieratic arrogance. It is not then to palliate persecution to note that

Catharism in decadence may have deserved some of the censure — though none of the abominable cruelties — that Catholicism launched against it.

There are however two more pieces of evidence which may throw light on the Catharist collapse. All history and especially our own critical time may learn from a negative and positive factor which is evident in the Provençal civilization. The negative factor is the same which is present in Tibet. In both societies, instead of a caste system there are only two completely contrasted classes, *perfecti* and Hearers. So, instead of a self-irrigatory social system whereby the loftiest insight may be continually transmitted, delegated and applied, there is one class too far removed from life and the other too little enlightened and inspired. In consequence there arises that division which is fatal to an evolving society — a monasticism in which all the higher types become involved, wherein dead to the world they tend increasingly to concentrate wholly on death, and a laity who in consequence can only think of the religious life and mind-training as being exclusively concerned with death and therefore only of concern to the fully living when they must face dying.

The positive factor is the intense development among the laity of Lyric Love and erotic passion which in Provence in those centuries of the Catharist ascendancy, reached the highest pitch known in the West. This attained such ecstatic intensity that, as W. B. Yeats has suggested[1] the mistress (who of course was completely separate from the wife and mother) seems to have become the vehicle or medium for

[1] *Criterion*, July 1935, p. 555.

that type of mystical experience which attempts to use and sublimate physical passion in order thereby to attain mystical experience of union with all being and loss of the self. This of course is the Tantric method and is often associated with Hathi Yoga exercises. It is certainly extremely dangerous for two reasons. In the first place it too often makes the experimenter lose all social responsibility. The exquisite experience — 'the flight of the alone to the alone' — becomes an end in itself. The lover, even when a lover of the divine, may become completely centred on his passion. In the second place, not so often but far too frequently, the passion, having attained a too private, lyric intensity and having adored its object and the object's symbol (the mistress) as above all thought of physical union, seems to leave the physical organism uncontrolled. Hence startling relapses into sensualism, pure physicalism. Here again it looks as though there were some interference with the circulatory growth. As the individual has ceased to yield the community his contribution of devotion, so also he has made a fissure between his spirit and body. So individual and community and spirit and body, neither of these two aspects of being is reciprocating.

This, we know, was the charge brought against Gnosticism, Manichaeanism and Catharism — that each tended in the end to treat the body as so insignificant as to be a matter of compete indifference — when they became uncontrolled sensualists. There was undoubtedly some truth in the charge. It looks, then, as though the Catharists failed to make their psychological discoveries and knowledge work out in a real social invention. They could not keep the two sides of experience together in one reciprocating organism. So the *perfecti* became a Life Fearing, Death Desiring order — proclaiming, sometimes, that all continuation of the human race was evil. And the Hearers became lyricists who attaining love-ecstasy failed to bring their devotion into the service of the community and they themselves, when this ecstasy gave out, as give out it must, relapsed often into pure physical satisfaction — which gives out even quicker.

Here again then we have illustrated the important psycho-social principle: that the Apollonian religion, or rather the Raj-Yoga mental training is the way on which society must advance, but that advance — that spreading stream of living water — must be carried on the five-arched aqueduct of a caste system. Otherwise the vision of the seer never enlightens the ordinary man. If this social aqueduct of delegation does not exist then the individual is tempted and often driven to the Dionysian religion, or the Hathi Yoga mental training. In a single life, by every means, psychological, physiological and environmental, he attempts to desert mankind and make certain his private deliverance. This he may strive to do either by asceticism or by lyricism. He may go into a monastery and then flee from that to make even faster advance in the eremite's cell. The convent is only a step to the solitary anchorite's life. Or he may by lyric passion, as private and as self-centred, attempt to find the same solitary escape. Whether he succeeds, because

Down to Gehenna or up to the Throne
He travels the fastest who travels alone.

357

Or whether, as most authorities maintain, he must fail, that problem is not our immediate concern here. It is not for us to judge these explorers but only to study their influence on society. All that we can say on that point is that the solitary does desert society. So he fails to bring his knowledge to its help in building up its organism with that psychological discovery necessary to balance its economic and physical discoveries, necessary to permit the human state to exist without constant violence. So deserted society must collapse.

4. THE REPLY OF THE INDIVIDUALIST WEST

The actual crusade is one of the horrors of history. The fanatical Domenic, finding he can make no impression by preaching, openly declares he will use violence. The rapacious Simon de Montfort is given, as a hawk is loosed at a heron, the papal blessing to devastate this pleasant countryside. The pathetic transitional people caught between dependence on the sword and on enlightenment became that dangerous animal which defends itself when attacked. Brilliant towns were exterminated as though the Hun was again in Europe. It was an insane action on the Church's part. Yet this appalling atrocity, equal to the Armenian massacres of Abdul the Damned, did not suffice. The religion was real. De Montfort's own chaplain was found to be a Catharist. As all terrorists discover, martial law is not enough. The informer, the spy, the secret tribunal, torture, refusal to confront the accused with his accusers, all these outrages, not merely against common pity but against common justice, were mobilized.

The effect was inevitable. A nightmare suspicion spread among the people. What had been the gayest countryside became the most haunted. Every man suspected his neighbour, as well he might. Heresy became a horror and the houses of those denounced and murdered were pulled down and left in ruins as sites possessed.[1] The corruption spread naturally to judges as well as to the judged. The victims became paranoiic: the executioners pitiless. Time and again the pope had to intervene to remove inquisitors who were getting rid of people in order to seize their property. We know from the history of oppression how for one injustice which reaches the ear and touches the heart of authority a hundred go unheeded. Such things are ghastly but inevitable. Violence once loosed will, if it can, rid itself of all restraints and, once rid, all pretence of preserving justice or faith disappears. As Buddha the Enlightened said — it is an eternal commonplace — Evil must breed true: it cannot produce good. Violence, for whatever end employed, sooner or later must attain its own end. Criminal means result in criminal ends.

The Provençal civilization was shattered. Next the Catharist faith was driven into the forests and hills. Its last glimmer seems to have been among the Waldensian communities in the Alpine valleys of Dauphiny. There, practising the only true communism (the community of goods which arises naturally from a community of ideals, an economic unity

[1] These became so extensive that finally petitions were made that owing to the need of more cultivatable land some of these abandoned areas might be reclaimed.

because a psychological unity has been established), these gentle people clung on until persecution sought them out there also and the bones of 'the slaughtered saints' lay 'scattered in the Alpine wild'.[1]

---

[1] It is essential to understand how inevitable, how natural was the action of all authorities depending on violence, when faced with this alternative way of social life, with this foundation of a self-sanctioning civilization. All rulers hated it because they saw its success was the end of their authority but they honestly felt – in their ignorance of their own nature they could not help feeling – that its success would mean not only the elimination of themselves but of all order, and society's collapse directly into anarchy.

CHAPTER XVIII

THE EVAPORATION OF VALUES

1. DARKNESS FROM THE EAST

WHILE, then, Illumination had failed in Europe and the Church had, in stamping it out, aided the collapse of Western civilization, again on the outer fringes, the consistent specialized violence of the nomad was preparing to call civilization to ordeal by battle, to see whether the culture that would not face the fact that violence was the absolute reality and yet would find no other way, could stand up against an organization which frankly confessed this fact.

When tracing the Mesopotamian arc of civilization to its extinction we saw that the final annihilating blow was dealt by a completely specialized sword power from the steppes, the Tatars. We must now trace that storm to its source. Ghenghis, who starts life as a small chieftain in the Karakorum, dies having launched a war machine of unprecedented destructiveness. It smashes its way into the heart of China, into Mesopotamia, which, as we have seen, perished completely, and into Europe as far as Hungary. Had Ghenghis himself lived he might have razed the Vatican and cut down into a common squalor of savagery, Mohammedan and Catholic. As it was his armies saw the Baltic and the Adriatic.

Such explosions of destructive energy are, however, so pure that they cannot last; so consistent, that compromising human nature finds them almost as difficult to pursue as the way of enlightenment. Ghenghis was a monomaniac genius. All his diplomatic cunning, all his great and original intelligence went in organizing and discharging violence. He employed Greek engineers, the most advanced technicians civilization had produced, to make civilization's destruction complete. The Venetians sold themselves as the spies of his generals in Europe. A Chinaman became his supreme Minister of Munitions. It is necessary to repeat, for though historians for the last fifty years have recognized the fact, it is one we have reasons for burking: the forces he employed were not overwhelming. Victory was due to three things: consistency: these specialists cared only and purely for destruction, they knew war was a pure state, an absolute activity: strategical and tactical genius, which best possesses people whose intelligence is restricted wholly to activity and whose reflective capacity is atrophied: balked inventiveness[1] which sees every device and instrument as a tool to make war more efficient.

When at the height of his power this inevitable development of the partial intelligence, the truly unbalanced mind was asked why he so behaved — destroying and not accumulating? (He sacked and burnt almost all cities and his favourite activity after that was to make as big a pyramid as possible of freshly severed human heads, and when his empire became immense, embracing half the known world,

---

[1] It has been said above, war ends inventiveness. It certainly does so in the free mind of the layman, who then driven by natural selection can only think of flight or 'freeze' like a fright-paralysed rabbit. The soldier also is generally uninventive, even Napoleon, as Bainville points out, only exploiting others' inventions. On rare occasions native untapped energy such as the Tatars can be monomaniacly inventive.

still he only organized in order to make cavalry depots from which to raid and wreck further). His pure, unchecked, degenerative activity could of course find no answer and he had to say, as Atilla before him and Timur after him, that he was sent by God to punish the human race. Though his empire, being even more consistently martial than Alexander's, was even less enduring (as it was vaster), a century after the same explosion takes place under 'the little lame man' Timur. The violence and track of this human typhoon is so closely similar to its predecessor's that we can recognize the same source of unbalanced energy. Mesopotamia being, however, destroyed and a new force lying across the Near East the actual conflicts vary. Timur finds the Ottoman Turks under the Sultan Bayazit, having become Moslems, having swept over the Seljuk Turks, about to overwhelm Constantinople. So a more savage, more specialized destroyer saves the Eastern Empire from a less extreme but more pressing danger. Timur puts Bayazit in a cage instead of killing him outright. Probably he had seen the great rock-carved picture of the Sassanian Shapur mounted on his horse with the captive Roman Emperor Valerian crouched before him. Tradition said the Persian used his rival as his mounting block and after death had his victim stuffed as a footstool. Certainly these gloatings show a reflective state, if not a high one. The human tornado is no longer wholly content with activity. He is looking back on his great moments. So hard, evidently, is it even for a monomaniac to be wholly true to his one-sided obsession. The native hue of resolution is sicklied o'er with the first penumbra of the pale cast of thought.

Even if these conquerors had not died on the brink of world victory, another change might have caused cessation of such frantic degenerative activity. The conqueror himself may wake up out of his orgiastic nightmare. Timur was brought up a Muslim and his conquests were far more restricted than Ghenghis's. Even if the conqueror himself does not tire his abetters, 'the ingenious engineers', the spies and diplomatic agents who have put the inventions of civilization at his disposal for pay, may feel that, having opened the world oyster and split its shell, he is really going too far by stamping on the oyster itself. Often the master of the Terror such as Robespierre is himself killed by those assistants who feel his pure incorruptible monomania will soon destroy them also.

2. THE FOSSILIZATION OF CHINA

These blasts from the desert therefore die down. They were, however, a warning, a warning civilization would not take. Civilization East and West was now united. A common military peril, through new inventions, could reach and strike down both. Civilization in the East was becoming static. After the great Sung culture which Ghenghis wounded, China became increasingly conservative, new ideas were no longer acceptable, foreigners were 'devils'. This degeneration and 'loss of nerve' was natural enough. China was more and more concerned with military defence. Her devastations made her think only in terms of arms. But deeper and behind this decay was the slow descent which the choice of Confucianism, of the religion of authority and precedent instead of the religion of experience and exploration, made inevitable. What had seemed an alternative, Taoism, that too had lost its insight, its realization that psychological exploration was the path and the widening of consciousness the only way to get the sword out of the side of society and give man a true sanction for his values. Taoism itself had become individualized. It accepted the objective mind's picture of reality as complete. It ceased to explore the mind and sought unceasingly only to coerce this 'outer nature', to work magic that would turn common stuff into gold and give the individual — grotesque misapprehension of his nature — an undying body. Chinese judicial punishments become increasingly elaborate and ghastly. Violence is present everywhere in the State; therefore violence alone can direct the State's relationship with other States.

3. THE ANARCHIZING OF CHRISTENDOM

The same symptoms are present in Europe. The states inflict severer and severer punishments as their rules are not kept. The Church calls for the Inquisition to be extended. In 1404 when the English Lancastrian usurper Henry IV has too poor a claim and too small forces to be sure of his throne without spiritual aid, the Church exacts as price the *de heretico comburendo*. The Church is attempting to assert a European authority and to have a united civilization at its disposal. In the eleventh century Hildebrand had used a mixture of diplomacy and excommunication, balance of forces and spells to hold the Imperial power which depended solely on the sword. He won. Next Innocent III in the thirteenth century pushes even further this control. The Emperor's sword power is to be the Church's instrument. He also initiates, as we have seen, the Inquisition. Finally Boniface VIII — consistent if extravagant — holds both swords in his hands and cries 'I am Pope, I am Emperor'. In fact, however, he was nothing of the sort. But his failure to become emperor — a real theocrat — undoubtedly caused his failure even to die peacefully as pope. He had shown that the papacy could not stay where it was: either it must eschew violence and find some really spiritual way to men's wills or it must take all violence directly into its own hands. It could not wince away from the consequences of its dependence on violence, hand over the offender 'to the secular arm' as the final instrument and not expect that secular arm ultimately to act on its own.

This was the state of moral confusion, spiritual anarchy, which gave rise to the Reformation. Men rushed to the Bible to see what authority Authority really had for its endless appeals to violence, its persecutions, its exactions, its squalid struggle for power, for political dominion, for wealth. Why should not religion be simple and government simple? Was not one's own salvation to be obtained by direct access to God and one's own government by whole and single allegiance to one's local king? Why all this complication and confusion — of salvation only through the Roman hierarchy, and law and order only through a balance between the national ruler who had the power and a distant potentate who exercised authority through threats? What had a power which reigned with territorial commitments in Central Italy to do with the soul's salvation and how could psychological and moral questions depend on political conveniences?

Clearly there was an immense confusion and things had come to a deadlock. Unfortunately Reformers as much as Conservatives, completely underrated the difficulty of clearing it up. They misapprehended the nature of the problem. If it was to be straightened out, they must go deep. The fault was not in events or institutions but in men's selves, in their misunderstanding of their own nature, a misunderstanding which Catholic and Protestant shared equally. The mistake was not that the Church had misrepresented, suppressed or been disloyal to her foundation documents, the Scriptures. She had naturally not been anxious to discuss these openly with the Laity. They did present grave difficulties, as the Reformers were to find. Nor was it even that these documents conflicted, and that the Old Testament morality could not be reconciled with the Sermon on the Mount. The Church had never denied that the source of all her teaching was Jesus of Nazareth and that the essence of his doctrine lay in the Sermon on the Mount.

The real problem, which was bringing the Church to an impasse, and to the solution of which the Reformers were contributing and did contribute nothing, was how, if you abstained from violence, the Sermon on the Mount, or even the *lex talionis* and the ten commandments were to be made actual. If the Sermon on the Mount was simply a set of instructions, without means to carry them out, then the quandary was hopeless. At the very first step in your attempt to fulfil the teaching, you had to violate it and so you must continue, until, instead of the Kingdom of God coming on earth, you had, through even more violence, created a kingdom of the devil.

4. THE REFORMATION ENDS COMPROMISE

The Reformation itself was, we now see, not an effort to solve the profound problem that faced Western civilization, it was not even a symptom that problem was approaching solution. On the contrary it was a symptom that the crisis was about to become acute. That one-sided development of the human mind, which we have seen creates the purely physico-economic world, was now accelerating its growth. The compromise which Catholicism had tried to impose, by maintaining that there was an external Deity who could, if properly approached, change the order of the mechanism of nature — that compromise was collapsing, and, like a river bursting through an ice jam, men's minds were rushing headlong to the logical conclusion. The premise, that there was outside them this mechanic world going by inevitable laws, was not challenged by either side as reality. The only point at issue was whether there was beside the vast machine a machine-maker and minder to whom one might and could appeal to intervene. The compromise of Catholicism rested on this basis. It was true you had to use violence every now and then, regrettably often in point of fact. Jehovah on many occasions, it had to be owned, was as unwilling to plead for himself and avenge his own quarrel as Baal had been. In default, man had to intervene to uphold the divine honour.

Still, there were the words, 'Vengeance is Mine', saith the Lord, 'I will repay'. God was patient, man had often to give provisional sanction, hold back injustice by inflicting injustice, but in the end God himself would assert himself. That hope of the ultimate intervention, the Great Assize, Protestants no more questioned than Catholics. Both sides then accepted the machine of outer nature and the machine-maker and minder, external both from the machine and from themselves.

What Protestantism knew that it was doing — though it did not fully realize the implication — was that, negatively, it was beginning to doubt whether miracles — divine interventions — ever took place, and positively, it was beginning deliberately to make inventions, to research. There was, as Catholicism felt, a real connection between these two attitudes of mind. They were complementary and supplementary aspects of a new stage in the individualizing of consciousness, in the hardening of the threshold between the objective mind and the subjective mind, so that man mistook the cut-off, individualized part of his consciousness as the only consciousness and the picture it gave of the world as the whole of reality. The Church had delayed, though not resolved, this narrowing of consciousness, by maintaining miracles continued to the present day, God revealed himself when there was any real need: hence (which on this premise is true) research was unnecessary, impertinent, asking questions which would have been answered if there were real need; asking questions which were either intended to embarrass authority or arose from 'idle curiosity', a dangerous state of mind. This Catholic defence we see

could not last, for it was misstating, in anthropomorphic cosmological terms, what was really a psychological problem and which could only be satisfactorily
established on psychological premises.

Catholic conservative intuition was however correct.
The disfavour with which Roger Bacon was viewed,
the repression and punishment which Galileo drew
upon himself, had this perfectly sound reason. Research and invention showed a frame of mind which
already doubted miracles and was getting ready to
equip itself with such powers that miracles, divine
intervention would be otiose. Protestantism would
inevitably become a non-miraculous Deism, next a
natural Theology in which the god was increasingly
merged in the machine and finally the mechanism
which, as La Place, the astronomer, said to Napoleon,
had no need of the Deistic hypothesis. God might be
there but he never appeared outside the machinery.
All you had to deal with was mechanism.

5. THE SMOTHERING OF THE SUBCONSCIOUS

It is not then coincidence that the first great Protestant century, the seventeenth, is also the Century
of Invention as Dr. Whitehead has called it. Increased,
almost exclusive, concentration on the data given by
the objective mind, led to rapidly increasing power
over nature, a nature conceived, with every victory, as
increasingly, completely outside the observer. Reci-
procally, each victory confirmed the objective mind
in its mistake that it saw things at last as they really
were, that it could use them as it would and could

turn them to such effect that it need, neither for its own protection nor out of reverence, consider any power beyond itself. Nature, its inventions would let it hold at bay. Divinity, its theories showed, was a shadow to which it need pay no tribute.

Catholicism attempted to oppose this advance and for a short time the Counter Reformation won back much. For men were almost as much dismayed as elated at the new advance. It is significant that no eminent scientist in the seventeenth century is an atheist while Descartes who composes the philosophy which will end in materialism remains a Catholic. All thinkers realized that too swift progress, progress that could not be controlled, would upset the social order. Luther completely lost his nerve and humanity when he saw the peasants throwing off their oppressors and besought the princes to 'Kill, Kill'. Below the concern for the social order, was the profounder misgiving for the meaning of life and all values. What if men had to pay, for this new freedom and these new powers, by all design vanishing out of life, all morality, all purpose, save the physical satisfaction of those who had the strongest physique and physical equipment?

The Counter Reformation had then a weakened Protestantism to attack: an enemy which did not feel free to take up his strongest position.

Post-Trentine Catholicism, however, was equally limited by weakness of position. The Church was rationalized. In it, too, the unbalanced development of the objective mind had gone on, as it had to go on, in any religion which adopts anthropomorphism as its expression, and cosmology (instead of psychology) as its demonstration. St. John of the Cross, was a true mystic, comprehending that exploration from within, *introrsum aścendere*, is the real religious method, the way to solve both the problem of social sanctions and the problem of a world which seems, to the partial, objective mind, blind, mechanical, dead.[1] He was naturally put in prison by the Church and died, worn out by his hardships, finally confined strictly in a monastery. His real offence was that he taught that the popular method of devotion which Ignatius made the basis of his *Exercises*, of raising in the mind visual images, was not the way to gain illumination and recover union: on the contrary such a method would only increase and inflame individuality.

Yet, as we have seen, it was just this method which the Jesuits, because they themselves were so infected with individualism, so completely shut up in the objective mind, had to adopt. They were fighting individualism by a method which aggravated it. To use violence to advocate religion is to wound religion more deeply than its supposed enemy. To use an individualism, which made crudely concrete God, Heaven and Hell, was to fight the new individualism on its own ground where it was bound to win. The mechanistic cosmology, a partial construction of the partial objective consciousness, was accepted as fully real, a complete account of facts and theologically satisfactory, if to it you added a series of fully condensed anthropomorphs, the saints, the Queen of Heaven, her Son, his Father and the Dove.

[1] In his aphorisms he says, 'Without Labour shall you subject the peoples, and things shall be subject to you, if you forget both them and yoursèlf', i.e. if you can transcend your individualism which separates you from the common Life of all. He was not preaching magic but the power of subconscious influence. Cf. p. 3c4.

Mysticism, the wish to explore and expand consciousness, is everywhere under increasing suspicion.
Through the Middle Ages such explorations had
been pursued with almost scientific care, a real 'field-
naturalist study', and without ecclesiastical censure
in North-west Europe. Acton has pointed out how in
Ireland in the sixth and seventh centuries such exercises and enterprises were common and the thought of
Erigena, who went in the ninth century from Ireland
to the Carloving Court, is heretical, because it is based
on those extra-individual, anti-anthropomorphic experiences. This method or enterprise passes from
Ireland to North England and we have preserved, as
some of our earliest English, the description left by
Richard Rolle the mystic of Hampole in Yorkshire.
Later there are the reflections of Juliana the Anchoress
of Norwich, and indeed so common and approved
were these methods that in the *Ancren Riwle* we have
instructions for those who intend to adopt the recluse's
life. The Abbé Brémond believes that from this
British mysticism sprang the French, carried by one
refugee priest who, having studied the English four-
teenth-century work, introduced the method in
France. We know that Fénelon, in spite of his emin-
ence, was censured and Madame Guyon more severely
treated for their interest in this. In Rome Molinos is
tried by the Inquisition and condemned to lifelong
solitary confinement and so dies. The Jesuits are
always against such methods and rightly so, granted
their assumptions. Their assumptions are, however,
fatal.

Protestant and Catholic are then in reality being
carried to the same crisis, and the Jesuit, though he

thinks he is holding back the Protestant from destruction, is like a man pulling at his companion to draw him on to land while all the time both of them are in reality standing on a floe which is drifting them out to sea.

One peculiar effort of this time must also be mentioned. For although it failed it is of great significance. It shows that men realized that mental advance was becoming fatally one-sided and something must be done by thought to widen the whole terms of reference of thought. This is the rise, on the threshold of the Century of Invention (the seventeenth) of the Rosicrucians. Here was an attempt to make an Order which should not only work to combine all knowledge into a living system but should specifically welcome all the new physical knowledge and complement and balance it with that esoteric psychological knowledge which lurked degraded and corrupted because it was a persecuted thing. They would make the New Learning and the Experimental Method safe for Humanity by using that method on the old secret learning and making that too a science, a science of the mind which would balance the new, dangerously partial science of matter, which was about to give man such new immense power without increasing at all his knowledge of his own nature. There were great hopes of this programme and order but — sadly — it never came into the open and salvaged civilization.

---

[1] Burton in the *Anatomy of Melancholy* echoes the hope that scholars of his time felt in this movement.

CHAPTER XIX

THE AGE OF MEANS WITHOUT MEANING

THERE was, however, one movement which in the century of Protestantism, individualism and invention, attempted to close the growing gap. It would give the individual that extra-individual experience which would solve the three-sided riddle of the sphinx, any one side of which left unsolved would ruin all (*a*) the problem of the individual's double nature, his inner conflict between his deeds and his aspirations, (*b*) the problem of society, of sanctions and values, (*c*) the problem of the objective world: of a self-conscious creature which finds itself in what seems a blind mechanic universe.

I. THE LIGHT OF THE FRIENDS

That was the movement which was given definite shape under George Fox. It is certain that Fox himself acted by intuition and with no conscious realization of the path he was pursuing. He felt that the organized religion was dead — the new Reformed religion perhaps more so than the old, the Catholic. He felt that the various sects, which then started many new ways, were all, also, blind alleys. They were all passionately exclusive, individualistic, dogmatic. Even the 'Levellers' and the 'Diggers' (as the Communists to-day) were more fired by the thought of casting down

the mighty from their seats than by the vision of comprehensive union in which high and low would only
wish to be one. All these sects, we can say, could not
escape from individualism because they were clinging
to individualism's protection — an anthropomorphic
God, and not only a God in human shape, but one
whose use was as a sword-wielding judge.

Fox was certain of three things: That social justice
must be vastly improved: he preached continually
against the bitter wrongs of the time. He was certain
that there could be no improvement till men ceased to
fear and hate each other. He therefore preached
pacifism as the essential factor in social reform. The
practical man declared, then as now, that he had to be
brutal, for as society rested on Force, if you relaxed
Force then chaos would result. Fox like Lao Tzu saw
this was putting the cart before the horse. 'Why are the
people so restless?' asks the Chinese sage and answers
with insight 'Because there is so much government'.
Fox, too, saw to the centre of this confusion. If you
trust human beings and treat them justly and
generously then they will be lawful. If the State com-
mits crimes to secure itself, its constituents will commit crimes to secure themselves. They will feel free of
moral compunction and indeed will feel a very active
resentment against authority's coercion.

The third intuition which possessed Fox was that if
you were to have social justice and the agreed peace,
which is the only condition in which there can be
social justice, you must find some way other than
violence to persuade men that it is wise to co-operate.
He did not make the mistake of the individualist
rationalist Liberals who thought you could take the

first two steps and then you were at your goal. He saw the sword had stolen in and now was firmly planted in the body of society, because men had lost their original sense of kinship, their clear realization of their common life. As soon as they only knew themselves as individuals, they could only see their brother as a stranger. Mutual self-interest of individuals would never generate the moral capital, the devotion needed to keep a community alive. At best each would sit still waiting for the other to begin to pay into the common fund, ready no doubt to follow when the other led, but till then unwilling to risk anything. Such a society, like modern marriages of mutual convenience, cannot ever get under way. Neither party will or can provide the initial water needed to put down the pump before it will draw. At worst such a society soon throws up some individual who declares he has right and power to take an unequal share, and civil war and oppression follow.

Fox's intuitions formed Quakerism on these three successive layers: social justice, pacifism and the generating of the sense of his extra-individuality, the realization of his common uniting life, in every member. This final basic experience was obtained by the small groups which met together. This silence created a social psychic field in which the limen between the self-conscious individual and the common life was melted. The silence was essential, and the force so generated was such that as an early Quaker Robert Barclay said: 'When I came into the silent assemblies I felt a secret power among them', and the condition was more exactly diagnosed by a Red Indian who attending the early meetings in America and ignorant of English said he liked to sit in the silence from which words came, the silence which lay behind language, the silence in which the subconscious can rise, the will be creative and the intuition comprehensive.

Such a force is so powerful, the sense of *kind*ship, to those long benumbed by the current individualism of the age, is so overwhelming (as when blood comes back into a limb out of which the circulation had been driven), that the shock may be serious. Hence the trembling and quaking which these earlier empiricists took as the true symptom that the experience was being attained. Then, if the shock could be held in control, and the field was fully established, it was possible for any one member, being in telepathic communication with the rest, to speak the thought which was in their common mind, and, that voice speaking aloud to each his silent and profoundest conviction, clinched the process, by making the self-conscious individual consciousness, the objective mind of each, aware of his full nature and aware also that each of his fellows were sharing, were part of, that full nature. Such an experience made pacifism not merely possible but alone possible. Without such an experience pacifism may be desirable but it is not possible.

2. THE LIGHT ENVELOPED

Quakerism, however, was as we have seen, an intuition, an art, not a science. It had been stumbled on by a genius who himself did not realize the nature of his find. It was attempting to exist in an age of ever-intensifying individualism and it actually took on its organization in the generation which produced Hobbes, who taught fear and coercion to be the essential forces of society, and Mandeville who advanced the thesis that private vices were public virtues, that the greed, malice and fear of individuals preying on each other produced that by-product of profit which built up the State. Unless it understood better, more consciously, its unconscious working it would not be able to avoid being drawn along with individualism. A man with a crude case can always make it sound more sensible than one who has to defend behaviour which he senses to be wise but which he cannot defend against the charge of extravagance or superstition.

The Quakers, when sound and influential political guidance was offered by the powerful and adroit Penn; when a niche, if a lowly one, was offered by the State, when they could feel their extreme principles were granted toleration, when they could openly wear their dress, use their speech, confess their religious unconventionality and decline military service, the Friends then could hardly be concerned if they ceased to Quake. Hardly be concerned? Surely they must have felt almost a relief? They were openly showing forth their faith. They had won all they asked for. Now their principles must prevail. They would leaven the whole lump. All they had to do was to show the world they were not feckless, unstable fanatics but able by the Grace of God to make a success of this life as well as any worldlings. They threw themselves into just dealing with such enthusiasm that they became disproportionately influential in business. Again, was it not clear God had blessed them and justified them in the most practical way to the Generation of Reason and Commerce? Who could now doubt the Quaker way was at least as right as any other? Advancing this telling argument and pressing it home with such striking sustained success it was all the less necessary, all the more easy to be sensible about other things which might 'put off' reasonable men and which in any case did not seem to have any relevance. Pacifism, social justice, these things the Friends were advancing as fast as they could. Schools, charities, prison-visiting, yes, even work for lunatics showed remarkable success.[1] They were few and yet had done so much. As people saw how sensible was their way, how possible, how conscionable, how profitable, many would join, social reform and pacifism would leap forward and the Kingdom of God would be among men. The intense field of the small group, that field in which the experience of union might be so intense that individuals experiencing it could feel a joy equal to intoxication, all that enthusiasm was acutely jarring to the eighteenth-century mind. The Age of Reason was an age which was determined to get rid of the frantic argumentative fanaticism of the previous centuries (when men had tried to state and define in individualistic language psychological conditions

---

[1] It has been pointed out that until the modern psychiatry, which is based on the recognition of the subconscious mind, the only cures recorded among the insane were among those tended by the Quakers. At the same time it must be noted that a certain amount of the insanity was due to Quaker families themselves inter-breeding which was not only genetically dangerous but also showed a tendency to that very weakness, the materialistic belief in breeding, which ruined caste in India and which is clean contrary to the spirit behind the essential character of Quakerism and Yoga – that no man can say into what family or class will be born a spirit who has the gift to follow the supreme path of enlightenment.

which could not be expressed in such terms) by simply not talking about the emotional side of religion. Everyone's religion was to be the religion of every sensible man and that, it was equally agreed, was what every sensible man was to keep to himself. The eighteenth century was the forerunner of the nineteenth-century respectability. The one made religion indecent and the other went further and made sex.

The Quakers, anxious to commend their message to this age and succeeding beyond reasonable expectation, were naturally uninclined to stress the profoundly suspected 'enthusiasm' in their proceedings and, as we grow like those who like us, the more they were liked — the more men of the age said, 'A Friend, after all, could be in his way a sound fellow; his way, after all, paid, and there was, when you looked into it, really no nonsense about it' — the more any intense experience went out of their religious service. Unless the condition which the earlier gatherings precipitated — the heightened social field — is realized to be the essential factor in such a proceeding, individualized rationalism will and must take its place. The silence will become tense not with experience but with boredom and speech will be used not as a spontaneous expression of a common immense awareness but as a relief — a help, through argument and admonition, to keep the straying thoughts of many individual minds, struggling with their private pre-occupations, held to the exhausting task of thinking on noble, inhuman ideals and the austere necessity that one should live for others.

Certain it is that Quakerism steadily lost, throughout the Century of Reason, its power of creating fields

in which the extra-individuality, the collective consciousness could be experienced — steadily lost, as it
gained in national respect and wealth.

Quakerism was therefore failing because it could not
raise into terms of conscious procedure what had been
in origin an intuition. During the seventeenth century
while individualism was yet to forge its armour of
rationalism and so cut off completely any normal and
rhythmic communication between the self-conscious
objective mind and the subconscious (and so was to
make the subconscious only able to realize itself in
convulsive eruptions of 'enthusiasm') intuition could
serve. As reason was made into a logician's instrument, whereby all experiences which were not common
to the eighteenth-century individualized mind were
dismissed as illusory, the choice before Quakerism
became either to let lapse the experience or to render
it in terms of reason, i.e. psychologically. The latter
course being too difficult, the former was followed.
During these critical years we see Quakerism inevitably
defining more exactly its central tenet, the Inner
Light. The doctrine becomes individualized. The
illumination is not a field of widened consciousness
made possible by the group, rather it is turning back
to the central conviction of seventeenth-century
Protestantism, the individual's private inspiration, the
secessionist 'right of private judgment'. Here we see
definition inevitably proving itself limitation. The
eighteenth-century individualist-rationalist atmosphere
made this contraction all too natural. The Friends
were anxious to prove they could be rational and their
Inner Light had rid them of any dependence on
Christianity's miraculous and anthropomorphic past.

It was natural therefore for them to stress the Inner Light at this time. It was also natural that that stress could strengthen and condense, rather than relax and expand, the tense focus of consciousness. As inevitably, when, with the nineteenth century, Romanticism took the place of Reason (a reverence for the past as uncritical as had been the earlier century's contempt), the Quaker movement had to respond again.

So an Evangelical movement appears. The Inner Light had inevitably been too uninspired, too often only the individual's views. Back to Jesus of Nazareth seemed the only alternative. Such a return toward 'Fundamentalism' did not however solve the Society's problem. Many members left and joined specifically credal churches. The Friends did not enlarge with the enlarging population. The dress, the forms of speech were abandoned. Quakers seemed to have no real distinction from the State as a whole. Why should they remain as a peculiar people? As far as their technique was concerned, in what radical particular did it differ from any other Free-Church procedure? Silent prayer was not anything peculiar. Extempore prayer, particular petitions, silent individual petitions — that seemed a natural inevitable development among all nonconformist assemblies.

As far as their aims and objects were concerned, here, too, they seemed to have even less cause for difference, peculiarity, separateness. The victory of all they stood out for in the seventeenth century seemed won in the nineteenth. Elizabeth Fry had taken part already in rousing England to prison reform and the world looked with admiration at a State which produced women who would go into the gaols and gain a hearing for public enemies in the name of humanity. True, Industry was harsh and war still the accepted dealing of states. The Friends however were devoting themselves to adult education and were exempted from war. At any moment now the leaven would leaven the whole lump. Everyone paid lip-service to pacifism. War was simply a means, which, as the standard of life arose, and men became more comfortable, would be less and less needed. A really rich age could always be kept in order by fines and rewards, appeals to its property sense, and of course only poor uneducated states, which did not know the delights of ease and plenty and which needed these comforts, would go to war.

With this consummation before them an increasing number of Quakers left their organization. The flood was over: the ark, unneeded, stood stranded among the dry fields, and anyhow there seemed nothing in its structure which a critical rational eye could discover as making it more able to float than the houses and cities of earthy men. The timbers were as loosely bound as the meshes of a sieve. 'We are all socialists now', said the rich, powerful and aggressive individualist, the Cabinet Minister Vernon Harcourt. He meant we all wish everybody well, ultimately, and only delay making them comfortable until we can see how to do so without interfering with our own comfort. The pacifism from which all Liberals, including Quakers, hoped so much was not more real. We are all pacifists now so long as we see that security, honour, expansion, prestige, the getting of our way and the acknowledgment of our point of view can be obtained without violence.

So when the world war came there were found Quakers to say openly that, as the Allies were securing peace in the only possible way, every peace lover should support the war, and others who said that as the State tolerated their attitude, they should not protest against the war. Both points of view were quite natural, for once the society had lost its power to discover the only peaceful sanction for values, for law, order and peace itself, then, as individualism could not be given the evidence and experience of extra-individuality, society composed of individuals must fall back on the sword.

This sketch of Quakerism, short as it is, may seem disproportionate in an essay which tries to review the struggle which has lain behind the whole of human history. But the course of Quakerism illustrates in our own society a discovery, a conflict and a decline, all of which have been repeated throughout history with a constantly growing acuteness.

3. THE LATEST EVOLUTIONARY LINE
TO FOSSILIZE

The history of the Society of Friends is not a by-path in the field of English commercial development or a blind alley in the roadways of religion. It is a typical end-process of Evolution. It is what must always happen if at a certain stage psychological knowledge cannot keep abreast of physical knowledge — what must befall if a process (which till then has been able to work intuitionally) fails thereafter to work out deliberately and scientifically its technique. What lies behind all history, when we dissect to the core, is the struggle of two forces. We see, when we trace these forces back to their prehistoric divergence, that they arise from a profound crisis in man's consciousness. Man's consciousness, in its rapid development, tends to split into an objective mind and a subjective mind. The triumphs of his objective mind in dealing with that restricted aspect of reality which is all that it can compose or comprehend, are great. They lead to such powers that man is persuaded there can be no reality save this sector of reality. Such a belief means, first that man has to depend wholly on physical force to support the sanctions which he still feels subconsciously to be true, and, then as use of physical force makes such feeling to grow still fainter, he uses force for its own sake, to gain his individualized will and way.

This leads to the collapse of society, for the logical conclusion is, not a balance of power, but every man's hand turned against his fellow, anarchy. The powers of destruction have been, however, limited. Man so far cannot exterminate himself; even expert specialized monomaniacs such as Ghenghis fail. In consequence, after this demonstration, that it is not the sword which keeps peace but which destroys it, men question themselves whether their ideals and values may not be autonomous, whether men may not really belong to each other and to a higher order and so it may be natural for order and peace to exist as long as you abstain from using coercion and violence. They are willing to make this experiment because of the sorry pass to which violence has reduced them. A ruined man is not restrained by the caution which holds back the rich; a patient whom the surgeons have cut within

386

an inch of his life and left him still diseased will try a spiritual healer. Though the wish is not enough in itself, it may permit, and at times has permitted, men to make discoveries of various techniques suited more or less to their degree of individuality, whereby they might enlarge that individuality and become aware of their common consciousness. Such methods were however never sufficiently definite and flexible to allow for the psychology (which was so obtained) to continue to grow proportionately with the continued growth of physical knowledge, due to the steady intensification of the focus of the partial objective mind. Hence after peace and plenty increasing congestion, friction and finally a series of wars, at first defensive or preventive, and finally expressions of pure brigandage. So the world has rocked on its uneasy course.

'Still it progresses', say some. Gibbon concludes with the quiet glee of a rationalist that as there was now no reservoir of barbarians from which civilization might be flooded, civilization was safe. With its superior numbers and its still greater superiority in machines, it need never again fear the savage. Gibbon did not realize the savage is not an economic product but a state of mind, not a fossil creature safely buried far down in the deeper 'archaeological horizons' of history, but lurking just beneath the threshold of contemporary peoples' consciousness. Was not genteel Paris, a year or two after he laid down his complacent pen, to show how the latest enthusiasm could deal out mob violence and massacre to the educated, the urbane and the intelligent. He and his age could not grasp that the destroyer is not a primitive who has become extinct but a specialized aberrant, a social 'lethal mutation' which will always arise if the spiritual vitality of man fails and he shrink from the pain of always feeling — the price of progress.

4. THE FAILURE OF RATIONAL ECONOMIC PROGRESS

The eighteenth century with its code of deportment — its reaction from the emotionalism of the seventeenth century — had tried to rule war as a game, to make chivalry extend, not merely to individual combats, but to whole campaigns. Louis XIV's generals can let their soldiery drag the bodies of the Palatine bishops out of their cathedral graves and kick them down the street, but by the Great Wars of the Spanish succession, which close his reign, Marlborough and his rivals warn a town when they intend to bombard it, war is not against civilians. If they can keep out of the way they ought to be safe. War is a duel.

By the middle of the century crack regiments can request of their opponents that 'the gentlemen of the Guard fire first'. But by the end of the century French troops are giving no quarter and taking no prisoners. The Revolution has suddenly made violence real as the one apparent path to Reform.

Certainly there is no inevitable Progress. 'And none at all' add all Reactionaries. Yet — as was noted in the Introduction when stating our present dilemma — many Catholics who maintain progress is a Protestant myth will defend the brutalities of the Middle Ages on the old unsound argument that, considering the backward time, things then could not be done otherwise and churchmen often had to countenance and even advocate methods which would be unnecessary to-day, because then most men were much closer the savage.

Quite apart from the fact that this is a very dangerous argument to be used on behalf of a church which claims perpetual inspiration, it is clearly a mistaken historical judgment. No doubt at times men's individuality becomes inflamed and any, even the faintest, intuition of their complete and common nature is cut off. At such times men behave diabolically to one another. Such phases, however, as we have seen, generally lead to their own elimination. Pushing violence to the logical conclusion, the Men of Blood exterminate themselves. They have up to the present lacked the weapons to exterminate the race.

The picture of history which our psychological knowledge seems to give us to-day is then of a humanity which may at any time by specialization of its objective mind, growth of its physical, and atrophy of its psychic, intuition, become intensely callous and cruel, but which may quickly recover its sanity. This may take place at any date from the old Stone Age till now. The fact, however, that there is Progress, but that Progress is only possible if both sides of man's nature, his objective and his subjective minds — or aspects of his psychic — advance together, this fact does not make for complacency. For then — as is the case to-day — immense advance in physical mastery may be indicative of complete arrest of advance in psychological understanding. While the product of the physical advance gives weapons which can destroy the world, the lack of psychological advance may make men honestly believe there is no other way.

When then, we presume, as Gibbon, that no barbarians can overwhelm us, or comfort ourselves, as do many historians, Conservative as well as Liberal, that 'times' have become more humane and the heart 'of man is widened with the circling of the Suns' we are deluding ourselves.[1] The barbarian is the monomaniac in each of us ready to spring out armed the moment our intuition of general goodwill, of our whole and balanced being begins to fail. Historians have remarked repeatedly how wars which began with the decorum of a duel ended in shambles. You cannot appeal to Caesar and not go the whole way to Rome. The vague intuition of general goodwill, of moral progress, is the feeblest resistance. Let fear cause panic and in a short while everyone would be echoing the words of all realists from 'the Lord Shan' to Stalin 'men are bad'. And human nature given a bad name hangs itself. It needs only a minute decline of temperature and the ice sheet would come forward again and the Ice Age would be back. It needs only a slight rise in the number of those who are infected with malaria and malaria becomes endemic.

The Quakers it is clear struck on a method of deliberately heightening resistance, of raising the falling social temperature and so of fending off chaos and old night. They failed, it is equally clear, to make that method an assured technique. It disappeared.

To-day no one wants war. In the Middle Ages no one wanted the Tatars. Our social temperature is however steadily dropping. We want security and

---

[1] How extreme that doctrine is becoming can be seen from F. HARDIE'S *The Political Influence of Queen Victoria*, where the author says, 'It is unhistorical to take our stand in 1935 and condemn 1861-1901 by that standard'.

even goodwill because we can see what, with our present physical capacity for violence, the consequence must be to our individual comfort, and to that of those we love, if we use that violence. Violence, however, is given continually fresh opportunities.

Western civilization is split, not merely vertically but horizontally, and not only nations swear they will use all the resources of science for unlimited violence to re-establish what they believe to be their past fame, but classes also declare they will do no less to win what seems to them a perfect future.

5. PSYCHOLOGICAL KNOWLEDGE MUST BALANCE PHYSICAL KNOWLEDGE

It is clear that those who would refurbish an ancient culture and those who would enforce a new order are both playing into the hand of the monomaniac specialist expert who will finally so be given his opportunity to use all civilization's resources for his 'jolly game' (as Napoleon called it), the game which will crash civilization and break humanity's heart and nerve. The conclusion of the whole matter is: we must make clear as Eastern thought once made clear, the way, the technique by which the individual may enlarge his consciousness and realize he and his fellows are part of a general life. Our physical knowledge, our partial reality arising from our partial objective, individualized, isolated layer of consciousness, must be balanced by psychological knowledge, knowledge of that complementary aspect of reality which can only be obtained through our subjective, common, integrated depth of consciousness in which each one of us, our society and all Life are known in their true nature as one.

This is the only hope for civilization and without this even if we still advance in physical discovery and power this will but assure that, when, at last, our realism compels us to act in logical accord with its narrow but conscious principles, our civilization and our humanity will but fall with greater violence and disintegrate more completely.

CONCLUSION:

SUMMARY

It now only remains to summarize briefly the whole argument; to show how we have come to where we are and how with this new knowledge of our route and of the forces (the parallelogram of forces) which have driven us to this point, we may see what our actual position is, what we may still do.

We have found that the latest knowledge shows that we are not — as we assumed — sprung from a fighting stock. On the contrary our advance is wholly due to our having retained to the end, what all other forms of life to some degree lost, sensitiveness, awareness. For that purpose, for that essential requirement of progress, we have kept ourselves free of defensiveness and all narrowing specialization. As we have gone on in general capacity, receptiveness and adaptability we have had to keep on casting off any crust of custom, any unquestioned reaction, any quick, sure, hard efficiency, and constantly to break ourself out of any rut of safety. This is the principle of foetalization. It is not enough merely to remain uncommitted. As consciousness grows and becomes more intense, the living being has deliberately to open itself to new possibilities and impressions to which it has no prepared reply, to new riddles and questions to which it has no ready answer, to new interests which seem unwise, to new sympathies which seem unsafe. The man has to become continually as impressionable as is the child.

As long as man had no civilization, as long as his reflective objective mind had yet to be so condensed and focused as to make him capable of deliberate inventions and intentional discoveries (which should give him power), so long his innate unconscious sensitiveness and sympathetic need, his intuition of his union with his fellows, kept his society together — as all gregarious societies are kept together — without laws, still less police. And in man's case because of his supreme sensitiveness we may assume an even intenser tie which we call affection. The fact, however, that he could make inventions and began regularly to practise those crafts which made civilization possible, shows a specialization of one aspect of consciousness out of his complete psyche. This layer, the objective mind, made to act continually on its own, must in the end cause acute self-consciousness and a corresponding sinking of the remaining field of consciousness below a threshold or limen, where it would rapidly become inaccessible to the objective mind and to the individualized self-consciousness, to which that objective partial mind had given rise.

When man makes discoveries, or performs any process consciously, with a clear sense that it is a means to an end, then he must become aware of what he is doing and must ask why he does it and why it is worth his particular, individual while to do it.

There can be no doubt the proto-civilization made man think. No civilization is possible without reflection. Whether one mind or one small group of minds thought out the inter-related and interlocking

394

techniques, needed to make that civilization, every constituent who came into and under that civilization must have had his consciousness intensified. Intensified consciousness need not however mean intensified self-consciousness, a blinding awareness of one's own individuality to the loss of all other apprehension of any other quality or sort of consciousness. That has followed with us; we have therefore thought it inevitable. It is not. Yet it is true that if appropriate steps are not taken to balance up and counter-weight this one-sided advance, then intensified consciousness will and must give rise to an unquestioning individualism which will unhinge the constituent and derange society. Conscious progress in interference with the outer world must upset the unconscious relation with the inner world.

This dangerous crisis the proto-civilization seems however to have surmounted. Psychological discoveries seem to have been made which balanced the physical discoveries. The inventors who have made the new physical crafts seem also to have invented as deliberately and as consciously a psychical technique whereby they and their followers might still keep in touch with what would now otherwise have become the subconscious mind, a vague world of dreams, aspirations and unreal ideals, of inner conflict, not reconciliation. This technique need have been no more advanced, no more modernly conscious and 'scientific' than were the new physical crafts. The one essential was that the psychological method or praxis should be equal to, should balance the physical method, by advancing as far in *its* direction as the physical method (and the objective focus) had gone along the line of its specific departure. This the primitive Life Religion seems to have effected.

It was not then, therefore, that this break came in man's history. The first dangerous stage of his now rapid ascent was satisfactorily balanced. The next stage saw the fissure appear. The Indus arc of the primal culture seems to have surmounted that stage also. To match and balance the still more swift, more elaborate, more purposive, more conscious command over the physical world (a command which made the individual while so engrossed only able to think of this focus as complete reality), Yoga, in some early form, was the corresponding invention, a deliberate psychological method instead of tribal ritual. When the individualized mind had become cramped and even shrunken into its specialized absorption with means and the mastery of matter, then the psycho-physical exercises of reunion with its whole life, would again expand it to its full and right stature and dilate the narrowed focus of consciousness until it could again see the whole and itself as part. So self-consciousness in one direction would be complemented by increasing consciousness in the other and man would advance in awareness and yet remain whole: he would grow in deliberate power but also in deliberate purpose: he would gain knowledge and yet also attain wisdom.

The other two arcs of the proto-civilization seem to have failed to make the necessary proportionate advance. No doubt they hung on for some time with a psychology no longer adequate to their physics, i.e. a religion becoming anthropomorphic in idea and sensual or magical in practice. Then a stage was reached when unresolved individualism became no longer avoidable.

There, this fact of isolated self-consciousness, stood as gross as a stumbling block in the path of advance. There was no method of melting it. The most active individual completes this stage of the degenerative process, seizes power and the rest comply, because one master and some order seems better than many anarchs.

The State however is now completely unstable and war becomes a normal condition. The sword, which was permitted free play as the only possible sanctioner of justice and order, once free, begins to call justice whatever it can do, and the only order it allows is martial law — martial law, the essential step to spreading still further lawlessness and disorder. Even physical invention, the activity of the partial objective mind, is checked, as action becomes less and less long-sighted, more and more simple violence. Finally the most unbalanced specialist, the nomad military genius, using whatever of civilization's inventions will add most to destructive power, devastates civilization, which he hates for its constant checks on action and impulse, and humanity collapses.[1] He is too violent however. The drive he concentrates, scatters at his death, and this, added to the fact that he has (as yet) never had at his disposal machines and inventions which could really extirpate civilization everywhere in the short span of his life, has therefore permitted

[1] The feeling of deep hatred for civilization which the Nomad conqueror specialist feels has been in this essay illustrated from Ghenghis's life. It must also be remembered that Mohammed said, 'Cursed is he who invented the plough'. He would dig down and collapse all society even below the proto-civilization.

recoveries after deluges. Before the conquering pest could reach the limit (and then all his legions turn on each other) the master monomaniac dies and the organization flies to pieces before it has done its work.

After this exhibition of what violence can do and must do, men begin again to trust intuition. The trust in the sword as the guardian of order led to this anarchy. The reaction from violence is however no more than an emotional wish that it might be dispensed with. Men do not attempt to find an alternative. They do not diagnose the difficulty and see that the sword's point is only the ultimate condensation and focus of their unresolved individualism. Hence mere disgust at carnage and chaos leads to no solution. After the shock has worn off the same degenerative processes gain increasing free play. Good wishes only lead to another collapse into 'realism'.

This then has been the degenerative history of civilization, first in the West and then in the East. Time and again new psychological techniques ventured into the open, tried to get hold of the controls of the car of civilization and present man with a spiritual praxis proportionate to his physical power and individualized intensity. Buddhism in India; Taoism in China; those three tongues of psycho-physical religion which pushed into Europe as Gnosticism, Manichaeanism and Catharism, all these attempts won temporary success and then failed.

Meanwhile as these salvations failed, and, at the other extreme, the destroyers Attila, Ghenghis, and Timur also fail, Humanity, tormented and distressed, staggers along to its goal. Its technical physical knowledge is recovered and with these mnemonics in his hand, man begins once again to work at those partial formulae, products of a partial mind, which gave him power over an outer indifferent world, ever more means at the price of ever narrower, meaner ends.

Looking back three hundred years, we can see men throw off the last inadequate construction that medieval man had tried to make so as to give him a crude balance between means and ends, facts and values. The Catholic cosmology discarded, an intensification of individualism and invention takes place. Europe breaks up, while the scientific powers the European fragments jointly inherit and develop, become such that a complete disintegration of society by use of physical violence at last becomes possible. At least one remarkable effort, to make intuition real and find a technique of getting into touch with the subconscious, is attempted, in the Society of Friends. The drift of the time is too powerful however. The current individualism prevents the Quakers from realizing what they have done and what they must do much more clearly — scientifically — if at so late a date they are to save society.

I. THE PATH OF PROGRESS

Here then we find ourselves at the time of crisis. This is the course we have come, the forces which have driven us and the task we have to achieve if civilization is to be saved. Otherwise it will do to itself what the monomaniac destroyer desired but lacked the power, what to-day we dread, but have the power and lack the will to avert, because we can see no other way, no way out. We are like panic-stricken horses which burn to death in a blazing stable. We are terrified, too terrified to escape.

Yet though the peril is desperate there is hope. As the danger had increased, the way out has become clearer. We see there is no doom written in our nature. We are not made naturally to behave in this way. We have only to advance, to find we have left the horror of to-day behind as the waker leaves behind, and wholly dissipates, his nightmare. For to-day 300 years of ever-intensifying analyses has brought man to the intensive study of himself. He sees then what nature intended him to be—receptive, sensitive. He sees how he is to obey this command of nature by keeping his nature open and by balancing all his advances in control and understanding of 'the outer world' by an equal control and understanding of the 'inner world'. He realizes, after having suffered for some 6000 years from a fissured consciousness, that this is the explanation of what he took to be the insuperable difficulties of his social life, its political injustices and economic hardships; here in the depths of himself lay the source of all his troubles. It was to bridge this gap and counter-balance this instability that religions have been so constantly made and, as the gap grew, have so constantly had to be widened. His misapprehension of his nature and outer nature, his feeling that fact and value were in irreconcilable conflict, these things also arose from the fault in his consciousness.

The fact that this is the cause of all his miseries, mental and physical, shows him that it is here he must bring about reconciliation, that once reconciliation is effected at this centre the outer conflicts will resolve themselves and that, by advancing psychological knowledge and experience to the degree which physical knowledge and power have been — disproportionately — advanced, he will again become sane, his society happy, his civilization advance and Life go forward to its destiny and goal.

2. TRADITIONAL RELIGION, ACADEMIC PSYCHOLOGY AND PSYCHICAL RESEARCH ARE NONE SUFFICIENT

Some people think this may be effected by nothing more than our present psychological knowledge of the subconscious. Here is demonstration that man is much more than an individual and disregards his greater self at peril of the sanity of even his lower self. Knowledge of a fact, however, is not sufficient. To know that the pain and helplessness of a limb is due to a broken bone is not to have set and knit the fracture.

Others, aware of the progress in 'field studies' or 'field exploration' in psychology think that psychical research, yielding as it does evidence of telepathy, clairvoyance and prevision, gives the necessary evidence of the larger state of consciousness to which we all belong. This again does not seem sufficient. Such states of consciousness are, in psychical research, only made evident through the dissociated condition to which those rare, and often far from impressive people, sensitives, can reduce themselves. This is allowed by those who build most on evidence so obtained. Spiritualists maintain that the data must be

CC   401

put together and framed in a hypothesis of another after-death life. This, in nearly all such accounts, resembles closely in its vivid anthropomorphism much of the cosmological imagery used by the religions which we have seen have been developed by the individualized civilizations which sprang from the Sumerian and Egyptian cultures. It is clear that these after-death religions, though they may have acted as a slight brake on the dissolution of society, through its appeal to naked violence, did not solve the problem which produced the appeal to violence, the isolated individualized consciousness with its partial, 'menial' view of reality. Hence, though they might give the individual a bad conscience after he had committed his crimes, they could scarcely ever restrain him before. They could add internal conflict to external chaos and make the murderers, Macbeth and his wife, little happier than their victims, Duncan and Banquo. They could not check Macbeth's desperate plunge forward into deeper bloodshed. Had he hesitated, then only tougher creatures would have taken on. The devils that believe and tremble are superseded by those who believe nothing and never know remorse.

The final argument, that after-death religions and the rewards and threats they can advance, are not sufficient to preserve society, is that these religions have themselves allowed they could not dispense with the sword. Not only have none of them declared the sword to be unnecessary so long as rewards and punishments after death were proclaimed to be certain; the special advocates of these, the Zoroastrian Magi, the Mohammedan Mufti, the Catholic clergy, have all called on the government to use unlimited violence against any member of the state who might question not general morality but any of their peculiar and far from evident opinions.

What then both our experiences and history establish is that the community requires, not a proof for individuals that in the end it does not pay to behave as an individual, but some psychological technique whereby the individual may be able to transcend his individuality. That, no anthropological cosmological religion, no religion focused on a life after death, aims at giving — though individuals practising such religions may attain the condition, as it were accidentally.

3. THE REQUIREMENT: A PSYCHOLOGICAL PRAXIS

The cure for the fissure in consciousness, that is what we require and that cannot be wrought by any of the religions which arose when man was already individualized and which therefore, with their anthropomorphic god and his interventions on an outer order of nature, with their last Judgments and otherworldly final rewards and punishments, only 'project' and fix the condition which spiritual insight should cure. The task before the individual and civilization is simple, drastic, but not — as the world assumes — impossible. We have to recover the direct awareness of our extra-individuality. This is not a matter of belief or dogma. It is an empirical procedure. It is an advanced psychology. It is true it requires some belief that it is a valid procedure — or the experiment

CONCLUSION

will not be undertaken — but it does not require any
assumptions about the nature of the universe or
definitions of the character of the forces which may
help that progress.

The people who made the first steps in this technique — record of which has come down to us — were,
it seems clear, Indians. That does not mean that we
are to adopt any of their many varieties of method in
detail, any more than when the West took over the
mathematics of India we adopted the Indian notation.
All we have to do, but what we must do, is to recognize
that our psychological advance must be brought to the
same pitch, so as to balance our physical advance, and
that proportionate advance can only be through a
method of changing the aperture of consciousness,
enlarging and shifting the field of awareness above
and beyond that restricted field, which has given us
the present world of means and facts, that restricted
field, to-day so fatally inadequate and yet, a field so
long brooded upon exclusively, that we cannot
imagine any other.

4. WHY YOGA FAILED

It only remains to ask, if this is the way and this
way is possible, why we have had to get to such
extremity before coming in sight of it and why those,
who actually had their feet on the first steps, should
not have opened up a royal road for all mankind.
India has, it is true, endured better than Europe,
but its sufferings have been as squalid and its achievement, in giving enlightenment to all its inhabitants,
has not been superior. The ryot is as tied to economics

as is the moujik, and there are not only mill hands in Bombay and other big cities but 'indigenous' wasteland tribes in India which have as little insight into their relationship with the whole of life and reality as an occidental slum-dweller. The same must be said of China where the psycho-physical technique was also explored.

The answer very briefly seems to be that the East may have something to learn from the West as the West has much to take from the East. There is progress, man does advance. The body of psychophysical discoveries made in Asia, whereby the individual consciousness could be enlarged, was beyond anything Europe has so far known, far beyond such happy accidents as Quakerism, but it was still more of an art than a science, more of a tradition than an empiricism. It, too, settled and became authoritative, became more of a privilege, an escape for the few, rather than an essential deliverance and development for all.

(a) *Caste*

The caste system, which is a specific device to extend the benefits of such a procedure throughout the community, when it was to have become a constantly supplying and integrating organism (as the transmitter of values, the system through which the whole social life is irrigated from its head-waters) becomes rigid. Instead of picking adepts in whatever class of the community they might appear, the Brahmin made himself an hereditary stock. This was obviously a grave mistake, so grave that we are astonished at it. Our astonishment may lead us to

405

explore further and then we may discover the reason for the mistake.

(b) Psycho-Physical Dangers

These experiments and techniques in the expansion of consciousness are, we have seen, like all real powers, dangerous. To-day we know that our impression of the outer world, what we call objective reality, is not a direct apprehension. Our senses are only responsive to a very narrow belt of all the form-energy which radiates around us. But that is not all. Our senses take this restricted amount of the fundamental data and instantaneously make out of it a construction which we call the world of sense. This construction seems to be of a threefold texture. First there are the narrow apprehensions and interpretations of the animal, which serve its survival. These apprehensions are a little confused by those random observations of curiosity which a creature, as sensitive as our animal stock, must endure. Next there are the current attentions and interpretations of our society — common sense. Finally there are the personal interests, aversions or insensitivenesses of each individual. These three wefts make that mixture of fact and judgment which we call reality.

It is this tissue of cross-threads, loosely ravelled, which we, in the West, assumed embraced and held all Reality. Now that we have come to examine this net we are surprised that it could hold anything or that we could have any certainty that anything we picked out of it came from the sea and was not fragments of the net itself. Nevertheless it has until now served. It is a balance between bodily needs and general awareness, between what the individual likes and society demands. It is a possible construction allowing us to live as animals and yet take in just that selvedge of observation which is of no practical present use to us but which allows that play and possible expansion of apprehension, which we must have, if we are to continue to be Life's favourite, the creature that always takes in more than it actually at the moment needs, and so can continue uneasily to evolve.

So we have shuffled along. Now, however, we have to enlarge greatly that border and take in much more if we are to prevent ourselves coming to a dead-end. To turn the flank of our present obstacle we have to feel out into apprehensions which are not merely those which we have considered useless but which we have thought illusory or non-existent. This is not only a difficult task. It is one which is highly dangerous as well. We have our traditional construction of things which has worked in its way. To change the simile from net to viaduct, to take to pieces the bricks of this simple little arch and try to throw another arch of much wider span, this is to attempt something which the uninformed think impossible and the informed, though they know it to be possible, know to be both intensely difficult and dangerous. As our information grows we realize that the impossibility of shifting consciousness and bringing it to another clear focus (and so gaining the apprehension of a fuller and more harmonious reality) is not the real difficulty. That realized, Western minds are apt to think the way then is open. If there is something there, if the missing side of reality can now be found, well, men will now find it and that will be the happy end of the matter. The West, with its advance in 'material knowledge' — a knowledge which is neutral, neither good nor bad, but depending whether it is good or bad, on how it is used, for what end and for what values it is the means — the West cannot yet think of knowledge being in itself dangerous. How can the actual finding of new knowledge imperil man? This is, however, the real difficulty that now confronts us in our advance: There is a further sphere of reality to be found: we must find it, or our present knowledge is so incomplete that with it alone we shall ruin our civilization and ourselves: this further sphere of reality is nevertheless only to be attained with great risk. How is this?

In the first place all changes are dangerous, not merely because new powers may make ill acts more grave but because we human beings — in spite of the fact of our unequalled adaptability — are nevertheless animals and all animals are adapted to live only under very restricted circumstances. Change suddenly the water's temperature by a degree or two or its salinity by a grain or two and most fish life would perish in the sea. Innumerable insects can only live on the leaf of a particular shrub or tree. Man forgets his restrictions, so ingeniously has he managed to live within them, but many animals hold to life by firmer grapples than he. He cannot live on grass as the herbivores, but has to have them as a link, or grow a few special grasses, extract their seed and cook them. The termites have even a firmer hold, being able to live on dry wood.

What is even more precarious in his position is that the moment he moves outside the particular level in the film of atmosphere in which he must live he begins to disturb his consciousness. He is adapted to live with an atmospheric pressure upon him of some 14 lb. to the square inch. Raise him only some 20,000 feet and he is already in considerable distress and frequently suffers from hallucinations, i.e. begins to have impressions which he cannot correlate with his sea-level normal experience, but which bear some relation to his experiences when his consciousness is disturbed by fever or by drugs. Move him at a pace accelerating more than 32 feet a second and, again, he begins to fail to make automatically that synthetic construction of impressions — of data — which give him the picture of the outer world and of himself moving as an independent consciousness in it.

And these disturbances are not merely disconcerting: they are dangerous. Keep him at over 20,000 feet and he will probably die, he will certainly undergo great distress. Sustain his acceleration at 32 feet a second for a few minutes and he will probably also die. In either case it is certain he will fail completely to 'make sense of' and 'act sensibly to' his impressions. He will be deranged.

5. PHYSIOLOGICAL RISKS

Now this rapid change of his impressions is what he must be prepared to face if he is going to attempt, what is even more radical than a change of bodily condition, a complete change of mental construction, i.e. if he is going (first) to realize by conscious analysis how he composes, from the impressions yielded by his senses, the common-sense picture of objective reality, (second) what are the data actually given him (before he has worked them into constructions and concepts), and (third), what additional data he can bring into consciousness, add to the earlier data he has cleansed of their patina of concept and, from these the sum of data accessible to him, make into a new comprehensive concept and 'sense'.

Granted that our present field and focus, our present construction which we make with our present capacities out of the energy around us (which construction is for us the outer objective world and ourselves in it), is partial, is to-day dangerously, critically inadequate, to make another is going to be difficult and dangerous. In fact we shall have to take this lower normal gear out of mesh and put it into neutral before we can engage the higher gear. We shall have to throw this field out of focus before we can find the other wider field. We know that the picture we have made of the unknown which is around us, and which we call reality, is a workable construction, a construction which although proving inadequate is nevertheless one which most people consider to be obvious common sense. With the new apprehensions, facts, can we make another coherent picture, or will we find ourselves surrounded by an incoherent limbo, a lunatic's outlook? This is a most serious question. Reality is a construction, a selection made by tradition out of a, literally, overwhelming mass and deluge of possible data. If we see through and discard that construction, we are compelled to make another. But only a great artist possessed of masterly technique and creative power of composition, can make a vast design, including an enormous extent of new material. Are we such master artists?

CONCLUSION

It is not enough to perceive one completely new fact or to have one profoundly original idea. If fact and idea are really original they certainly will not 'bond' with all the rest of our current 'reality'. He who so sees will have to discontinue such seeing or he will find, in the clear field of accepted common sense, he alone suffers from an intrusion which deranges his outlook and makes him doubt what all the rest know to be all of reality. He will find he is an 'idiotes', a creature outside the pack, on his own, unable to make sense of and to convey his irrelevant apprehension. The more we study history the more we see — as the proto-civilization and the Indus Culture have shown — that ideas to be accepted and not to be fatally disruptive must be fully comprehensive, a complete way of living, and that only those facts can be accepted which work in with and sustain (and, may be, consistently enlarge) a community's entire pattern and design of life.

The dangers, then, should now be obvious: In the first place there are the physiological dangers. We now know that our power of attention is that amount and degree of consciousness which can be left over when all the other essential attentions (attentions essential for consciousness to exist in a body) have been met. Deep hypnosis has shown that a degree of consciousness is required to keep the heart beating and the lungs selecting how much oxygen, how much carbon dioxide the blood will need. The big nerve ganglia such as the medulla oblongata and the solar plexus, it seems increasingly likely, have round them a field of consciousness appropriate to the functions they perform; as the self-conscious, analytic intelligence seems mainly based on the seventh cortex of the fore-brain. These routine attentions needed for heart, lungs, etc., are, in us, cut down to the minimum in order that the conscious power of attention should be as free as possible. We run our bodies on the minimum of consciousness and we do that by making the running a routine. We shall only expect of the body normal behaviour. What then will happen (*a*) if we require and demand a greater intensity of attention than we normally exact; (*b*) if we require and demand of the body behaviours which our lower layers of conscious-ness are not accustomed to provide?

To draw on the subconscious in order to widen and extend consciousness is then first and foremost to starve the supply of subconscious attention needed to keep the body going. That is the difficulty and danger, the physical danger, of the first step, of putting the gear into neutral — a preliminary step. The process is one of heightened attention and is brought about by drawing on the reserves or garrisons of attention scattered through the body (through alteration of the breathing rhythm, the heart beat, etc.). In this state, the practiser may suffer from collapse owing to the failure of the nerve impulse needed to keep a vital organ functioning.

6. MENTAL RISKS

Granted, however, that he can attain the neutral state and yet keep the body functioning, we have seen he now has to build up consciously, from the wider data of consciousness which he now experiences, a coherent construction. This is the psychological peril.

For to make this construction he requires an additional increase of mental energy. The dangers here are (1) that having picked to pieces common sense he may not be able to make any other sense — with the disjointed pieces and a lot more added, he may be completely unable to compose his widened impressions; (2) or, that he may be content to contemplate merely, having got out of the wood just to stay out of it, having surmounted the pass to be content to stay in the fresh air of the tableland and not go back to the confusion and squalor in the valley he has left behind.

The new explorer then has to take physical risks. His body may break down: mental risks, his mind may not be good enough to make the generalization — the linkage which will combine common-sense experience, which is come to a dead end, with this higher complementary experience: he may become an incomprehensible mystic or a logomachic word-spinner. He has moral or psychological risks: he may desert humanity, and having found the way out go off and leave his fellows: he may learn how to be completely superior to the world and cease to care whether anyone else has the secret. These dangers have undoubtedly taken such a vast toll of explorers that one cannot be surprised 'that those who know do not say' or only say you must go singly and slowly and each with an accredited guide. These are the dangers. Surely they are real enough.

This, very briefly, seems the reason why this expansion has been slow and indeed tends to languish, even in places where it is known, especially whenever social conditions become sufficiently settled that man can persuade himself there is really no vital need why he should leave his present position and attempt the supreme effort of crossing the pass, when he wishes to settle down and evolve no more. What is certain is that the dangers of this method are such that general scientific exploration, 'for curiosity's sake' was strongly discouraged. In consequence the methods could not become scientific, generalized principles but were and had to be passed on by Guru to Chela, fed by master to pupil, as the teacher saw how the student responded to the various disciplines and methods.[1]

Hence conservatism, authoritarianism, profound psycho-physical discoveries mixed with worthless inert tradition: the accidents of time and place mixed with the substance of reality itself. It is as though radium naturally occurred in great clots but was always too dangerous to be extracted and so masses of pitch-blende had to be used, sometimes giving radio-therapeutic effects and sometimes nothing.

7 . WE MUST ADVANCE

To-day it is clear the risk must be taken. Stable societies forbid all exploration either into the nature of the outer or that of the inner world. We have permitted, have urged forward the former until our world is splitting asunder under our feet. We cannot then, because of the danger, any longer delay. When, of two climbers, roped and balancing their way along a knife-edge 'aret', one suddenly slips and falls to the left the only course of safety for either is for the other

---

[1] This procedure the empirical scientist need not dismiss as a cover for obscurantist incompetence. Many powerful and useful drugs are so idiosyncratic that no general instructions as to their use can be given. The reaction of each patient to them has first to be tried out.

to fling himself headlong down the precipice to the right. To-day our science, which has mined our society and put the match in our trembling fingers, must penetrate into our minds and at any risk find for us the controls which have slipped from us. Then, using this knowledge of the East, we may again, by a bold and daring plunge of advance into the subconscious, suddenly rebalance and hold in control our other advance which is already falling headlong into the abyss. It is a dangerous, perhaps a desperate, step but it is the only possible one adequate to our peril.

Some would say it is better this civilization go down in agony and futility than that fresh psychological powers, it may misuse as grossly as it has misused its physical powers, be given it. Those who wish to know can be saved. The rest must perish. It is the way of Life. Only a remnant ever survives any of the great crises and carries on the purpose of Life. Yet to-day even a remnant might not survive, and so many seem willing to advance, if only some one could show them the way, a real path, not a rainbow bridge. Let but this way be opened up and then a new social order will at once crystallize it. Let picked researchers and adepts find the way through, give clear proof that here is the sanction of values for peace and creative order, that here within us is 'the Kingdom', we can if we will directly experience the whole life of which we individuals are all interdependent units, and the nightmare will vanish, the sword which is at our throats will fall, as the razor drops from the hand of the suicide maniac when he suddenly realizes he need not die.

8. WHY ADVANCE ALONE IS POSSIBLE

Only one point remains. Though the illuminated may see this reality and so realize that the kinship of all is the union of all, that peace and not violence is what unites men, how can they, simply because they are illuminated and pacific make others who are blind see the light and know peace? This has been the millennial objection to pacifism, the objection ever since men, through knowing of no technique to solve their individuality, thought of peace as an individual convenience, not as a consequence of having transcended individualism, and of values and goodwill as aspirations which needed reality to make them actual, not as reality itself.

This objection we have seen is answered by the facts of history and present experience. Undefended, Pope Leo was able to meet Attila and win from the conqueror what defence could not have secured. Undefended, the Quakers were able to make friends with the Red Indians. To-day anthropologists have yet to find a people which cannot be approached and associated with, if a defensive attitude is abandoned and the advance is obviously friendly. The homicidal lunatic may attack but he is much less likely to do so if whoever goes up to him goes with complete defencelessness and with complete interest, not in their safety but in his welfare. He is nearly always a paranoic, longing to be protected. The wild animal, the large carnivore it too may attack but, as already mentioned, such naturalists and animal breeders as Elliot S. Humphrey have proved that the carnivore, if without hunger, attacks because it fears to be attacked. It is not, however, enough for the tamer to show no outward sign of aggressive defence. If the animal is to be peaceable with him he must not only act peaceably and quietly, he must feel it. This case of animal training, the approach to the savage beast, seems all too mystical and superrational. Yet, although it gives the most unequivocal support to the dynamic pacifism of the Yogic or psycho-physical morality, we have seen (p. 294) it is capable of a simple physiological explanation. We have here a vivid illustration of how when we are dealing with creatures incapable of rational deduction, our feeling-tone is wholly decisive. The pacifism, which is not a timid shrinking from the risk of personal pain but a vivid sense of union with and reverence for all Life, can 'shut the mouths of lions'.

Apply this to the problem of human pacifism and the principle can be enormously expanded. Human beings are not as 'physiologically paranoiic' as the carnivores. We have also seen (p. 112) we have anatomical proof of this as well. In the carnivores (who also are mainly solitary and not gregarious — in whom therefore suspicion must be a more natural state than trust), the suprarenal glands, 'the glands of combat' as they have been rightly called, have been highly developed. The temperament is then, one which is unstable. It tends to break down into frantic, unreflective action at any stimulant. Man on the other hand has the predominant balance given to his emotional nature not by the glands of combat but by the thyroid, the gland of the persistent effort, the gland, the secretions of which tend to make the creature patient, persistent, reflective.

CONCLUSION

We have then at the physiological end a basis on which to make approach to one another. If adrenalin-charged carnivores can be approached, *a fortiori* can we make contact and make our dominant mood prevail, our obvious good faith carry over to thyroid-controlled humans. Further, humans being intensely gregarious, there is always open an approach, lacking in contact attempts with non-gregarious animals. If the non-gregarious carnivore has mainly to judge your good will, or the reverse, by your smell, the gregarious human can judge it by many other factors. These may be, and probably are, all unconscious, and all the more powerful and instantaneous for that, but they need not be physiological. The physiological appeal is limited obviously by the range of the senses. Gregarious ties are, it seems increasingly clear, psychological, not physiological.

It is here we see disclosed the final argument for the psychological approach to pacifism and the complete abandonment of the false way of physical coercion. If the body-mind attitude, and unconscious psycho-physical expression of the human being influences and shapes the reaction of the carnivore he approaches, how much more the state of mind, the degree of the enlargement of consciousness, the adept has attained, invades the subconscious of those other humans whom he would release, and, percolating up through the limen, enters as an assurance and conviction of goodwill and good faith into their consciousness. We are learning how much more our eye and ear tell us than we consciously realize. Further, the evidence of telepathy shows beyond further doubt how moods and feeling-tones spread unconsciously

418

from mind to mind — far quicker than specific images or messages; and the evidence of crowd psychology, of mass movements and national and international enthusiasms, shows how certain states of mind can run rapidly through millions of people and over immense areas.

There is then no inherent impossibility in this method. The rescue of humanity, through teaching men how to enlarge their consciousness, is not, at least it need not and should not be, the rescue of a few anchorites out of a foundering civilization and from a doomed species. It is not a private salvation. It is a way whereby those who have found their way over the pass may hold it open, so that a new trust and confidence may spread throughout our race and our deadly paranoia which has reached panic proportions may be healed. Poor humanity which is to-day bursting its shackles (of security by armament), naked, self-wounded, haunting the sepulchres of a dead past; when requested its name, crying out, 'our name is legion for we are many': when, presented with hope of release, howling with fear against the peace-bringer, ' "What hast thou to do with us? Depart. Why hast thou come to torment us before the time,..." why are you trying to bring on the dreadful crisis toward which we are helplessly stumbling': this poor, possessed and splintered personality may then at the approach of the spirit, which does not fear it but has compassion on it and understands it, suddenly find itself made one, at rest, at peace, 'seated, clothed and in his right mind'.

Nor is the temper of men's minds to-day really unfriendly to such an approach. As a modern alienist would diagnose, the Gadarene maniac really wanted to be made sane: below the frantic surface conflict and defiance, of the 'splintered personality', there was a root of unity imploring the courage which dared help it, to bind it together again and give it a single sane expression and power of contact with its fellows. So to-day, behind the paranoiic fear, we have a pathetic wish to be understood, a sense, whether it be among Japanese, Germans, Italians, Chinese, Russians or Turks that they have been looked down on and have, for civilization's sake, to prove they are as fine as anyone. But more than that, there is to-day widespread through our civilization, a humanitarianism, a sensibility, which was probably never surpassed by any other age. Millions honestly dread and detest war because they hate cruelty quite as much as they fear pain and ruin. They have a real and vivid compassion for the weak, the defenceless and the broken of any race and of any sentient species. This feeling has gathered like a tide rising under the threshold of consciousness. Men drift nearer toward war but hate it the more, in spite of the wish to 'brave it out'. Their heart detests what their hand finds to do and what their narrow head tells them is inescapable.

Tell them there is a way out, and the force of compassion that is in them may well drive them to scale that way, however steep. Let them drift on to war and then the horror at what they have done, the fact that they felt so keenly for others and yet committed this crime against mankind, that keen sensibility may well drive them to despair. Their present humanitarianism (though, without a new psychology to back it and make it reasonable, it may be dismissed as sentimentality and so fail to arrest cataclysm) is both a symptom that, below the level of consciousness, there does gather a force which would respond to a new explanation, interpretation and line of conduct, and also a presage that, if cataclysm is not averted, then, even if it does not at the first blow destroy man physically, it will destroy, unhinge him, mentally. He will come to, from his paranoiic violence, to find that the enemy he wounded mortally was his brother, himself. Remorse and despair at his own madness will drive him to abandon his fatal bloodstained civilization. His consciousness will be completely fissured and unhinged between what he feels and what he does. Only a subhuman type will be able to survive and flourish.

A psychological revolution is therefore our only escape from material destruction and mental derangement. There is no other way, that is clear. This is what men mean when they say 'We must have a new growth of religion'. To-day we see rapidly working itself out the inevitable process whereby the sword of security becomes the weapon of suicide. To resuscitate social responsibility and respect, Mussolini has to become yearly more aggressive in his appeals. Hitler, attempting the same *resorgimento*, is rushing headlong down the same path. The Dictator, to keep the devotion of his followers, has to become unquestioned, inspired, and at the same time has to murder his opponents. The man who has to be always right, has also by the same inevitability, to commit crimes which reduce his rightness to no more than what he can do and what he must do. Whatever is, whatever happens, is right. Whatever expediency, megalomania, and, finally, paranoia, may drive upon one poor human creature, incapable of owning—forbidden to own—he can be mistaken; cut off from the kindly, co-operative judgment of his fellows — whatever ignorant and violent acts this sad and sorry aberrant may do, they are right, this is justice and wisdom, this is what must be and should be.

Thirty years ago Europe would have believed that such insane superstition could only exist among savages spellbound by sorcery and degraded through a nightmare cult of human sacrifice and demonology. Our reasonable light, our sane use of the sword had only to cut into these miasmic jungles and these last septic spots would be cleaned up. That word 'clean up' has, however, itself to-day been acquired, climatized by our insane epoch. The 'reasonable sword' has not cleaned up Africa. It has spread the horror of the witch doctor, a broadening shadow across Europe, where the pretence of justice becomes the assassin's weapon, where the nightmare panic about the community's safety urges everyone to denounce the stranger, and finally his fellow, until a universal suspicion and hatred infects all civilization.

9. ALL OTHER WAYS NOW STRAIGHT FOR DESTRUCTION

In the U.S.S.R., which claims to be making actual, through the same use of unlimited violence and unrestricted suspicion, a new order of manifest justice, there too we see the same degenerative process which those means assure. First it was realized that Communism was not to be achieved, but State Capitalism. The appeal then, having to be to individual human beings (whose individualism was of course inflamed, not reduced by suspicion and violence), the State has to abandon the Socialist slogan 'From all according to his capacity: to all according to his need'. Piece rates, bonuses, class distinctions (the industrial worker, the soldier, the secret police official), all methods of acting through individualism had to be adopted. The appeal to the private wish to be more secure than one's fellows is, however, by itself not enough. The fear of the class-enemy — *that*, through the using up of nearly all the available fuel, is dying down. Another fear must be found. That of course is always present in the foreigner, the neighbouring nations. Hence to-day the acute increase of patriotism and the preparation for war. Voroshiloff, or some other general who can be the Red Army's Master, must grow daily in power. Many people think that Russia, because internal conditions are becoming easier, is becoming more stable, more peaceable. What is actually taking place is the shifting of violence from the hands of amateurs, who thought they could make it build a new social order (if only the end was right, the old means would serve and carry humanity to the goal it had never before attained), into the hands of specialists who will use it just for the old conventional national ends. Voroshiloff, or whoever is the Red Army's Commander-in-Chief, will challenge the Japanese and 'wipe out' Russia's disgrace in 1905,[1] and then the next step down — some

[1] See Stalin's speech when he pointed out how Russia had, throughout her history down to 1905, been defeated because she was not 'ready'. It is worth noting that as the Revolutionary enthusiasm dies down in Russia and the country becomes increasingly only one of the Great Powers once more, not only is patriotism encouraged (the 'enemy' becomes the different national and not the different class and alliances are made with capitalist powers so as to secure national advantages), but internally the pure revolutionary and the social worker is edged out of power and the pure militarist takes his place. Kaganovitch, the young pure Red Jew party organizer, or Voroshiloff,

monomaniac specialist, successor to Ghenghis and Napoleon, will use the excuse of universal empire for indefinite campaigns of wreckage round the world.

It is not suggested that this degenerative process has at any moment been pursued consciously by Russia's rulers. It is an inevitable process inherent in the means used and therefore able to work itself out, whether the conscious aims are capitalist or communist. The deadly result is no more intended than was the fatal dermatitis and the cancer that resulted from the first free employment of X-rays and radium. In both cases men fail to notice that they are handling a force which will destroy them.

The same nobility of aim, the same 'realist' consistency and the same inherent disaster are present in the proclaimed policy of Japan.[1] Here is the appeal

[1] See 'The Determination of the Japanese People toward the Crisis', pamphlet published by the Newspaper Section of the Japanese War Office, on March 10th, 1935, summarized in *The Times*, April 10th, 1935. Even later information (July, 1935) reports the purging of the army of those officers, mainly young, who had combined social reform with militarism. So with Hitler getting rid of his revolutionaries, we see in Germany, Russia and Japan fanaticism which used violence being dismissed and its place taken by the pure expert specialist for whom war is not a means but an end.

the pure Russian generalissimo – between the sides these two represent, all informed opinion holds the succession lies. When the present autocrat of the Soviet ceases to rule, to which of these will the centre of power shift? Stalin lately married Kaganovitch's sister. Even more lately Kaganovitch left the centre of the party machine to be appointed commissar of communications, a task, which if it is not to prove the grave of his, as of his predecessors' reputations, must take him away from the secret levers of power: while the popularity of Voroshiloff, the pure Russian, among people who think of themselves increasingly as first and foremost Russians, the soldier, in a nation which thinks itself as about to become great and honoured among nations by arms – that popularity grows and must grow. Voroshiloff himself may be too fond of show to play out the part, but that he sees himself playing it was shown by his melodramatic presentation of himself at the last Moscow review of the Army when after the forces were put to attention, a fanfare was blown and the gates of the Kremlin thereupon being thrown open Voroshiloff appeared before his legions alone on a white horse – a forecasting shadow flung by Marengo? That the amateurs of violence are being shelved, the dissolution of the old Bolsheviks' and the old convicts' society, the picked clubs of strictly orthodox Revolutionaries early this summer (1935) is proof.

to men to sacrifice themselves to aims nobler than personal indulgence and individual satisfaction, here is the denunciation of that mixture of self and society, of state advance through private profit (the Mandevillian recipe) which is the unstable compromise of rationalistic individualistic Liberalism. Here is the comparison between their own culture, and its claim to lead East Asia, and the incoherence of outlook and trespass of influence of which capitalistic Liberalism is guilty. Japan — as Russia — must be armed as no one else, and prepared to go to greater lengths than anyone else, for it is clear she has a loftier message to give the world than anyone else and because of her loftiness she is envied by and in danger of aggression from all the other nations who are lower beings.

There remain the shattered remnants of the Liberal individualist tradition. They have lasted on and preserved greater freedom for their constituents, there is less cruelty in their ways than in those of the more consistent, new-model states, because of their inconsistency. They have not found out any technique whereby to develop and resolve the individual, but they have not yet crushed him. They thought he might be left to himself. They imagined he might be an end in himself and just as he is. This is, of course, a mistake. The technique must be given him to develop himself, or he must and will quickly be suppressed. He is a transitional being and the states which sustain him in an unresolved condition can also only be transitional. To-day, after the short period in which they used his private vices, his greed and fear and unrestrained competition, to build up for them their wealth, they have increasingly to restrict his activity, to abandon the hope that the utmost wild freedom, the freedom of individuals who had lost their social sense, could lead to national and international profit and order,[1] and to start on that specialization in armament, in ever intensified violence and suspicion, which will make them capable of competing with the consistent tyranny states, and which must also make them so crush their own constituent individuals that they, too, the capitalist-liberal states, will become dictatorships—tyrannies.

10. ALL AT STAKE AND JUST TIME

Thus, then, in this year of crisis, we see violence, having almost completed its degenerative process, and ready to throw off its pretence of being protector of values, of being the guarantor of peace and the sanctioner of justice. At a touch we shall see paranoiics, armed as dynamitards, flung at each other, and, after the first explosion, if forces can again be focused, we shall see the monomaniac expert, the degenerative specialist, gather round him his merry men — they to loot the ruins and he (a purer more advanced decadent) to stamp those ruins into dust.

There is then open to us no other way — at least all the other ways are broad and wide and open as the brink of a precipice. There is this one way, the only way out, strait and narrow, almost precipitously steep and exacting. It is evident, it is so hard, no other age could bring itself to take it. But we have reached a pass

---

[1] News comes that the United States' most famous gangster still practising, Dutch Schultz (Flegenheimer), has been acquitted in New York. The U.S. Attorney General and the Judge declare this 'a terrible miscarriage of Justice'. August 2nd, 1935.

when, if any way is open, we must attempt it — or go over the brink at our feet. We cannot deny there is this way out. We are suicides if we do not attempt it. Our desperate peril may make us scale the cliff as paralytics will sometimes, if the house is on fire, rise from their beds and clamber both to safety and to a new life of freedom.

We now see it is the partial, hopelessly disproportionate development of one aspect of our consciousness, of our objective minds, which makes us to-day stand with our fingers on a weapon which now at last can destroy us. We realize we could rouse ourselves to see that this sense of deadly propulsion to edge nearer the abyss, this awful sense of obsessive necessity and helplessness, is an obsession, is due to the fact that we have become blinded to the part of our nature which would dispel the nightmare conviction of that necessity and reveal us to ourselves, whole and free. We realize if we could see things in this sane way we should be then at the end of this delirium tremens of tyranny.

We are then free. We can then hope that we shall ' act on our freedom. We still have time, and the pressure is sufficient to make even the most sluggish act. If we so act we have saved ourselves, civilization, humanity and the vast hope that Life has worked to bring to fruition in us — the whole object of evolution. If we fail, then we are set for destruction, not merely of our society but of our whole species and it well may be of the whole adventure and effort of Life itself. That is the choice: We may . . .

INDEX

INDEX

Ford, Henry, 157
Fortune, Dr., 159
Fossils, 75, 76, 77, 84, 85, 103
Foxe; George, 375, 376
'Foxhall jaw', the, 108 *note*
Freedom, 250
Friends, Society of, 17, 18, 377ff., 390, 405, 416
Fry, Elizabeth, 383
—— Roger, 129
Future, the, 188, 189, 212ff., 299, 305, 306, 391, 392, 414ff.

GAIUS, EMPEROR, 317
Galileo, 370
Galley Hill, 107, 108
Geddes, Professor, 56
Genetists, the, 62, 63
Germany, 40, 43, 260 *note*
Ghenghis, 165, 361, 362, 397 *note*
Gibbon, Edward, 184, 387, 390
Gibbon, the, 86, 87, 88, 89, 94
Gibraltar skull, the, 103
Glands, 112-113
Gnosticism, 281, 328, 329, 358
Goat, the, 128
God-idea, 162, 174, 180
Goering, General, 309
Gorilla, the, 82, 83, 84, 85, 86
Great Britain, 39
Greece, 273, 278 *note*
Group-suggestibility, 192,193
Guyon, Madame, 373
Hadrian, emperor, 321
Hammurabi, 180, 250
Hands, 91, 93, 111, 128
Hardie, F., 390 *note*
Harrison, J. 102
Herdrelka, Dr., 105 *note*
Hildebrand, pope, 365
Hinduism, 277
History, defined, 20
Hitler, Adolf, 43
Hobbes, Thomas, 117, 118, 215, 379
Horse, the, 73, 90
Hulagu, 170, 171
Hungary, 361
Huxley, T. H., 62
Hylici, the, 328

ICE AGE, THE, 108
India, 209, 273, 275ff., 310, 327, 349, 353
Indian Survey, 207
Individualism, 179, 240, 296 *et passim*
Indus Civilization, The, 146, 162 *note*, 198, 199, 201, 207 *note*
Indus Culture, the, 144, 145, 146, 148, 149, 158, 161, 190, 191, 192, 198, 201, 208, 210, 220, 221, 224, 233, 404, 411

Inferno, The, 148
Inge, Dr. W. R., 67
Innocent III, pope, 366
Inquisition, the, 33, 34, 346, 365
Instinct, 13, 14, 22
Instincts of the Herd, 242
Introduction to Egyptian Religion, 264 *note*
Iron, 168
Islam, 341, 350
Italy, 40, 43, 44, 278

JAMES, WILLIAM, 266
Jehoshaphat, 258, 259
Jemnet Nasir culture, 144
Jesuits, 372, 373
Jews, 252, 258
John of Cappadocia, 366 *note*
John of the Cross, St., 371
Judaism, 350
Juliana of Norwich, 373
Justice, 29, 46, 47, 53, 246, 259, 262, 376
Justin Martyr, 332

KABBALISTS, 350
Keith, Sir Arthur, 109 *note*, 115 *note*
Khaled, 170
Khyan the Hyksos, 165
Kiesow, 238 *note*
King-idea, 162, 180, 248
Kol Deja, 144
Koran, the, 341, 343ff.
Krapina, 103

LAO TZU, 299, 300, 303, 305, 306, 376
La Place, P.-S., 370
'Law', sociological, 136, 137
Leakey, Dr. L. S. B., 108, 109
Le Moustier, 103
Levant, the, 182
Life, 80, 208
Life Religion, 225, 226, 324
Love, 120, 121
Luther, Martin, 45, 371
Lydia, 252, 253

MCALISTER, DR., 102
Mace, Egyptian, 146, 147, 148
Macedonia, 312
Mackey, E., 146, 162, 201, 207 *note*
Magdalenian culture, 104, 122
Magic, 20, 123, 182, 197, 268 *note*, 297, 328
Magism, 347
Malaya, 95, 284
Malthus, T. R., 58
Mammals, 70, 71, 73, 74, 81, 90
Man, ancestry of, 82ff., 97, 99-101
Man, his mind and character, 80, 81, 82, 91, 154, 155, 159, 308, 309, 310, 318, 393

Mandeville, B. de, 215, 379
Manichaeanism,345, 347,348, 349, 356
Marcion of Sinope, 329
Marcus Aurelius, 321
Marius, 314, 335
Marmoset, the, 85, 86, 95
Marshall, Sir John, 161, 207 *note*, 223 *note*, 224 *note*
Mathematics, 276, 325
Megiddo, 258, 259
Mencius, 295, 296
Mendel, Gregory, 62
Menhirs, 265 *note*
Mesopotamia, 144, 145, 146, 148, 149, 158, 166, 168, 169, 170, 172, 174, 179, 191, 248, 249, 250, 273, 361, 363
Metals, knowledge of, 158 *note*, 161
Mexico, 159
Militarism, 47, 160, 291ff.
Milk, 128
Mill, J. S., 285
Milo, 314
Miracles, 257
Mohammedanism, 202, 340 (*see also* Islam)
Mohenjo Daro culture, 144, 146, 201
Mohenjo Daro and the Indus Civilization, 223 *note*, 224 *note*
Moir, Reid, 102
Money making, 209
Monkeys, 85
Morality, 152, 153, 178, 181, 194, 199 *note*, 256, 268 *note*, 280, 282, 288, 290
Moret, 187
Mo Ti, 296
Music, primitive, 88, 124
Mussolini, Benno, 42, 43, 421
Mutationism, 62
Mysticism, 19, 373

NAPOLEON, ON WAR, 153
Narim Sin, 182, 250
Nationalism, 37
Nations, 249
Natural Selection, 23, 24, 55, 56, 58, 59 *et passim*
Nazis, 297
Neanderthal skull, the, 103, 104, 105, 106, 107, 108
Neolithic Age, the, 127
Neo-Pagan revival, 260 *note*
Nero, emperor, 317, 320
New Guinea, 159
New Light on the most Ancient East, 158, 168, 223 *note*
Nietzsche, Frederick, 353
Nile civilization, 159, 161, 181 (*see also* Egypt)
Nirvana, 282 *note*
Nubia, 182
Nyanza, 108

430

INDEX

431